James Constantine Pilling

**Bibliography of the Eskimo Language**

James Constantine Pilling

**Bibliography of the Eskimo Language**

ISBN/EAN: 9783743388796

Manufactured in Europe, USA, Canada, Australia, Japa

Cover: Foto ©Thomas Meinert / pixelio.de

Manufactured and distributed by brebook publishing software
(www.brebook.com)

James Constantine Pilling

**Bibliography of the Eskimo Language**

SMITHSONIAN INSTITUTION

BUREAU OF ETHNOLOGY: J. W. POWELL, DIRECTOR

.

# BIBLIOGRAPHY

OF THE

# ESKIMO LANGUAGE

BY

## JAMES CONSTANTINE PILLING

.

WASHINGTON
GOVERNMENT PRINTING OFFICE
1887

# PREFACE.

A number of years ago the writer undertook the compilation of a bibliography of North American languages, and in the course of his work visited the principal public and private libraries of the United States, Canada, and Northern Mexico; carried on an extensive correspondence with librarians, missionaries, and generally with persons interested in the subject, and examined such printed authorities as were at hand. The results of these researches were embodied in a volume of which a limited number of copies were printed and distributed—an author's catalogue which included all the material at that time in his possession.[1] Since its issue he has had an opportunity to visit the national libraries of England and France, as well as a number of private ones in both these countries, and a sufficient amount of new material has been collected to lead to the belief that a fairly complete catalogue of the works relating to each of the more important linguistic stocks of North America may be prepared. The first of such catalogues is the present; the second, which it is hoped to issue shortly, will be the Siouan.

The people speaking the Eskimo language are more widely scattered, and, with perhaps two or three exceptions, cover a wider range of territory than those of any other of the linguistic stocks of North America. From Labrador, on the east, their habitations dot the coast line to the Aleutian Islands, on the west, and a dialect of the language is spoken on the coast of Northeastern Asia. As far north as the white man has gone remains of their deserted habitations are found, and southward they extend, on the east coast to latitude 50° and on the west coast to latitude 60°. Within this area a number of dialects are spoken, the principal of which will be found entered herein in their alphabetic order.

Some difficulty has been encountered in deciding upon the claim of certain titles to admission into the bibliography. There are certain districts, notably in Alaska and Northeastern Asia, visited or inhabited by Eskimo or people closely allied to them and by other tribes not Eskimo. A vocabulary collected in such a district may be purely Eskimo, or purely not Eskimo, or a mixture containing words in different languages and dialects. The vocabularies collected by Norden-

---

[1] Proof-sheets of a Bibliography of the Languages of the North American Indians, Washington, 1885, pp. i-xl, 1-1135, 4°.

# BIBLIOGRAPHY OF THE ESKIMO LANGUAGE.

## BY JAMES C. PILLING.

## A.

[A B C card in the Greenland language.]
1 p. 16°. No title or caption; begins: a e
i o u, and ends: tau mau lan.
*Copies seen:* Pilling, Powell.
My copy, procured of the Unitäts-Buchhandlung, Gnadau, Saxony, cost 10 pf.

[Abécédaire ou Premier Livre de lecture.
Hanniame, 1849.] *
20 pp. sm. 8°. In the Eskimo language.
Title from the Pinart sale catalogue, No. 352,
where it brought, with eight other works in Eskimo, 16 fr.

Abecedarium:
Aleut.                      See Aleutian.
Eskimo.                     Abécédaire.
Greenland.                  A B C card,
                            Abecedarium,
                            Gronlandsk,
                            Kattitsomarsut.

[Abecedarium in the Greenland language.]
*Colophon:* Budissime, Nakkitarsima-
put E. M. Monsemit. [1861.]
Pp. 1-8, 16°. No title-page or caption; the
page begins: a e i o u, and ends: tau mau lau
1861.
*Copies seen:* Pilling, Powell.
My copy, bought of the Unitäts-Buchhandlung, Gnadau, Saxony, cost 20 pf.

Abel ( Iwarus ). Schediasma hocce
etymologico-philologicum prodromum
Americauo-Grönlandicum in patronis
appropriatum insinuat I. A.
Havniæ, 1783. *
12°. Title from the British Museum Catalogue of Printed Books. London, 1882.

[Acts of the Apostles, translated into the
Language of the Esquimaux Indians ou
the Coast of Labrador, by the Mission
aries of the United Brethren.
London, 1816. ] *
160 pp. 12°. Title from Trübner's catalogue,
August, 1874, p. 115, where it is priced 7s. 6d.
See Apostelit.

Adam (Lucien). En quoi la langue esquimaude diffère-t-elle grammaticale-
ment des autres langues de l'Amérique
du Nord ?
In Congrès International des Américanistes,
Compte-Rendu, fifth session, pp. 337-355, Copenhague, 1884, 8°. *
The subject is treated under the following
heads: Gender, Number, Pronominal suffixes,
Declension of nouns and of separate personal
pronouns, Declension of adverbs of place and
of demonstrative pronouns, Postpositions,
Verb, Incorporation, and Polysynthesis.
The communication to the Congress was
only an analysis of a memoir on the subject.
I am informed by the author that the article
was also issued separately; whether with title-
page or not I do not know.

Adelung (Johann Christoph) and Vater
(*Dr.* Johann Severin). Mithridates |
oder | allgemeine | Sprachenkunde |
mit | dem Vater Unser als Sprach-
probe | in bey nahe | fünf hundert
Sprachen und Mundarten, | von | Jo-
hann Christoph Adelung, | Churfürstl.
Sächsischem Hofrath und Ober-Biblio-
thekar. | [Two lines quotation.] | Er-
ster[-Vierter] Theil. |
Berlin, | in der Vossischen Buchhand-
lung, | 1806[-1817].
4 vols. (vol. 3 in 3 parts), 8°.
Aleut numerals, vol. 4, p. 253.—Vocabularies,
vol. 3, pt. 2, pp. 340-341; vol. 4, pp. 251-252.
Andreanowski Island vocabulary, vol. 3, pt.
3, p. 459.
Eskimo grammatic comments, vol. 3, pt. 3,
pp. 425-448.—Numerals, vol. 4, p. 253.—Vocabularies, vol. 3, pt. 2, pp. 340-341; pt. 3, pp. 238, 454-
455 (from Dobbs and Long), 461 (from Cook);
vol. 4, pp. 251-252.
Greenland grammatic comments, vol. 3, pt. 3,
pp. 435-448, 452-454.—Lord's Prayer (six versions), vol. 3, pt. 3, pp. 448-452 (from Anderson,
Egede, and others).—Numerals, vol. 4, p. 253.—
Vocabularies, vol. 3, pt. 2, pp. 340-341; pt. 3,
pp. 454-455 (from Egede and Anderson), 461;
vol. 4, pp. 251-252.

1

**Adelung (J. C.)**—Continued.

Kadjak numerals, vol. 4, p. 253.—Vocabularies, vol. 3, pt. 2, pp. 340–341; pt. 3, pp. 458–459 (from Resanoff), 466–468 (from Robek and Sauer); and vol. 4, pp. 251–252, 254.

Konægen grammatic comments, vol. 3, pt. 3, pp. 456–465.

Labrador grammatic comments, vol. 3, pt. 3, pp. 430–433.

Norton Sound grammatic comments, vol. 3, pt. 3, pp. 456–465.—Vocabularies, vol. 3, pt. 3, pp. 461, 466 (from Cook).

Tschugazzen grammatic comments, vol. 3, pt. 3, pp. 456–465.—Numerals, vol. 4, p. 253.—Vocabularies, vol. 3, pt. 2, pp. 340–341; pt. 3, pp. 458–459, 466 (from Resanoff), vol. 4, pp. 251–252.

Ugaljachmutzi grammatic comments, vol. 3, pt. 3, pp. 232–235.—Vocabularies, vol. 3, pt. 3, pp. 212–213, 230–231, 235, 237, 238 (from Resanoff).

Uualaschka vocabularies, vol. 3, pt. 3, pp. 458–459 (from Resanoff); vol. 4, p. 255.

*Copies seen:* Astor, Bancroft, British Museum, Bureau of Ethnology, Congress, Eames, Trumbull, Watkinson.

Sold at the Fischer sale, No. 17, for £1; another copy, No. 2042, for 16 shillings. At the Field sale, No. 16, it brought $11 88; at the Squier sale, No. 9, $5. Leclerc (1878) prices it, No. 2042, at 50 francs. At the Pinart sale, No. 1322, it sold for 25 francs; and at the Murphy sale, No. 24, a half-calf, marble-edged copy brought $4.

**Aglegmut:**

| | |
|---|---|
| Texts. | See Pinart (A. L.). |
| Vocabulary. | Balbi (A.), |
| | Pinart (A. L.), |
| | Wowodsky (—). |
| Words. | Schombargk (R. H.). |

**Ajokærsoutit** oppersartuit Gudimik pekkossænigdlo, tamaessa Luterij katekismusiugvætta ok'äuse.

Havniame, 1849.                    *

*Literal translation:* Teachings by God, such are Luther's his Catechism, its words. At Copenhagen, 1849.

125 pp. 8°, in Greenland Eskimo. Title from Dr. H. J. Rink, Christiania, Norway.

**Ajokærsutit** | illuartut Gudimik | Pekkorsejniglo Innungnut;, Koïsimarsudlo Koïsituksædlo | Iliniægeksejt Nalengniægeksejdlo, Pidluarsinnäungorkudlugit.

Kiöbenhavnime, | Aipeksäuik nakkittarsimarsut | 1797. | J. R. Thielmit.

*Literal translation:* Instructions | holy by God | and according to his will, to men; | that the baptized and candidates for baptism | scholars and all-sorts-of-people | may now be blessed. | At Copenhagen, | a second time pressed | 1797. | By J. R. Thiel.

Title verso blank 1 l. half-title: I. Katekismusim, &c. (a 2) verso blank 1 l. text, entirely in Greenland, pp. 3–150, 16°. At p. 131 is a half-

**Ajokærsutit**—Continued.

title: II. Kalkkorsun, &c. verso blank. The questions and answers are numbered in Part 1, 1–393; in Part II, 1–222. Catechism in the Eskimo language of Greenland.

*Copies seen:* Maisonneuve.

Leclerc, 1878, No. 2220, prices this work at 40 francs; he attributes the authorship to Fabricius.

**Ajokærsutit** | illuartut Gudimik | Pekkorsèjuiglo Innungnut; | Koïsimarsudlo Koïsituksædlo | Iliniægeksèjt Nalengniægeksèjdlo, ' Pidluarsinnäungorkudlugit. |

Kiöbenhavnime, | Pingajueksänik nakkittarsimarsut | 1818. | Illiarsuïn igloænne C. F. Skubartimit.

*Literal translation of imprint:* At Copenhagen, | a third time pressed, | 1818. | At the orphans their houses ["Wausenhaus"] from C. F. Schubart.

Pp. 1–158, 16°.

*Copies seen:* Congress.

A later edition as follows:

**Ajokærsutit** | illuartut Gudimik | Pekkorsèjniglo Innungnut; | Koïsimarsudlo Koisituksædlo | Iliniægeksèjt Nalengniægeksèjdlo, | Pidluarsinnäungorkudlugit. |

Kiøbenhavnime, | Sissameksämik nakkittarsimarsut | 1833. | P. T. Bruunikimit. |

Pp. 1–158, 16°. "A fourth time pressed."

*Copies seen:* British Museum.

**Ajokertutsit** pijarialiksuit. See **Erdmann** (F.).

**Ajokoersoirsun** Atuagekseit. See **Egede** (Paul).

**Akudnirmiut** Songs, Tales. See Boas (F.).

**Aleut.** Russkie Aleutskie slovar.      *

Manuscript, 2 vols. 4°. Russian-Aleut vocabulary. In possession of Mr. A. L. Pinart, who says it is a very important work, written about the year 1850.

**Aleut.** Russkie Aleutskie slovar.      *

Manuscript, 36 pp. folio. Russian-Aleut vocabulary, dialect of Atkha. In possession of Mr. A. L. Pinart.

**Aleut.** Russkie Aleutskie slovar.      *

Manuscript, 62 pp. folio. Russian-Aleut vocabulary. In possession of Mr. A. L. Pinart, who says it is a very important document, and has on it many pencil notes by Radloff.

**Aleut:**

| | |
|---|---|
| Abecedarium. | See Aleutian. |
| Biblo, Matthew. | Tishnoff (E.), |
| | Veniaminoff (J.) and |
| | Netzvietoff (J.). |

**Aleut—Continued.**

Catechism. See Jean (*Père*), Tishnoff (E.), Veniaminoff (J.) and Netzvietoff (J.).
Christian guide book. Tishnoff (E.).
Christian creed. Veniaminoff (J.) and Netzvietoff (J.).
Dictionary. Pinart (A. L.).
Grammar. Houry (V.), Veniaminoff (J.).
Grammatic comments. Buynitzky (S. N.), Furuhelm (H.), Pinart (A. L.), Voniaminoff (J.).
Grammatic treatise. Houry (V.), Pflzmaier (A.).
Guide to the Heavenly Kingdom. Veniaminoff (J.).
Notes on the Unalaskan Islands.
Numerals. Veniaminoff (J.).
Adelung (J. C.) and Vater (J. S.), Buynitzky (S. N.), Coxe (W.), Erman (G. A.), Latham (R. G.), Pott (A. F.),
Primer. Aleutian, Tishnoff (E.).
Relationships. Oppert (G.).
Remarks. Lowe (F.).
Sacred history. Veniaminoff (J.) and Netzvietoff (J.).
Songs. Pinart (A. L.), Veniaminoff (J.).
Texts. Pinart (A. L.).
Vocabulary. Baer (K. E. von), Balbi (A.), Balitz (A.), Bancroft (H. H.), Buynitzky (S. N.), Drake (S. G.), Everetto (W. E.), Gallatin (A.), Herzog (W.), Lowe (F.), Müller (F.), Robeck (—), Russkie, Sauer (M.).
Words. Campbell (J.), Coxe (W.), Pinart (A. L.), Umery (J.).

**[Aleutian Abecedarium.**

St. Petersburg, 1839 or 1840.] •
8°. Without place or date. Title from Ludewig, p. 4, who copies from Vater's Litteratur der Grammatiken, p. 454.

**Aleutian.** Алеутскій | букварь. |

Москва. | Въ Сунодальной Типографіи. | 1846.

*Translation:* Aleutian | Abecedarium. | Moscow. | Synod Press. | 1846.

**Aleutian—Continued.**

Title 1 l. pp. 1-30, 8°. Partly in Cyrillic type, partly in Russian.
*Copies seen:* British Museum, Pilling, Powell.

**American Bible Society:** These words following a title indicate that a copy of the work referred to was seen by the compiler in the library of that institution, New York City.

**American Bible Society.** Specimen verses | from versions in different | languages and dialects | in which the | Holy Scriptures | have been printed and circulated by the | American Bible Society | and the | British and Foreign Bible Society. | [Picture, and one line quotation.] |
New York: | American Bible Society, | Instituted in the Year MDCCCXVI. | 1876.
Pp. 1-48, 16°.—John iii, 16, in the language of Greenland, and in the Esquimaux [of Labrador], p. 36.
*Copies seen:* American Bible Society, Eames, Powell, Trumbull.
An edition, similar except in date, appeared in 1879 (Powell); and another, "Second edition, enlarged," in 1885. (Powell.)

**American Tract Society:** These words following a title indicate that a copy of the work referred to was seen by the compiler in the library of that institution, New York City.

**Anderson** (Johann). Herrn Johann Anderson, | I. V. D. | und weyland ersten Bürgermeisters der freyen Kayserlichen | Reichstadt Hamburg, | Nachrichten | von Island, | Grönland und der Strasse Davis, | zum wahren Nutzen der Wissenschaften | und der Handlung. | Mit Kupfern, und einer nach den neuesten und in diesem Werke ange- | gebenen Entdeckungen, genau eingerichteten Landcharte. | Nebst einem Vorberichte | von den Lebensumständen des Herrn Verfassers. |
Hamburg, | verlegts Georg Christian Grund, Buchdr. 1746.
Title verso blank 1 l. 14 other p. ll. text pp. 1-328, register 3 ll. map, 8°.—Dictionariolum, pp. 285-299.—Formularum loquendi usitatissimarum, pp. 300-303.--Formvla conivgandi verbum, pp. 304-314.—Ten Commandments, Prayers, &c. pp. 314-325. All in Greenland.
*Copies seen:* Astor, British Museum, Brown, Congress.
Priced by Leclerc, 1878, No. 649, at 25 fr.

—— Herrn Johann Anderson, | I. V. D. | und wieland ersten Bürgermeisters der freyen Kayserl. | Reichstadt Hamburg, | Nachrichten | von | Island, | Grönland

**Anderson (J.)**—Continued.

| und der | Strasse Davis, | zum wahren Nützen der Wissenschaften | und der Handlung. | Mit Kupfern, und einer nach den neuesten und in diesem Werke | angegebenen Entdeckungen, genau eingerichteten Landcharte. | Nebst einem Vorberichte | von den | Lebensumständen des Herrn Verfassers. | Frankfurt und Leipzig 1747.

Title verso blank and 14 other p. ll. text pp. 1–388, register 4 ll. 12°.—Linguistics as in 1746 edition, pp. 321–337, 337–341, 342–353, 353–368.

*Copies seen:* Brown, Trumbull.

There is an edition: Kiöbenhavn, 1748, 12°, which does not contain the linguistics. (British Museum, Brown.)

—— Beschryving | van Ysland, | Groenland | en de | Straat Davis. | Tot nut der wetenschappen en den | koophandel. | Door den Heer | Johan Anderson, | Doctor der beide Rechten, en in leven eerste Burgermeester der | vrye keizerlyke Rykstad Hamburg. | Verrykt met Platen en een nieuwe naauwkeurige Landkaart der ontdek-. | kingen, waar van in dit werk gesproken word. | Benevens een voorbericht, bevattende de levensbyzonderheden | van den geleerden schryver. | Uit het hoogduitsch vertaalt. | Door | J. D. J. |

Te Amsterdam, | By Steven van Esveldt, | Boekverkoper | in de Beurs-Steeg, 1750.

9 p. ll. pp. 1–289, map, sm. 4°.—Linguistics, pp. 244–258, 258–262, 262–273, 274–286.

*Copies seen:* British Museum, Brown.

—— Histoire | Naturelle | de L'Islande, | du Groenland, | du Détroit de Davis, | Et d'autres Pays situés sous le Nord, | traduite de l'Allemand | de M. Anderson, de l'Académie | Impériale, Bourgmestre en Chef | de la Ville de Hambourg. | Par M** [J. P. Rousselot de Surgy], de l'Académie Impériale, & | de la Société Royale de Londres. | Tome Premier [–Second]. | [Design.] |

A Paris, | Chez Sebastien Jorry, Imprimeur- | Libraire, Quai des Augustins, près | le Pont S. Michel, aux Cigognes. | M. DCC. L [1750]. | Avec Approbation & Priyilége du Roi.

2 vols.: pp. i–xl, 1–314; i–iv, 1–391, 16°.—Supplément contenant un petit Dictionnaire et quelques Principes de la Grammaire Groenlandoise, vol 2, pp. 295–386.

**Anderson (J.)**—Continued.

*Copies seen:* Brown, Congress.

Priced by Leclerc, 1878, No. 650, at 12 fr.

Sabin's Dictionary, No. 1408, mentions an edition: Paris, Jorry, 1754.

—— Beschryving | van | Ysland, | Groenland | en de | Straat Davis. | Bevattende zo wel ene bestipte bepaling van de ligging en | grote van die Eilanden, als een volledige ontvouwing van hunne | inwendige gesteltenis, vuurbrakende Bergen, heete en war- | me Bronnen enz. een omstandig Bericht van de Vruchten | en Kruiden des Lands; van de wilde en tamme Landdie- | ren, Vogelen en Visschen, de Visvangst der Yslanders | en hunne onderscheide behandeling, toebereiding en | drogen der Visschen, voorts het getal der Inwoon- | ders, hunnen Aart, Levenswyze en Bezigheden, | Woningen, Kledingen, Handteering, Arbeid, | Veehoedery, Koophandel, Maten en Ge- | wichten, Huwelyks Plechtigheden, Opvoe- ' ding hunner Kinderen, Godsdienst, Ker- | ken en Kerkenbestuur, Burgerlyke Rege- | ring, Wetten, Strafoeffeningen en wat | wyders tot de kennis van een Land | vereischt word. | Door den Heer | Johan Anderson, | Doctor der Beide Rechten, en in Leven eerste Burgermeester | der vrye Keizerlyke Ryksstad Hamburg. | Verrykt met Platen en een nieuwe naauwkeurige Landkaart der | ontdekkinge, waar van in dit Werk gesproken word. | Uit het Hoogduits vertaalt. | Door | J. D. J. | Waar by gevoegt zyn de Verbeteringen | Door den Heer Niels Horrebow, | Opgemaakt in zyn tweejarig verblyf op Ysland. | [Design.] |

Te Amsterdam, | By Jan van Dalen, Boekverkoper op de Colvéniersburgwal | by de Staalstraat. 1756.

Engraved frontispiece 1 l. title verso blank 1 l. 7 other p. ll. pp. 1–286, index 3 ll. map, sm. 4°.—Linguistics, pp. 244–258, 258–262, 262–273, 274–286.

*Copies seen:* Brown, Congress.

**Anderson (William).** Vocabulary of the language of Prince William's Sound.

In Cook (J.) and King (J.), Voyages to the Pacific Ocean, vol. 2, pp. 375–376, London, 1784, 3 vols. and atlas, 4°.

Mr. Anderson died at sea, August, 1778, before the expedition returned to England.

This vocabulary is reprinted in the following editions of Cook and King's Voyages:

**Anderson (W.)** — Continued.

London, Nicol, 1784, 3 vols. 4°. Linguistics, vol. 2, pp. 375-376.

Dublin, Chamberlaine, 1784, 3 vols. 8°. Linguistics, vol. 2, pp. 375-376.

London, Stockdale, 1784, 4 vols. 8°. Prince William's Land Vocabulary, vol. 3, pp. 310-311.

London, Nicol, 1785, "second edition," 3 vols. 4°. Linguistics, vol. 2, pp. 375-376.

Paris, 1785, 4 vols. 4°. Linguistics, vol. 3, p. 105.

Paris, 1785, 4 vols. 8°. Linguistics, vol. 3, p. 129.

Perth, Morrison & Son, 1785, 4 vols. 16°.

Perth, Morrison & Son, 1787, 4 vols. 16°.

Berlin, Hande und Spener, 1787-1788, 2 vols. 4°. Linguistics, vol. 2, pp. 89-90.

There is an edition in Russian, St. Petersburg, 1805-1810, which I have not seen; and one, Philadelphia, De Silver, 1818, 2 vols. 8°, which contains no linguistics.

The work is reprinted in Kerr (R.), General History and Collection of Voyages, vol. 15, pp. 115-514; vol. 16; and vol. 17, pp. 1-311. The linguistics appear in vol. 16, pp. 285-286.

Extracts from the work are printed in Pinkerton and Pelham, but they do not contain the linguistics.

The vocabularies are also reprinted in Fry (E.), Pantographia, London, 1799, 8°, and in Voyages of Capt. James Cook, London, 1842, vol 2, p. 305. (*)

**Andreanowski:**

Vocabulary.     See Adelung (J. C.) and Vater (J. S.), Robeck (—).

**Anner' lâb innuagorsimasub pârinek'arneranik.** See **Rudolph** (—).

**Antrim** (Benajah J.). Pantography, | or | universal drawings, | in the comparison of their natural and arbitrary laws, | with the nature and importance of | Pasigraphy, | as | the science of letters; | being particularly adapted to the orthoepic accuracy | requisite in international correspondences, and | the study of foreign languages. | With Specimens of more than Fifty Different Alphabets, including a concise description | of almost all others known generally throughout the World. | [Design.] | By Benajah J. Antrim. |

Philadelphia: | Published by the author, and for sale by | Thomas, Cowperthwait & Co. | 1843

Pp. i-vi, 7-162, 12°.—Numerals 1-10 of the Esquimaux and of Greenland. p. 153.

*Copies seen:* Astor, Congress.

**aperssûtit | okalugtnarissanut | tastamantitorkamigdlo tastaman- | titâmigdlo agdlagsimassunut.**

---

**aperssûtit** — Continued.

Druck von Gustav Winter in Stolpen. | 1877.

*Literal translation:* Questions | telling of the | Old Testament and of the New | Testament written.

Title verso blank 1 l. contents 1 l. text pp. 1-68, 12°. Questions and answers in the language of Greenland; based on Tastamantitorkamik.

*Copies seen:* Pilling, Powell.

My copy, procured of the Unitäts-Buchhandlung, Gnadau, Saxony, cost 1 M.

**Apersûtit** kigutsillo unipkantsinut. See **Bourquin** (T.).

**Apostelit** Piniarningit. | Lucasib Aglaktangit.

*Colophon:* W. McDowallib, Nenilauktangit. [1819.]

*Literal translation:* · The Apostles (their Acts. | Luke his writings. | W. McDowall, his pressings.

No title-page; heading as above; pp. 1-160, 16'. Acts of the Apostles in the Eskimo of Labrador. The British Museum catalogue (the copy described therein I have seen) gives it the date of 1819, which is probably correct, as Bagster's Bible of Every Land mentions an edition of that date.

There is sometimes issued separately, with heading as above, a portion (pp. 277-637) of the work, titled Testamentetak tamedsa, London, 1840, which is probably the "Acts, Epistles, and Revelations in Eskimo-Labrador, completed in 1839," mentioned by Bagster. The first part of Testamentetak tamedsa (pp. 1-276), containing the four gospels, was also issued separately with the title beginning Tamedsa Matthæusib.

See Acts.

**Apostles' Creed:**

Greenland.     See Egede (H.).

Hudson Bay.     Peck (E. J.).

Arctic Vocabulary.     See Everette (W. E.), Petitot (E. F. S. J.).

Argaluxamut Vocabulary. See Hoffman (W. J.).

Arithmetic, Greenland. See Wandall (E. A.).

**Arkiksutiksak** Pollesiunnut. See **Fabricius** (O.).

Asiagmut Vocabulary.     See Vocabularies.

Astor: This word following a title indicates that a copy of the work referred to was seen by the compiler in the Astor Library, New York City.

**Atka:**

Christian creed.     See Veniaminoff (J.) and Netzvietoff (J.).

Gospel of Matthew.     Veniaminoff (J.) and Netzvietoff (J.).

Notes on the Unalaska   Veniaminoff (J.). Islands.

**Atka**—Continued.

Vocabulary.            See Dall (W. II.),
                       Gibbs (G.),
                       Veniaminoff (J.).

**Atkinson** (*Rev.* Christopher). The | Emigrant's Guide | to | New Brunswick, | British North America. | By | the Rev. Christ. Atkinson, A. M., | Late Pastor of Mascreen Kirk, St. George, New Brunswick. | [Quotation six lines.] | Berwick-upon-Tweed : | Printed at the Warder Office, 57, High Street. | 1842.            *

Pp. i–iv, 1–124, map and plates, 16°. — The Lord's Prayer in Eskimo, p. 98.

—— A | Guide | to | New Brunswick, | British North America, &c. | By the Rev. Christopher W. Atkinson, A. M. | Late Pastor of Mascreen Kirk, St. George, New Brunswick. | Second Edition. | [Quotation, five lines.] | Edinburgh : | Printed by Anderson & Bryce, High-street. | 1843.            *

Pp. i–iv, 1–2, 1–220, map and plate, 16°. — Lord's Prayer in Eskimo, pp. 137–138.

The third edition: Edinburgh, 1844, pp. i–xvi, 13–284, 16°, contains no linguistics.            *

Titles and notes of the three editions of this work from Mr. W. Eames.

**Attuægaùtit** Evangeliumit sukniǎntòjt. See **Kragh** (P.).

**Attuækkæn** illuarsautiksæt. See **Kragh** (P.).

**Atuagagdliutit.** | Nalinginarnik | tusaruminasaṡsunik únivkǎt. | No. 1–45. |

Nũngme Nũnap Nalagaṫa | Nakiterivianuĕ Nakitat. | L. Möllermit. | 1861–1865.

*Literal translation:* The means for furnishing reading. | About all sorts of | things heard, narrations. | No. 1–45. | At the Point [Godthaab] on the country its ruler's [the Inspector's] | his printing press pressed. | From L. Möller.

An illustrated eight-page quarto paper, two columns to the page, printed in Eskimo at Godthaab, Greenland, in a small printing office, founded by Dr. H. J. Rink in connection with the inspector's office. First issued January, 1861, and continued at irregular intervals. Up to and including the issue of April, 1874 (No. 193), the columns were numbered consecutively to 3,081. This is followed by 24 columns index. Since that time there have been six volumes issued to April 15, 1880, each containing 192 columns, making in all 4,257 columns. This is the last I have seen. Dr. Rink informs me the publication was continued until 1885, the whole numbering 5,162 columns, with more than 250 leaves of illustrations in addition.

**Atuagagdliutit**—Continued.

*Copies seen:* British Museum, Congress, Powell.

Parts 1–4, Jan.–April, 1865, at the Fischer sale, No. 2,343, brought £1.

**Auer** (Alois).  *Outside title:* Sprachenhalle. |

N. B.  Die erste Abtheilung, das Vater Unser in 608 Sprachen und Mundarten, enthält den Adelung'schen Mithridates sammt 86 von mir beigefügten Vater-Unser-Formeln, in getreuen Abdrucke nach den | Quellen, und zwar in tabellarischer Aufstellung, um alle Mängel und Fehler der Originalien deutlicher zu veranschaulichen, und dadurch die Verbesserung zu erzielen. | Die zweite Abtheilung, das Vater Unser in 206 Sprachen und Mundarten, enthält die von mir neuerdings gesammelten verbesserten Vater-Unser in den Völkern eigenthümlichen Schriftzügen mit der | betreffenden Aussprache und wörtlichen Uebersetzung, | A. Auer.

*First engraved title:* Das | Vater Unser

*Second engraved title:* Das | Vater Unser | in mehr als 200 Sprachen und Mundarten | mit | Originaltypen.

[ Wien : 1844–1847. ]

Outside title, reverse, a short description, 1 sheet ; 17 other sheets printed on one side only, in portfolio ; oblong folio. Part I, dated 1844, has the caption : Das Vater-Unser in mehr als sechshundert Sprachen und Mundarten, typometrische aufgestellt. Part II, dated 1847, has the caption : Das Vater-Unser in 206 Sprachen und Mundarten, neuerdings gesammelt und aufgestellt von A. Auer. Zweite Abtheilung. Mit 55 verschiedenen den Völkern eigenthümlichen Schriftzügen abgedruckt.

The Lord's Prayer in the Greenland is numbered 602–607.

*Copies seen:* Astor, British Museum, Congress, Harvard.

Sabin's Dictionary, No. 57438, gives brief title of an edition : Viennæ e Typographia Imp. 1851, royal 8°. (*)

Authorities        See Catalogue,
                   Dall (W. H.) and Baker (M.),
                   De Schweinitz (E.),
                   Giesing (C.),
                   Leclerc (C.),
                   Ludewig (H. E.),
                   Nyerup (R.),
                   Pick (B.),
                   Quaritch (B.),
                   Reichelt (G. T.),
                · Rink (H. J.),
                   Sabin (J.).
                   Steiger (E.),
                   Vater (J. S.),

# ESKIMO LANGUAGE.

# B.

**Baer (John).** Comparative vocabulary of the Yerigen and Chucklock.

Manuscript, 3 ll. folio, in the Bureau of Ethnology; printed form of 180 words. A note as follows: "The foregoing were taken by John Baer, U. S. Marines, belonging to Commander Rodgers' N. Pacific Exploring Expedition, and were collected in Glasenop Harbor, Straits of Seniavine, west side of Behrings Straits." The "Chucklock" is Eskimoan; the Yerigen is probably a Siberian language.

**Baer (Karl Ernst von).** Statistische und ethnographische Nachrichten | über | die Russischen Besitzungen | an der | Nordwestküste von Amerika. | Gesammelt | von dem ehemaligen Oberverwalter dieser Besitzungen, | Contre-Admiral v. Wrangell. | Auf Kosten der Kaiserl. Akademie der Wissenschaften | herausgegeben | und mit den Berechnungen aus Wrangell's Witterungsbeobachtungen | und andern Zusätzen vermehrt | von | K. E. v. Baer. | St. Petersburg, 1839. | Buchdruckerei der Kaiserlichen Akademie der Wissenschaften.

Forms vol. 1 of Baer (K. E. von) and Helmersen (G. von), Beiträge zur Kenntniss des Russischen Reiches, St. Petersburg, 1839, 8°.

Short comparative vocabulary of the Atna, Ugalenzen, and Koloschen, p. 99.—Short vocabulary of the Inkülüchlüaten, pp.119-121.—A few words and numerals (1-5) of the Eskimo of Behring Strait, the Kadiak, Eskimo of Igloolik, and Unalaschkor, p. 123.—Names of the planets and months in Kuskokwim, pp. 134-135.—Comparative vocabulary of the Aleuten of Fox Island, Kadjack, Tschugatschen, Ugalenzen, Kuskokwim, and neighboring tongues not Eskimoan, pp. 259-270.

*Copies seen:* Congress.

—— Kuskutchewak vocabulary.

In Richardson (J.), Arctic Searching Expedition, vol. 2, pp. 369-382, London, 1851, 8°.
Reprinted in the edition: New York, Harpers, 1852, 8°, pp. 235-236. (Harvard.)

**Baffin Bay Vocabulary.** See Notice.

**[Bagster (Jonathan), editor.]** The Bible of Every Land. | A History of | the Sacred Scriptures | in every Language and Dialect | into which translations have been made: | illustrated with | specimen portions in native characters; | Series of Alphabets; | Coloured Ethnographical Maps, | Tables, Indexes, etc. | Dedicated by permission to his Grace the Archbishop of Canterbury. | [Vignette, and quotation, one line.] |

**Bagster (J.)—Continued.**

London: | Samuel Bagster and Sons, | 15, Paternoster Row; | Warehouse for Bibles, New Testaments, prayer books, lexicons, grammars, concordances, | and psalters, in ancient and modern languages. [1848-1851.]

Pp. i-xxviii, 1-3, 1-406, 1-12, maps, 4°.—Gospel of John i, 1-14, in the Esquimaux of Labrador, p. 359; in the language of Greenland, pp. 362-363.

*Copies seen:* American Bible Society, Boston Athenæum.

[——] The Bible of every Land; | or, | A History, Critical and Philological, | of all the Versions of the Sacred Scriptures, | in every language and dialect into which | translations have been made; | with | specimen portions in their own characters: | including, likewise, | the History of the original texts of Scripture, | and intelligence illustrative of the distribution and | results of each version: | with particular reference to the operations of the British and Foreign Bible Society, and kindred institutions, | as well as those of the missionary and other societies throughout the world. | Dedicated by permission to his Grace the Archbishop of Canterbury. | [Vignette.] |

London: | Samuel Bagster and Sons, | 15, Paternoster Row; | Warehouse for Bibles, New Testaments, prayer books, lexicons, grammars, concordances, and psalters, | in ancient and modern languages. | [Quotation, one line.] [1848-1851.]

11 p. ll. pp. xvii-lxiv, 4 ll. pp. 1-406, 1-4, 2 ll. pp. 1-12, 3 ll. 4°.—Linguistics as in previous title.

*Copies seen:* Astor.

[——] The Bible of Every Land. | A history of | the Sacred Scriptures | in every language and dialect | into which translations have been made: | illustrated by | specimen portions in native characters; | Series of Alphabets; | coloured ethnographical maps, | tables, indexes, etc. | New edition, enlarged and enriched. | [Design, and quotation, one line.] |

London: | Samuel Bagster and Sons: | at the warehouse for Bibles, New Testaments, church services, prayer

**Bagster** (J.)—Continued.

books, lexicons, grammars, | concordances, and psalters, in ancient and modern languages; | 15, Paternoster Row. [1860.]

27 p. ll. pp. 1-36, 1-480, maps, 4°.—Gospel of John i, 1-14, in the Esquimaux of Labrador, p. 438; in the Greenland (1790 version), p. 441; in the Greenland (1822 version), p. 443.

*Copies seen:* Boston Public, Congress, Eames.

**Baker** (Marcus). See **Dall** (W. H.) and **Baker** (M.).

**Balbi** (Adrien). Atlas | ethnographique du globe, | ou | classification des peuples | anciens et modernes | d'après leurs langues, | précédé d'un discours sur l'utilité et l'importance de l'étude des langues appliquée à plusieurs branches des connaissances humaines; d'un aperçu | sur les moyens graphiques employés par les différens peuples de la terre; d'un coup-d'œil sur l'histoire | de la langue slave, et sur la marche progressive de la civilisation | et de la littérature en Russie, | avec environ sept cents vocabulaires des.,principaux idiomes connus, | et suivi | du tableau physique, moral et politique | des cinq parties du monde, | Dédié à S. M. l'Empereur Alexandre, | par Adrien Balbi, | ancien professeur de géographie, de physique et de mathématiques, | membre correspondant de l'Athénée de Trévise, etc. etc. | [Design.] |

A Paris, | Chez Rey et Gravier, Libraires, Quai des Augustins, N° 55. | M. DCCC. XXVI [1826]. | Imprimé chez Paul Renouard, Rue Garencière, N° 5, F.-S.-G.

73 unnumbered ll. folio.

Langues de la région boréale de l'Amérique du Nord, formant la famille des idiomes eskimaux, plate xxxvi. — Tableau polyglotte des langues américaines, plate xli, contains a vocabulary of twenty-six words of a number of languages, among them the Ougaljakhmoutzi, Groënlandais (propre), Groenlandais (Ross ou de la Baie du Prince Régent), Groenlandais (Dobb), Groenlandais (Parry ou de l'Ile d'Hiver), Tchougatche-Konoga, Aleutien de l'Ile Ounalaska, Tchouktche-Améric. ou Aglemoute de l'Ile Nuniwok, Tchouktche-Améric. ou Aglemoute de l'Ile Saint-Laurent.

*Copies seen:* Astor, British Museum, Powell, Watkinson.

—— Introduction | à | l'atlas ethnographique | du globe, | contenant | un discours sur l'utilité et l'impor-

**Balbi** (A.)—Continued.

tance de l'étude des langues | appliquée à plusieurs branches des connaissances humaines; | un aperçu | sur les moyens graphiques employés par les différens peuples de la terre; | des observations sur la classification des idiomes | décrits dans l'atlas; | un coup-d'oeil sur l'histoire de la langue slave | et sur la marche progressive de la civilisation et de la littérature | en Russie, | dédié | à S. M. l'Empereur Alexandre, | par Adrien Balbi, | ancien professeur de géographie, de physique et de mathématiques, | membre correspondant de l'Athénée de Trévise, etc., etc. | Tome premier. | [Design.] |

A Paris, | chez Rey et Gravier, Libraires, | Quai des Augustins, N° 55. | M. DCCC. XXVI [1826].

Pp. i-cxliii, 1-416, 8°. Vol. I all that was published.—Langues de la région boréale de l'Amérique du Nord, formant la famille des idiomes esquimaux, pp. 317-321, contains (from Cranz) the conjugation of the verb *ernik* (to wash one's self), at first without suffixes, then with suffixes; also information on the literature of the language.

*Copies seen:* Astor, Boston Athenæum, British Museum, Congress, Watkinson.

The Atlas and Introduction together priced by Leclerc, 1878, No. 2044, at 30 fr. At the Murphy sale, No. 136*, they brought $3.50.

**Balitz** (Antoine). Vocabulary of the Aleuts.

Manuscript, 10 ll. 4°. In the library of the Bureau of Ethnology. Collected in the Aleutian Islands in 1860.

**Bancroft:** This word following a title indicates that a copy of the work referred to was seen by the compiler in the library of Mr. H. H. Bancroft, San Francisco, Cal.

**Bancroft** (Hubert Howe). The | Native Races | of | the Pacific States of North America. | By | Hubert Howe Bancroft. | Volume I. | Wild Tribes[V. Primitive History]. |

New York: | D. Appleton and Company. | 1874 [-1876].

5 vols. maps and plates, 8°. Vol. I. Wild Tribes; II. Civilized Nations; III. Myths and Languages; IV. Antiquities; V. Primitive History.

About one-third of vol. 3 of this work is devoted to the languages of the west coast, Chapter I giving a classification of languages and a general discussion. Chapter II is headed "Hyperborean Languages," and contains, pp. 574-580, Distinction between Eskimo and American, Eskimo pronunciation and declension,

**Bancroft** (H. H.)—Continued.

Dialects of the Koniagas and Aleuts, Dialects of the Atnahs and Ugalenzes compared; vocabulary of the Eskimo, Kuskokwigmute, Malemute, Aleut, and Kadiak.

*Copies seen:* Astor, Bancroft, Brinton, British Museum, Eames, Powell.

Priced by Leclerc, 1878, No. 49, at 150 fr. Bought by Quaritch at the Ramirez sale (catalogue No. 957) for £5 15s. and priced by him, No. 29917, at £5.

—— The | Native Races | of | the Pacific States | of | North America. | By | Hubert Howe Bancroft. | Volume I. | Wild Tribes[-V. Primitive History]. | Author's copy. | San Francisco. 1874 [-1876].

5 vols. 8°. Similar, except on title-page, to previous editions. One hundred copies issued.

*Copies seen:* Bancroft, British Museum.

In addition to the above this work has been issued with the imprint of Longmans, London; Maisonneuve, Paris; and Brockhaus, Leipzig; none of which have I seen.

—— The Works | of | Hubert Howe Bancroft. | Volume I[-V]. | The Native Races. | Vol. I. Wild Tribes[-V. Primitive History]. |

San Francisco: | A. L. Bancroft & Company, Publishers. | 1882.

5 vols. 8°. This series will include the History of Central America, History of Mexico, &c., each with its own system of numbering and also numbered consecutively in the series. Of these works there have been published vols. 1-7, 9-13, 15, 18-22, 27-29, 32, 33.

*Copies seen:* Bancroft, British Museum, Congress, Powell.

**Bannister** (Henry Martyn). Vocabulary of the Malimoot, Kotzebue Sound.

Manuscript of 200 words, 10 ll. 4°. In the library of the Bureau of Ethnology.

**Baptismal forms**, Greenland. See Egede (H.).

**Barth** (Johannes August). Pacis | annis MDCCCXIV et MDCCCXV | foederatis armis restitutae | monumentum | orbis terrarum | de | fortuna reduce gaudia | gentium linguis interpretans | principibus piis felicibus augustis | populisque | victoribus liberatoribus liberatis | dicatum. | [Engraving.] | Curante | Johanno Augusto Barth. |

Vratislaviae [Breslau], | Typis Grassii Barthii et Comp. 1816.

Outside title reading: Monumentum Pacis, 1 l. title above verso blank 1 l. 49 other unnumbered ll. folio.—An ode in the language of Greenland (over the name of J. Brodersen), 491..

**Barth** (J. A.)—Continued.

*Copies seen:* Astor, Congress, British Museum.

There is another edition, in 1818, with title exactly similar to the above, 81 ll. large folio. The Greenland ode occurs on the 73d l. (British Museum.)

**Bartholinus** (Caspar). Vocabula Grönlandica collecta á Casp. Bartholino, J. U. D.

In Bartholinus (Thomas), Acta medica & philosophica Hafniensia, vol. 2, pp. 71-77, Hafniæ, 1675, sm. 4°.

Contains about 250 Greenland words, arranged alphabetically, two columns to the page, with Latin equivalents.

**Barton** (Benjamin Smith). New Views | of the | Origin | of the | Tribes and Nations | of | America. | By Benjamin Smith Barton, M. D. | Correspondent-Member [&c. 10 lines]. |

Philadelphia: | Printed for the Author, | by John Bioren. | 1798.

1 p. l. pp. i-cix, 1-133, 1-32, 8°.—Vocabulary of the Greenlanders (from Cranz), and Eskimaux words scattered through the comparative vocabulary, which occupies pp. 1-132.

*Copies seen:* Astor, British Museum, Congress, Eames, Wisconsin Historical Society.

A copy at the Field sale, catalogue No. 107, brought $8. Leclerc, 1878, No. 809, prices an uncut copy at 40 fr. At the Murphy sale, catalogue No. 184, a half-morocco copy brought $9.50.

The first edition, Philadelphia, 1797, does not contain the Greenland vocabulary, but does include a few Eskimo words. (Congress.)

**Bastian** (Adolf). Ethnologie und vergleichende Linguistik.

In Zeitschrift für Ethnologie, vol. 4 (1872), pp. 137-162, 211-231, Berlin, [n. d.], 8°.

Contains examples in, and grammatic comments upon, a number of American languages, among them the Tschudi and Greenland, p. 157.

**Bathurst Vocabulary.** See Petitot (E. F. S. J.).

**Beck** (John). [Translations into the language of Greenland.]

"He translated the entire New Testament, with several portions of the Old, into the native tongue; and only a year before his departure [his death, which occurred in 1777] assisted brother Konigseer in revising a version of the Harmony of the Four Gospels."—*Cranz.*

**Beechey** (Capt. Frederic William). Narrative | of a | Voyage to the Pacific | and | Beering's Strait, | to co-operate with | the Polar Expeditions: | performed in | His Majesty's Ship Blossom, | under the command of | Captain

**Beechey** (F. W.)—Continued.

F.W. Beechey, R. N. | F. R. S., F. R. A. S., and F. R. G. S. | In the years 1825, 26, 27, 28. | Published by authority of the Lords Commissioners of the Admiralty. | In two parts. | Part I[–II]. | London: | Henry Colburn and Richard Bentley, | New Burlington Street. | MDCCCXXXI [1831].

2 vols. map, 4°.—Esquimaux names of animals, vol. 1, p. 299.—Vocabulary of words of the western Esquimaux, vol. 2, pp. 619–627.

The introductory remarks say: "This vocabulary contains a collection of words made by Mr. Collie, Mr. Osmer, and myself."

*Copies seen:* Bancroft, Boston Athenæum, British Museum, Congress.

A copy at the Field sale, catalogue No. 122, brought $6.

—— Narrative | of a | Voyage to the Pacific | and Beering's Strait | to co-operate with | the Polar Expeditions: | performed in His Majesty's Ship Blossom, | under the command of | Captain F. W. Beechey, R. N. | F. R. S., &c. | in the years 1825, 26, 27, 28. | Published by authority of the Lords Commissioners of | the Admiralty. | A new edition. | In two volumes. | Vol. I[–II]. | London: | Henry Colburn and Richard Bentley, | New Burlington Street. | 1831.

2 vols. maps, 8°.—Vocabulary of words of the western Esquimaux, pp. 366–383.

*Copies seen:* Astor, Bancroft, Eames.

Sabin's Dictionary, No. 4317, titles an edition: London, John Murray, 1831, 2 vols. 8°.

—— Narrative | of a | Voyage to the Pacific | and Beering's Strait, | to co-operate with | the Polar Expeditions: | performed in | his Majesty's Ship Blossom, | under the command of | Captain F. W. Beechey, R. N. | F. R. S. &c. | in the years 1825, 26, 27, 28. | Published by authority of the Lords Commissioners | of the Admiralty. | Philadelphia: | Carey & Lea—Chestnut Street. | 1832.

Pp. i-vi, 1 l. pp. i-xi, 13-493, 8°.—Esquimaux names of animals, pp. 255-256.

*Copies seen:* Boston Athenæum, British Museum, Congress.

A copy at the Field sale, catalogue No. 123, brought $2.50, and one at the Murphy sale, catalogue No. 205, $1.75.

Sabin's Dictionary, No. 4348, titles a German version: Weimar, 1832, 2 vols. 8°.

**Behring Strait Numerals.** See Baer (K. E. von).

**Benediction,** Hudson Bay. See Peck (E. J.).

**Bergholtz** (Gustaf Fredrik). The Lord's Prayer | in the | Principal Languages, Dialects and | Versions of the World, | printed in | Type and Vernaculars of the | Different Nations, | compiled and published by | G. F. Bergholtz. | Chicago, Illinois. | 1884.

Pp. 1-200, 12°.—The Lord's Prayer in the Esquimaux or Eskimo (Labrador and the Whale Rivers, Hudson's Bay, British America), p. 69.—Lord's Prayer in Greenland, p. 85.

*Copies seen:* Congress.

**Bergmann** (Gustav von). Das Gebeth des Herrn | oder | Vaterunsersammlung | in hundert zwey und fünfzig Sprachen. | Herausgegeben | von | Gustav von Bergmann | Prediger zu Ruien in Livland. | [Design.] | Gedruckt zu Ruien 1789.

Title and 6 other p. ll. pp. 1-58, 4 ll. 16°.—Lord's Prayer in Greenland, p. 6.

*Copies seen:* British Museum.

**Berthelsen** (R.) See **Kaladlit** Okalluktualliait.

**Beyer** (John Frederic). Grönland-German | Dictionar | By | John Frederic Beyer. | New Herrnhuth | Greenland | Apr. 16 1750.

Manuscript, 163 pp. 6½ x 8½ in. in size, averaging 32 words, with definitions, to the page. No preface or introduction. Preserved in the Moravian archives at Bethlehem, Pa. This description was kindly procured for me by Mr. John W. Jordan, of the Pennsylvania Historical Society, Philadelphia.

**Bibelib** | piviauarninga, saimanarningalo. | [Picture of Bible.] | [Druct von J. B. Steinkopf in Stuttgart.] 1851.

*Literal translation:* The Bible | its preciousness and its consolation.

1 p. l. pp. 1-8, 16°. Tract in the language of the Eskimo of Labrador.

*Copies seen:* American Tract Society.

**Bibelimit** ujarsimmassut. See **Stênborg** (K. J. O.).

**Bibelingoak** imalônêt: Gudim. See **Fabricius** (O.).

**Bibelingoak** Mordläinnut imaloneet. See **Fabricius** (O.).

| **Bible:** | Greenland. See Testamentetokak. |
|---|---|
| Old Testament. | Greenland. Beck (J.), (in part), |
| Old Testament. | Greenland. Brodersen (J.). (in part), |
| Pentateuch. | Labrador. Mosesil. |

**Bible—Continued.**

| | | |
|---|---|---|
| Genesis, | Greenland. | See Fabricius (O.). |
| Genesis, | Labrador. | Moscsib. |
| Exodus, | Greenland. | Kragh (P.). |
| Exodus, | Labrador. | Four Books. |
| Leviticus, | Greenland. | Kragh (P.). |
| Leviticus, | Labrador. | Four Books. |
| Numbers, | Labrador. | Four Books. |
| Deuteronomy, | Labrador. | Four Books. |
| Joshua, | Greenland. | Kragh (P.). |
| Joshua, | Labrador. | Erdmann (F.). |
| Judges, | Greenland. | Kragh (P.). |
| Judges, | Labrador. | Erdmann (F.). |
| Ruth, | Greenland. | Kragh (P.). |
| Ruth, | Labrador. | Erdmann (F.). |
| Samuel I-II, | Greenland. | Kragh (P.). |
| Samuel I-II, | Labrador. | Erdmann (F.). |
| Kings I-II, | Greenland. | Kragh (P.). |
| Kings I-II, | Labrador. | Erdmann (F.). |
| Chronicles, | Labrador. | Erdmann (F.). |
| Ezra, | Greenland. | Kragh (P.). |
| Ezra, | Labrador. | Erdmann (F.). |
| Nehemiah, | Greenland. | Kragh (P.). |
| Nehemiah, | Labrador. | Erdmann (F.). |
| Esther, | Greenland. | Kragh (P.). |
| Esther, | Labrador. | Erdmann (F.). |
| Job, | Labrador. | Erdmann (F.). |
| Psalms, | Greenland. | Brun (R.), |
| Psalms, | Greenland. | Egede (Paul), |
| Psalms, | Greenland. | Egede (Peter), |
| Psalms, | Greenland. | Fabricius (O.), |
| Psalms, | Greenland. | Jörensen (T.), |
| Psalms, | Greenland. | Kjer (K.), |
| Psalms, | Greenland. | Kristunmintut, |
| Psalms, | Greenland. | Muller (V.), |
| Psalms, | Greenland. | Wolf (N. G.). |
| Psalms, | Labrador. | Davidib, |
| Psalms, | Labrador. | Erdmann (F.). |
| Proverbs, | Greenland. | Wolf (N. G.), |
| Proverbs, | Labrador. | Erdmann (F.), |
| Proverbs, | Labrador. | Salomonib. |
| Ecclesiastes, | Labrador. | Erdmann (F.). |
| Song of Solomon, | Labrador. | Erdmann (F.). |
| Isaiah, | Greenland. | Brodersen (J.), |
| Isaiah, | Greenland. | Wolf (N. G.). |
| Isaiah, | Labrador. | Prophetib. |
| Jeremiah, | Labrador. | Salomonib. |
| Ezekiel, | Labrador. | Salomonib. |
| Daniel, | Greenland. | Kragh (P.). |
| Daniel, | Labrador. | Salomonib. |
| Minor prophets, | Greenland. | Kragh (P.). |
| Minor prophets, | Labrador. | Salomonib. |
| Apocrypha (pt.), | Greenland. | Kragh (P.). |
| New Testament, | Greenland. | Beck (J.), |
| New Testament, | Greenland. | Egede (Paul), |
| New Testament, | Greenland. | Fabricius (O.), |
| New Testament, | Greenland. | Kleinschmidt (J. C.), |
| New Testament, | Greenland. | Testamento- tak terssa. |
| New Testament, | Labrador. | Testamento- tak tamedsa. |
| Four Gospels, | Greenland. | Egede (Paul), Gospels. |
| Four Gospels, | Greenland. | |

**Bible—Continued.**

| | | |
|---|---|---|
| Four Gospels, | Labrador. | See Burghardt (C. F.), |
| Four Gospels, | Labrador. | Tamedsa Mat- thæusib, |
| Four Gospels, | Labrador. | Testamonti- tak tamædsa. |
| Matthew, | Alout. | Tishnoff (E.), |
| Matthew, | Alout. | Voniamino ff (J.) and Notz- victoff (J.). |
| Matthew (pt.), | Greenland. | Warden (D.B.), |
| Matthew (pt.), | Labrador. | Warden (D.B.), |
| Luke, | Greenland. | Apostolit. |
| Luke, | Hudson Bay. | Peck (E. J.). |
| John (part), | Eskimo. | Church. |
| John (part), | Greenland. | American Bi- ble Society, |
| John (part), | Greenland. | Apostolit, |
| John (part), | Greenland. | Bagster (J.), |
| John (part), | Greenland. | Bible Society, |
| John (part), | Greenland. | British and Foreign Bi- ble Society, |
| John (part), | Greenland. | Warden (D.B.). |
| John (part), | Hudson Bay. | Peck (E. J.). |
| John (part), | Labrador. | American Bi- ble Society, |
| John (part), | Labrador. | Bagster (J.), |
| John (part), | Labrador. | Bible Society, |
| John (part), | Labrador. | British and Foreign Bi- ble Society, |
| John, | Labrador. | Kohlmeister (G. B.), |
| John (part), | Labrador. | Warden (D.B.). |
| Acts, | Labrador. | Acts, |
| Acts, | Labrador. | Apostolit, |
| Acts, | Labrador. | Testamonti- tak tamædsa. |
| Epistles, | Greenland. | Apostolit, |
| Epistles, | Greenland. | Gospels. |
| Epistles, | Labrador. | Acts, |
| Epistles, | Labrador. | Epistles. |
| Epistle, Romans (pt.), | Hudson Bay. | Peck (E. J.), |
| Epistles, Corinthians (pt.), | Hudson Bay. | Peck (E. J.), |
| Epistles, John (pt.), | Hudson Bay. | Peck (E. J.). |
| Revelation, | Greenland. | Apostolit. |
| Revelation, | Hudson Bay. | Peck (E. J.). |
| Revelation, | Labrador. | Acts. |

Bible (small), Greenland. See Fabricius (O.).

Bible lessons:
Greenland. See Fabricius (O.), Kaumarsok, Kjer (K.), Kragh (P.), Jeausib, Nalekub, Tamerssa.
Labrador. Jerusalemib, Josuse,

**Bible lessons—Continued.**

Labrador.　　　See Kanmajok,
　　　　　　　Nálekam,
　　　　　　　Nalungiak,
　　　　　　　Naughtawkkoa,
　　　　　　　Nauk taipkoa,
　　　　　　　Nukakpiak,
　　　　　　　Nukakpiarkœk,
　　　　　　　Tamedsa Gudib,
　　　　　　　Tussajungnik,
　　　　　　　Ussornakaut.

**Bible Society.** Specimen verses | in 164 | Languages and Dialects | in which the | Holy Scriptures | have been printed and circulated by the | Bible Society. | [Design, and one line quotation.] |

Bible House, | Corner Walnut and Seventh Streets. Philadelphia. [1876?]

Printed covers, pp. 3–46, 18°.—St. John iii, 16, in the language of Greenland and of the Esquimaux, p. 36.

*Copies seen:* Eames, Pilling, Powell.

—— Specimen verses | in 215 | languages and dialects | in which the Holy Scriptures | have been printed and circulated by the | Bible Society. | [Design, and one line quotation.] | .

Bible House, | Corner Walnut and Seventh Streets, | Philadelphia. | Craig, Finley & Co., Prs., 1020 Arch St. | [n. d.]

Printed covers, pp. 1–48, 16°.—St. John iii, 16, in the Eskimo of Labrador and of Greenland, p. 26.

*Copies seen:* Eames, Powell.

＇ Some copies of this edition have printed cover, the title being printed in type differing from the above, and the line beginning with the word *Craig* is omitted. (Eames, Powell.)

**Bible stories:**

Greenland.　　　See Fabricius (O.),
　　　　　　　Gutip,
　　　　　　　Kragh (P.),
　　　　　　　Mentzel (—),
　　　　　　　Okautsit,
　　　　　　　Senfkornesntépok,
　　　　　　　Stênberg (K. J. O.),
　　　　　　　Steenholdt (W. F.),
　　　　　　　Tamersaa,
　　　　　　　Tastamentitorkamik.

Labrador.　　　Okpernermik.
　　　　　　　Pillitikset,
　　　　　　　Pingortitsinermik,
　　　　　　　Senfkornetnn-ipok,
　　　　　　　Unipkautsit.

**Boas (Dr. Franz).** [Tales and songs of the Okomiut and Akudnirmiut, the Eskimo of Cumberland Sound and Davis Strait ; collected by Dr. Franz Boas.] ＊

**Boas (F.)—Continued.**

Manuscript; recorded in blank books. Information from the author. Contents as follows :

I. Old tales.

1. Yjimarasukdjukdjuak.
2. Sednalo Kakodlulo (Sedna and the mollimoke).
3. Ytitaija (tale and song).
4. Origin of the white men (tale and song).
5. Unikartua (old story).
6. Arnalukalo kaggim innualo (the woman and the spirit of the sing house).
7–12. Short tales.
13. Grandmother and grandchild.
14. Tigang.

II. Old songs.

1. Song of the Innuit traveling to Lake Nettilling.
2. Song of a man who watches the seal at its hole.
3. Mocking the Torguak.
4–7. Songs of the Fornit.
8. Old song in the language of the Angekut.
9. Song of Kodln's sister.
10. Terrieniarlo arnalukalo (fox and woman).
11. Kaudjukdjuam nulianga (song of the Kaudjukdjuak's wife).
12. Tulugam pissinga (song of the raven).
13. Avignakulum pissinga (song of the lemming).
14. Terrieniak (song of the fox).
15. Nettik (song of the seal).
16. The young man who was lost in his Kajak.
17. Song of a man who had lost his way home.
18. Pissaik (song).
19–21. Yglukitaktung (playing at ball).
22. Arlum pissinga (song of the killer).
23. Suluitung.
24. Adlam pissinga (song of the adla).
25. Kallopallirg.
26. Song of the sun.

III. Fables.

1. Avignarlo terrieniarlo (lemming and fox).
2. Tulugarlo nanjalo (raven and gull).
3. Opikdjnarlo avignakululo (owl and lemming).
4. Opikdjuarlo kopernuarlo (owl and snowbird).
5. Opikdjuarlo tulugarlo (owl and raven).

IV. New songs.

1. Beauties of summer.
2. Journey to Pileing.
3. The returning hunter.
4. The desperate hunter.
5. Song of a man who went adrift on the ice.
6. Kidloaping's song.

This material was collected by Dr. Boas in 1883–'84. A copy was sent to Dr. Rink, of Christiania, Norway, and the original retained by the author.

In addition to the above, Dr. Boas informs me that he has collected a vocabulary of perhaps a thousand words and some slight account of the grammar of the language. See Rink (H. J.).

**Bock** (Carl Wilhelm). Analysis Verbi | oder | Nachweisung der Entstehung | der | Formen des Zeitwortes | für | Person, Tempus, Modus, Activum, Medium und Passivum; | namentlich im | Griechischen, Sanskrit, Lateinischen | und Türkischen; | von | Carl Wilhelm Bock, | Prediger zu Bergholz bei Löcknitz. |

Berlin. | A. Asher & Comp. | 1844.

Pp. i-viii, 1-172, 8°.—Grönländische Sprache, p. 34.

*Copies seen:* British Museum.

—— Erklärung | des Baues | der berühmtesten und merkwürdigsten älteren und | neueren Sprachen | Europa's, Asien's, Afrika's, Amerika's | und der Südsee-Inseln | von | C. W. Bock. |

Berlin. | Verlag der Plahn'schen Buchhandlung (Henri Sauvage). | 1853.

Pp. i-viii, 1 l. pp. v-vi, 1-98, folding diagrams, 8°. Followed by: Analysis Verbi | oder | Erklärung des Baues | älterer und neuerer Sprachen | alter Erdtheile.

1 p. l. pp. v-viii, 1-172, 1-24, 8°.—Grönländische Sprache, pp. 34, 81, 167.

*Copies seen:* Astor, Boston Public, British Museum, Congress.

[**Bodoni** (Jean-Baptiste), *editor.*] Oratio | Dominica | in | CLV. Lingvas | versa | et | Exoticis Characteribvs | plervmqve expressa. |

Parmae Typis Bodonianis MDCCCVI [1806].

3 p. ll. pp. i-ccxlix, folio.—Pars Quarta, Linguas Americanas complectens: Groenlandico (ex Evang. Groenl. Hafniæ edito), p. ccxvii.

*Copies seen:* British Museum, Lenox, Watkinson.

An "uncut, fine, clean copy," at the Fischer sale, catalogue No. 1272, brought 3s. 6d.

[**Böggild** (O.). Simonimik Syreniuiumik ... O. Böggild.

Nûngme, 1876.]

48 pp. 8°.—Bible story, Simon the Cyrenian, in the Eskimo of Greenland.—*Rink.*

[**Bompas** (*Rt. Rev.* William Carpenter).] Western Esquimaux Primer.

*Colophon:* London: Gilbert & Rivington, Whitefriars Street, and St. John's Square.

No title-page; pp. 1-23, 12°. Grammar lessons, prayers, hymns, and vocabulary, in double columns, English and Eskimo, alphabetically arranged according to the English words. I am informed by Archdeacon Kirkby that Mr. Bompas is the author.

**Bompas** (W. C.)—Continued.

*Copies seen:* Powell, Society for the Promotion of Christian Knowledge.

Boston Athenæum: These words following a title indicate that a copy of the work referred to was seen by the compiler in that library, Boston, Mass.

Boston Public: These words following a title indicate that a copy of the work referred to was seen by the compiler in that library, Boston, Mass.

[**Bourquin** (Theodor).] Apersûtit kigutsillo unipkautsinut aglaugne i hailiginêtunut | apostelillo | kingornganno pijokalaurtunut | illingajut. | IllautitannuajoKarivoK oKautsit tussarngartat | sunatuinait tukkingita nellonarnugnaertitauni- | ngannik. | Biblische | und kirchengeschichtliche | fragen und antworten | sowie | erklärung verschiedener fremdwörter; | gedruckt auf kosten der S. F. G. in London. |

[G. Winterib Stolpenemêtub nenilaurtangit.] 1872.

*Literal translation:* Questions and Answers | (relating) to the stories in writing | holy (?) | and the apostles' | afterwards their histories (?) | made so. It explains words strange various their sense. | G. Winter's Stolpen printing press. | 1872.

Title 1 l. preface 1 l. vorwort, signed by Bourquin, pp. i-xiii, text pp. 1-99, reverse of p. 99 Berichtigung, 16°.

A catechism of Bible history in the language of Labrador.

In his preliminary remarks the author asks for criticisms on his work, in order that improvements may be made in a subsequent edition.

*Copies seen:* Pilling, Powell.

My copy, procured from the Unitäts-Buchhandlung, Gnadau, Saxony, cost 1 M. 30 pf.

—— [Esquimau Grammar.]

"At the present time [1885] Theodore Bourquin is preparing an Esquimau Grammar which will be published in 1886 or 1887."—*Reichelt.*

Bourquin is superintendent of the Moravian Missions in Labrador.

**Brandt** (R. J.). See **Kragh** (P.).

Brinley: This word following a title indicates that a copy of the work referred to was seen by the compiler-at the sale of books belonging to the late George Brinley, of Hartford, Conn.

Brinton: This word following a title indicates that a copy of the work referred to was seen by the compiler in the library of Dr. D. G. Brinton, Media, Pa.

Bristol Bay Vocabulary. See Johnson (J. W.), Vocabularies.

British and Foreign Bible Society: Those words following a title indicate that a copy of the work referred to was seen by the compiler in the library of that institution, London, England.

**British and Foreign Bible Society.** Specimens of some of the languages and dialects | in which | The British and Foreign Bible Society | has printed or circulated | the Holy Scriptures. |

*Colophon:* London: Printed by Messrs. Gilbert & Rivington, for the British and Foreign Bible Society, Queen Victoria Street, E. C., where all information concerning the society's work may be obtained. [n. d.]

1 sheet, large folio, 28 x 38 inches, 6 columns.—Contains St. John iii, 16, in Greenland, No. 126, and in Esquimaux [of Labrador], No. 127.

*Copies seen:* British and Foreign Bible Society, Pilling, Powell.

—— Specimens | of some of the | languages and dialects | in which the | British and Foreign Bible Society | has printed and circulated the Holy Scriptures. | [Picture.] |

No. 10, Earl Street, Blackfriars, London. | Printed by W. M. Watts, Crown Court, Temple Bar, London, | from types principally prepared at his foundry. | [1865?]

Pp. 1–16, 8°.—Contains Acts ii, 8, in Greenland and Esquimaux [of Labrador], p. 15.

*Copies seen:* British and Foreign Bible Society, Powell.

—— Specimens | of some of the | languages and dialects | in which the | British and Foreign Bible Society | has printed and circulated the Holy Scriptures. | [Picture, and one line.] |

London. | 1868. | Printed by W. M. Watts, 80, Gray's-Inn Road, from types | principally prepared at his foundry.

Pp. 1–16, 18°.—Contains Acts ii, 8, in Greenland and Esquimaux [of Labrador], p. 15.

Though agreeing in most respects with the [1865] edition, this is not from the same plates.

*Copies seen:* British and Foreign Bible Society, Powell.

—— St. John iii. 16 | in some of the | languages and dialects | in which the | British & Foreign Bible Society | has printed or circulated the Holy Scriptures. | [Picture, and one line quotation.] |

London: | Printed for the British and Foreign Bible Society, | By Gilbert &

British and Foreign — Continued.
Rivington, 52, St. John's Square, E. C. | 1875.

Pp. 1–30, 1 l. 1 6°.—Contains St. John iii, 16, in Greenland and Esq uimaux [of Labrador], p. 29.

*Copies seen:* British and Foreign Bible Society, Pilling, P owell.

Some copies are date d 1868. (*)

—— St. John I II. 16 | in some of the | languages and dialects | in which the | British and F oreign | Bible Society | has printed and circulated | the Holy Scriptures. |

London : | Brit ish and Foreign Bible Society, Queen Victoria Street. | Philadelphia Bible Society, cor. Walnut and Seventh Sts , | Philadelphia. | [n. d.]

Printed title on cover, pp. 3–30, 12°.—Contains St. John iii, 16, in the Greenland and Esquimaux [of Labrador], p. 29.

*Copies seen:* Eames, Powell.

—— St. John iii. 16 | in most of the | languages and dialects | in which the | British & Forei gn Bible Society | has printed or cir culated the Holy Script ures. | [Design, and one line quotation.] | Enlarged edition. |

London : | Printed for the British and Foreign Bible Society, | By Gilbert & Rivington, 52, St. John's Square, E. C. | 1878.

1 p. l. pp. 1–50, 1 6°.—St. John iii, 16, Eskimo [of Labrador], and Greenland, p. 26.

*Copies seen:* A merican Bible Society, Powell.

—— St. John iii. 16 | in most of the | languages and dialects | in which the | British & Foreign Bible Society | has printed or circulate d the Holy Script ures. | [Design, and one line quotation.] | Enlarged e dition. |

London: | Printe d for the British and Foreign Bible Society, | By Gilbert & Rivington, 52, St. John's Square, E. C. | 1882.

1 p. l. pp. 1–48, 1 l. 16°.—St. John iii, 16, in Eskimo [of Labrador] and Greenland, p. 26.

*Copies seen:* British and Foreign Bible Society, British Museum, Pilling, Powell.

—— Ev. St. Joh. iii. 16. | in den meisten der | Sprachen und Dialecte , in welchen die | Britische und Ausländische Bibelgesellschaft | die heilige Schrift druckt und verbreitet. | [Design, and one line quotation.] | Vermehrte Auflage. |

London: | Britische und Ausländische Bibelgesellschaft, | 146 Queen Victoria Street, E. C. | 1885.

**British** and Foreign—Continued.

Printed cover as above, pp. 1–68, 3 ll. 16°.—St. John iii, 16, in Esquimaux, p. 20; in Greenland, p. 25.

*Copies seen:* Powell.

—— Еванг. отъ Іоанна, гл. 3й ст. 16. | Образцы | переводовъ священнаго писанія, | изданныхъ | великобританскимъ и иностраннымъ | библейскимъ обществомъ. | [Design, and one line quotation.] |

Печатано для британскаго и иностранаго библейскаго | общества, | у Гильберта и Ривингтона (Limited), 52, Ст. Джонсъ Скверъ, Лондонъ, | 1885.

*Literal translation:* The gospel by John, 3d chapter, 16th verse. | Samples | of the translations of the holy scripture, | published | by the British and Foreign Bible Society. | ' God's word endureth forever" | Printed for the British and Foreign Bible | Society | at Gilbert and Rivington's (Limited) St. John's Square, London, | 1885.

No inside title, printed cover in Russian as above, reverse quotation and notes, pp. 5–68, 1 l. 16°.—St. John iii, 16, in Eskimo [of Labrador] and Greenland, p. 36 (Nos. 105 and 106).

*Copies seen:* Powell.

—— St. Jean III. 16, &c. | Spécimens | de la traduction de ce passage dans la plupart | des langues et dialectes | dans lesquels la | Société Biblique Britannique et Étrangère | a imprimé ou mis en circulation les saintes écritures. | [Design, and one line quotation.] |

Londres: | Société Biblique Britannique et Étrangère, | 146, Queen Victoria Street, E. C. | 1885.

Title on outside cover as above, pp. 1–68, 2 ll. 16°.—St. John iii, 16, in Esquimaux, p. 20; in Greenland, p. 25.

*Copies seen:* British and Foreign Bible Society, Pilling, Powell.

—— St. John iii. 16, &c. | in most of the | languages and dialects | in which the | British and Foreign Bible Society | has printed or circulated the Holy Scriptures. | [Design, and one line quotation.] | Enlarged edition. |

London: | The British and Foreign Bible Society, | 146, Queen Victoria Street, London, E. C. | 1885.

Printed cover, pp. 1–68, 2 ll. 16°.—St. John iii, 16, in Esquimaux [of Labrador], p. 20; in Greenland, p. 25.

In this edition the "specimens" are arranged alphabetically instead of geographically.

*Copies seen:* British and Foreign Bible Society, Pilling, Powell.

**British Museum:** These words following a title indicate that a copy of the work referred to was seen by the compiler in the library of the British Museum, London, England.

**Brodersen** (Jaspar). [An ode in the language of Greenland.]

In **Barth** (J. A.), Pacis annis MDCCCXIV et MDCCCXV, &c. l. 49. Vratislaviæ [Breslau], [1816], folio.

Reprinted in another edition of Barth's work, with title similar to above, Vratislaviæ, [1818], 81 ll., large folio, the ode occurring on the 73d l. (British Museum.)

—— [Translations into the Greenland language.]

"Brother Konigseer, departing this life in 1786, was succeeded in his office as superintendent of the mission by Brother Jaspar Brodersen, a student of theology, who had already lived several years in the country. * * * Being firmly persuaded that the best service he could render to his flock would be to extend their acquaintance with the inspired volume, he employed his leisure hours in translating select portions of the historical part of the Old Testament and of the prophecies of Isaiah. Besides this he compiled a new collection of hymns for the use of the Greenlanders, and, having brought a small printing-press with him from Europe, he struck off a few copies for immediate circulation till a larger impression could be printed in Germany. * * * A severe fit of illness in April, 1792, * * * caused his return to Europe with his family in 1794."—*Cranz.*

**Brown:** This word following a title indicates that a copy of the work referred to was seen by the compiler in the library of the late John Carter Brown, Providence, R. I.

**Brown** (Dr. Robert). On the History and Geographical Relations of the Cetacea frequenting Davis Strait and Baffin's •Bay.

In Royal Society [of London], Manual of the Nat. Hist. Geol. and Physics of Greenland, &c. pp. 69–93, London, 1875, 8°.

Greenland and Eskimo (of western shores of Davis Strait) names for whales, pp. 70, 91.

Reprinted from the Zoöl. Soc. Proc., No. 35, pp. 533–556.

**Brun** *or* **Bruun** (Rasmus). [Grønlandst Psalmebog.

Kiobh. 1761.]

Title from Nyerup's Dansk-norsk Litteratur-lexicon, vol. 1, p. 98.

**Bryant** (——). Table to shew the Affinity between the Languages spoken at Oonalashka and Norton Sound, and those of the Greenlanders and Esquimaux.

**Bryant**—Continued.

In Cook (J.) and King (I.), Voyage to the Pacific Ocean, vol. 3, pp. 552-553, London, 1784, 4°.

Contains vocabularies of Oonalashka, Norton Sound, Greenland (from Cranz), and Esquimaux.

These vocabularies are reprinted in the following editions of Cook and King's Voyages:

London, Nicol, 1784, 3 vols. 4°. Linguistics, vol. 3, pp. 554-555.

Dublin, Chamberlaine, 1784, 3 vols. 8°. Linguistics, vol. 3, pp. 554-555.

The second edition: London, Nicol, 1785, 3 vols. 4°. Linguistics, vol. 3, pp. 554-555.

Paris, 1785, 4 vols. 4°. Linguistics, vol. 4, pp. 538-539.

Paris, 1785, 4 vols. 4°. Linguistics, vol. 4, appendix, pp. 99-160.

Perth, Munson & Son, 1785-?, 4 vols. 16°.

Perth, Munson & Son, 1787, 4 vols. 16°.

There is an edition in Russian, St. Petersburg, 1805-1810, which I have not seen; and one, Philadelphia, De Silver, which contains no linguistics.

The voyages reprinted in Kerr (R.), General History and Collection of Voyages, vol. 15, pp. 114-514, vol. 16, and vol. 17, pp. 1-311. The linguistics occur in vol. 16, pp. 310-311.

Extracts from the work occur in Pinkerton and Pelham, but they contain no linguistics.

The vocabularies are reprinted also in Voyages of Capt. James Cook, vol. 2, pp. 553-554, London, 1842, 8° (*), and in Fry (E.), Pantography, London, 1799, 8°.

**Bureau of Ethnology:** These words following a title indicate that a copy of the work referred to was seen by the compiler in the library of the Bureau of Ethnology, Washington, D. C.

**[Burghardt** (*Rev.* C. F.).]   The | Gospels | according to | St. Matthew, St. Mark, St. Luke, | and | St. John, | translated into the language | of | the Esquimaux Indians, | on the coast of | Labrador; | by the | Missionaries | of the | Unitas Fratrum; or, United Brethren. | residing | at Nain, Okkak, and Hopedale. | Printed | For the use of the Mission, | by | The British and Foreign Bible Society. |

London: | Printed by W. M'Dowall, Pemberton Row, Gough Square. | 1813.

1 p. l. pp. 1-416, 12°. The work does not contain the Gospel of John. One thousand copies printed for the British and Foreign Bible Society, to correspond with the Gospel of St. John, with which it was intended to be bound.

*Copies seen:* American Bible Society, Astor, Congress, Powell, Trumbull.

Priced by Leclerc, 1878, No. 2232, at 20 fr. The Brinley copy, catalogue No. 5641, brought

**Burghardt (C. F.)**—Continued.

$3.25; the Murphy copy, catalogue No. 2914*, $3.50; and a copy is priced by Quaritch, catalogue No. 30046, at 3s. 6d.

The Report of the British and Foreign Bible Society, vol. 1, gives the title: The Four Gospels in Esquimaux. British and Foreign Bible Society, 1811 & 1813. Bagster's Bible of Every Land says John was published in 1810, the remaining three in 1813. See Kohlmeister (B. G.) for the former.

**Buschmann** (Johann Carl Eduard). Über den Naturlaut. Von Hrn. Buschmann.

In Königliche Akad. der Wiss. zu Berlin, Abhandlungen aus dem Jahre 1852, pt. 3, pp. 391-423, Berlin, 1853, 4°.

Contains a few words of Kadjak, Eskimo, Grönländisch, and Inklik.

Issued separately as follows:

—— Über | den | Naturlaut, | von | Joh. Carl Ed. Buschmann. |

Berlin, | In Ferd. Dümmler's Verlags-Buchhandlung. | 1853. | Gedruckt in der Druckerei der königlichen Akademie | der Wissenschaften. |

1 p. l. pp. 1-34, 4°.

*Copies seen:* Astor, British Museum.

Translated and reprinted as follows:

—— "On Natural Sounds," by Professor J. C. E. Buschmann. Translated by Campbell Clarke, Esq., from the Abhandlungen Königlichen Akademie der Wissenschaften zu Berlin, aus dem Jahre 1852.

In Philological Society [of London?], vol. 6, pp. 188-206. [London, 1855], 8°.

—— Der athapaskische Sprachstamm, dargestellt von Hrn. Buschmann.

In Königliche Akad. der Wiss. zu Berlin, Abhandlungen aus dem Jahre 1855, pp. 144-319, Berlin, 1856, 4°.

Comparative vocabularies of a number of languages occur on pp. 242-313, among them the Ugaleuzen, Inkalik, Inkalit, and Koltschanen.

Separately issued as follows:

—— Der | athapaskische Sprachstamm | dargestellt | von | Joh. Carl Ed. Buschmann. | Aus den Abhandlungen der Königl. Akademie der Wissenschaften | zu Berlin 1855. |

Berlin. | Gedruckt in der Druckerei der königl. Akademie | der Wissenschaften | 1856. | In Commission bei F. Dümmler's Verlags-Buchhandlung.

Printed cover 1 l. pp. 149-320, 4°.

*Copies seen:* Astor, Brinton, British Museum, Trumbull.

**Buschmann (J. C. E.)**—Continued.

Trübner's catalogue, 1856, No. 639, prices it at 6s.; the Fischer copy, catalogue No. 273, brought 11s.; the Squier copy, catalogue No. 142, $1.13; priced by Leclerc, 1878, No. 2050, at 10 fr.; the Murphy copy, catalogue No. 2850, brought $2; priced by Quaritch, No. 30031, at 7s. 6d.

—— Die Pima-Sprache und die Sprache der Koloschen, dargestellt von Hrn. Buschmann.

In Königliche Akad. der Wiss. zu Berlin, Abhandlungen, aus dem Jahre 1856, pt. 3, pp. 321-432, Berlin, 1857, 4°.

A short comparative vocabulary of the Kolosch and Eskimo, p. 389.

Separately issued as follows:

—— Die Pima-Sprache und die Sprache der Koloschen | dargestellt | von | Joh. Carl Ed. Buschmann. | Aus den Abhandlungen der Königl. Akademie der Wissenschaften [ zu Berlin aus dem Jahre 1856. | Berlin. | Gedruckt in der Druckerei der Königl. Akademie | der Wissenschaften | 1857. | In Commission bei F. Dümmler's Verlags-Buchhandlung.

1 p. l. pp. 321-432.

Copies seen: Astor, British Museum, Trumbull.

At the Fischer sale, a copy, catalogue No. 274, brought 6s.; priced by Leclerc, 1878, No. 2053, at 10 fr. and by Trübner, 1882, No. 122, at 4s. 6d.

—— Die Völker und Sprachen Neu-Mexiko's und der Westseite des britischen Nordamerika's, dargestellt von Hrn. Buschmann.

In Königliche Akad. der Wiss. zu Berlin, Abhandlungen, aus dem Jahre 1857, pp. 209-414, Berlin, 1858, 4°.

Numerals of Prince William's Sound, p. 326.— A few words of Nutka and Eskimo, p. 367.

Separately issued as follows:

—— Die Völker und Sprachen | Neu-Mexico's | und | der Westseite | des | Britischen Nordamerika's dargestellt | von | Joh. Carl Ed. Buschmann. | Aus den Abhandlungen der Königl. Akademie der Wissenschaften | zu Berlin 1857. | Berlin. | Gedruckt in der Buchdruckerei der Königl. Akademie | der Wissenschaften | 1858. | In Commission bei F. Dümmler's Verlags-Buchhandlung.

Printed cover, title 1 l. pp. 209-414, 4°.

Copies seen: Astor, Congress, Trumbull, Watkinson.

ESK——2

**Buschmann (J. C. E.)**—Continued.

The copy at the Fischer sale, catalogue No. 270, brought 14s.; at the Field sale, catalogue No. 235, 75 cents; priced by Leclerc, 1878, No. 3012, at 12 fr. and by Trübner, 1882, at 15s.

—— Die Spuren der aztekischen Sprache im nördlichen Mexico und höheren amerikanischen Norden. Zugleich eine Musterung der Völker und Sprachen des nördlichen Mexico's und der Westseite Nordamerika's von Guadalaxara an bis zum Eismeer. Von Joh. Carl Ed. Buschmann.

In Königliche Akad. der Wiss. zu Berlin, Abhandlungen, aus dem Jahre 1854, Zweiter Supp.-Band, pp. 1-819 (forms the whole volume), Berlin, 1859, 4°.

Comparison of terms of the Jakutat and Ugalenzen, p. 683.—Comparison of terms of the Ugaljachmutzi and Aztek, pp. 684-685.—Vocabulary of the Ugalenzen (from Resanoff and Wrangell), pp. 688-689.—Comparison of the language of Prince William Sound (from Portlock) with the Tschugatschen (from Wrangell), p. 693.—Comparison of the Tschugatschen (from Wrangell) with the Kadjak (from Wrangell) and the Innuit of Kotzebue Sound, pp. 693-694.—Comparison of the dialects of Stuart, Nuniwok, and Tschuakak Islands with Eskimo dialects, pp. 703,704.—Vocabulary of the Inkilik (from Sagoskin and Wassiljew), pp. 707, 708.—Vocabulary of the Inkalit-Jug-eljnut (from Sagoskin), p. 708.

Separately issued as follows:

—— Die | Spuren der aztekischen Sprache | im nördlichen Mexico | und höheren amerikanischen Norden. | Zugleich eine Musterung der Völker und Sprachen | des nördlichen Mexico's | und der Westseite Nordamerika's | von Guadalaxara an bis zum Eismeer. | Von Joh. Carl Ed. Buschmann. | Berlin. | Gedruckt in der Buchdruckerei der Königl. Akademie | der Wissenschaften. | 1859.

1 p. l. pp. vii-xii, 1-819, 4°.

Copies seen: Astor, Brinton, Maisonneuve, Quaritch, Trumbull.

Published at 20 marks. An uncut half-morocco copy was sold at the Fischer sale, catalogue No. 269, to Quaritch for £2 11s.; the latter prices 2 copies, catalogue No. 12552, one at £2 2s. the other at £2 10s.; the Pinart copy, catalogue No. 178, brought 9 fr.; Koehler, catalogue No. 440, prices it at 13 M. 50 pf.; priced by Quaritch, No. 30037, at £2.

—— Systematische Worttafel des athapaskischen Sprachstamms, aufgestellt und erläutert von Hrn. Buschmann. (Dritte Abtheilung des Apache.)

**Buschmann (J. C. E.)—Continued.**
In Königliche Akad. der Wiss. zu Berlin,
Abhandlungen, aus dem Jahre 1859. pt. 3, pp.
501–586, Berlin, 1860, 4°.
Comparative vocabulary of a number of languages, pp. 546–586, among them the Inkilik,
Inkalit Kinai, Ugalenzen oder Ugalachmjut.
Issued separately as follows:

— Systematische Worttafel | des athapaskischen Sprachstammus, | aufgestellt
und erläutert | von | Joh. Carl Ed.
Buschmann. | Dritte Abtheilung des
Apache. | Aus den Abhandlungen der
Königl. Akademie der Wissenschaften
zu Berlin 1859. |
Berlin. | Gedruckt in der Druckerei
der Königl. Akademie | der Wissenschaften. | 1860. | In Commission von
F. Dümmler's Verlags-Buchhandlung.
1 p. l. pp. 501–586, 4°.
Copies seen: Astor, Trumbull, Watkinson.
Published at 7 M. 80 pf.; a copy at the Fischer
sale, catalogue No. 277, brought 13s.; priced in
the Trübner catalogue of 1882 at 3s.

— Verwandtschaft der Kinai-Idiome
des russischen Nordamerika's mit dem
grossen athapaskischen Sprachstamme.

**Buschmann (J. C. E.)—Continued.**
In Königliche Akad. der Wiss. zu Berlin,
Bericht aus dem Jahre 1854, pp. 231–236, Berlin,
[n. d.], 8°.
Comparative vocabulary of the Kenai-Sprachen (Kenai, Atnah, Koltschanen, Inkilek,
Inkalit, and Ugalenzen), with the Athapaskische-Sprachen (Chepewyan, Tahkali, Kutchin, Sussee, Dogrib, Tlatskanai, and Umpqua), faces p. 236.

**Buynitzky** (Stephen Nestor). English-Aleutian | Vocabulary. | Prepared by |
Stephen N. Buynitzky. | Published by
the Alaska Commercial Company. |
San Francisco: | "Alta California"
Book and Job Printing House. | No 529
California street. | 1871.
Pp. i–iv, 5–13, 8°.—Preface, containing grammatic remarks and rules, pp. iii–iv.—Vocabulary, English and Aleutian, in parallel columns,
arranged alphabetically by English words, pp.
5–11.—Numerals 1–21, 30, 40, &c., 100, 200, &c.
1,000, 10,000, 103,000, pp. 12–13.
Copies of this little work have become very
scarce; I have seen but one, that belonging
to Major J. W. Powell, and know of but two
others.

## C.

[**Calendar** in Greenland-Eskimo, for the
year 1880.
Nungme, nakitigkat, L. Møller.]
[n. d.]
1 sheet folio.
Copies seen: Congress.

**Campbell** (Rev. John). On the origin of
some American Indian Tribes. By John
Campbell. [Second article.]
In Montreal Nat. Hist. Soc. Proc. vol. 9, pp.
103–212, Montreal, 1879, 8°.
Aleutian, Kadiak, and Unalashka words
compared with those of the peninsula, pp. 2.4–
205.—Kadiak and Aleutian words compared
with Dacotah, 205–206.—Kadiak and Aleutian
words compared with Wyandot-Iroquois, p.
206.—Kadiak and Aleutian words compared
with Cherokee-Choctaw, p. 207.

**Canticles,** Greenland. See Tuksiautit.

**Catalogue** | de | livres rares | et précieux | manuscrits et imprimés | principalement sur l'Amérique | et sur les
langues du monde entier | composant la
bibliothèque de | M. Alph.-L. Pinart |
et comprenant en totalité la bibliothèque Mexico-Guatémalienne de | M.
l'Abbé Brasseur de Bourbourg |
Paris | Vve Adolphe Labitte | libraire de la Bibliothèque Nationale | 4,
rue de Lille, 4 | 1883

**Catalogue—Continued.**
Outside title 1 l. pp. i–viii, 1–248, 8°.—Contains titles of a number of works in Eskimo,
of some of which I have seen no mention elsewhere.
Copies seen: Congress, Eames, Pilling.

Catechism:
Aleut.            See Jean (Père),
                  Tishnoff (E.).
Greenland.        Ajokærsoutit oppersartuit,
                  Ajokærsutit illuartut,
                  aperssûtit,
                  Egede (H.),
                  Egede (Paul),
                  Katekismuse,
                  Sapâme,
                  Tamersa,
                  Thorhallesen (E.),
                  Tuksiautit:.
Hudson Bay.       Peck (E. J.).
Labrador.         Bourquin (T.),
                  Erdmann (F.).

**Catechismus** Lutheri. See Egede (H.).

**Catechismus** Mingnek D. M. Lutherim.
See Egede (Paul).

Census:
Greenland.        See Piuiartut.
Pt. Barrow.       Ray (P. H.).

**Chappell** (Lieut. Edward). Narrative |
of a | voyage | to | Hudson's Bay | in |
his majesty's ship Rosamond | containing some account of | the north-eastern

**Chappell** (E.)—Continued.

coast of America | and | of the tribes | inhabiting | that remote region. | By | Lieut. Edward Chappell, R. N. | [Two lines quotation.] |

London: | Printed for J. Mawman, Ludgate street: | By R. Watts, Crown Court, Temple Bar. | 1817.

6 p. ll. pp. 1-279, map, 8°.—A short Esquimaux vocabulary (21 words), p. 116.

*Copies seen:* Astor, Boston Atheneum, British Museum, Congress, Powell, Trumbull.

A copy at the Brinley sale, catalogue No. 5647, brought $1.75, and one at the Murphy sale, catalogue No. 549, $1.25; priced by Quaritch, No. 21972, at 5s.

**Charencey** (Hyacinthe de). Recherches | sur les | noms des points de l'espace | par | M. le Cte de Charencey | membre [&c. two lines.] | [Design.] |

Caen | Imprimerie de F. le Blanc-Hardel | rue Froide, 2 et 4 | 1882

Printed cover 1 l. title 1 l. pp. 1-86, 8°.—Famille Esquimaude: Groënlandais, Tchiglit (des bouches du Mackenzie), pp. 11-14.

*Copies seen:* Brinton, Pilling, Powell.

**Chlagmiut Vocabulary.** See Zagoskin (L. A.).

**Christ:**

| | | |
|---|---|---|
| (Imitation of), | Greenland. | See Egede (P.). |
| (Life of), | Labrador. | Nalegapta. |
| (Salvation through), | Greenland. | Kragh (P.). |

**Christian**

| | | |
|---|---|---|
| Creed, | Aleut. | See Veniaminoff (J.) and Netzvietoff (J.). |
| Doctrine, | Greenland. | Jesusib, Jesusim, Konigseer (C. M.). |
| | Labrador. | Jesusib. |
| Faith (Elements of), | Greenland. | Egede (H.). |
| Guide Book, | Aleut. | Tishnoff (E.). |

**Christ's Passion,** Greenland. See Naleganta.

**Chronicles,** Labrador. See Erdmann (F.).

**Chugátchigmût Vocabulary.** See Dall (W. H.).

**Oho'klûkmût Vocabulary.** See Dall (W. H.).

**Church Missionary Gleaner.** Languages of N. W. America.

In Church Missionary Gleaner, No. 90, London, 1881, 4°.

St. John iii, 16, in Eskimo, p. 67.

**Church Missionary Society:** These words following a title indicate that a copy of the work referred to was seen by the compiler in the library of the above institution, London, Eng.

**Clare** (James R.). Terms of Relationship of the Eskimo, West of Hudson's Bay, collected by James R. Clare, York Factory, Hudson's Bay Ty.

**Clare** (J. R.)—Continued.

In Morgan (L. H.), Systems of consanguinity and affinity, line 78, pp. 293-382, Washington, 1871, 4°.

**Collie** (—). See **Beechey** (F. W.).

**Congress:** This word following a title indicates that a copy of the work referred to was seen by the compiler in the Library of Congress, Washington, D. C.

**Cook River** Numerals. See Dixon (G.).

**Court de Gebelin** (Antoine de). Monde primitif, | analysé et comparé | avec le monde moderne, | considéré | Dans divers Objets concernant l'Histoire, le Blason, les Mon- | noies, les Jeux, les Voyages des Phéniciens autour du | Monde, les Langues Américaines, &c. | ou | dissertations mêlées | Tome premier, | Remplies de Découvertes intéressantes ; | Avec une Carte, des Planches, & un Monument d'Amérique. | Par M. Court de Gebelin, | de diverses Académies, Censeur Royal. | [Design.] |

A Paris, | Chez | L'Auteur, rue Poupée, Maison de M. Boucher, Secrétaire du Roi. | Valeyre l'aîné, Imprimeur-Libraire, rue de la vieille Bouclerie. | Sorin, Libraire, rue Saint Jacques. | M. DCC. LXXXI [1781]. | Avec approbation et privilége du Roi.

Forms vol. 8 of Monde Primitif, Paris, 1777-1782, 9 vols. 8°. The volumes have title-pages slightly differing one from another.—Essai sur les rapports des mots, entre les langues du Nouveau Monde et celles de l'Ancien, pp. 489-560, contains: Langue des Esquimaux et des Groenlandois (with vocabulary), pp. 493-498.

*Copies seen:* Congress.

Trübner, 1856, No. 631, prices a copy of the full set (dated 1787) at £3 13s. 6d. ; at the Fischer sale, catalogue No. 1706, a copy (9 vols.) brought £1 10s. and at the Brinley sale, catalogue No. 5632, $20.25.

Sabin's Dictionary, No. 17174, titles an edition of the Monde Primitif, Paris, Boudet, 1775, 9 vols. 4°.

For a reprint of the Essai, see Scherer (J. B.).

**Coxe** (William). Account | of the Russian Discoveries | between | Asia and America. | To which are added | The Conquest of Siberia, | and | the History of the Transactions and | Commerce between Russia and China. | By William Coxe, A. M., Fellow of King's College-Cambridge, and Chaplain to his Grace the | Duke of Marlborough. |

London, | Printed by J. Nichols, | for T. Cadell, in the Strand. | M DCC L XXX [1780].

Coxe (W.)—Continued.

Pp. i–xxiii, 1–344, and index 13 unnumbered pp. maps, 4°.—Specimen of the Aleutian language (12 words, and numerals 1–10), appendix, p. 303.

Copies seen: Boston Athenæum, British Museum, Watkinson.

There is an edition of this work with title-page similar in all respects to the above, except the addition of: The second edition, revised and enlarged. (Boston Athenæum, British Museum, Congress.)

Third edition as follows:

—— Account | of the | Russian discoveries | between | Asia and America. | To which are added, | the conquest of Siberia, | and | the history of the transactions | and commerce between Russia and China. | By William Coxe, A. M. F. R. S. | One of the Senior Fellows of King's College, Cambridge; | Member of the Imperial Œconomical Society at St. Peters- | burg, of the Royal Academy of Sciences at Copenhagen; and | Chaplain to his Grace the Duke of Marlborough. | The third edition, revised and corrected. |

London, | Printed by J. Nichols, | for T. Cadell, in the Strand | MDCCLXXXVII [1787].

1 p. l. pp. i–xxviii, 1–454, 1 l. maps, 8°.—Specimen of the Aleütian language (12 words and numerals 1–10), appendix, p. 386.

Copies seen: Bancroft, Congress.

Priced by Quaritch, No. 11820, at 5s.

I have seen the following editions, which contain no linguistics: Neuchatel, 1781, 8°; Frankfurt und Leipzig, 1783, 8°; London, 1803, 8° and 4°; London, 1804, 8°.

Co-Yukon Vocabulary. See Everette (W. E.).

Cranz (David). David Cranz | Historie | von | Grönland | enthaltend | Die Beschreibung des Landes und | der Einwohner &c. | insbesondere | die | Geschichte | der dortigen | Mission | der | Evangelischen | Brüder | zu | Neu-Herrnhut | und | Lichtenfels. | Mit acht Kupfertafeln und einem Register. |

Barby bey Heinrich Detlef Ebers, und in Leipzig | in Commission bey Weidmanns Erben und Reich. | 1765.

17 p. ll. pp. 1–1132, 13 ll. maps, 12°.—VI. Abschnitt. Von den Wissenschaften der Grönländer, pp. 277–304, contains remarks on the grammatic construction of the language of Greenland, with examples, and the Creed.—A Greenland song, with German translation, pp. 969–972.—Letters written by the Natives, with German translation, pp. 1096–1100.

Copies seen: Astor, Congress, Watkinson.

Priced by Leclerc, 1878, No. 2730, at 40 fr.

Cranz (D.)—Continued.

—— Historie | van | Groenland | Behelzende | Eene nauwkeurige Beschrijvinge | van | 's Lands ligging, gesteldheid, en natuurlijke Zeldzaamheden ; | Den Aart, Zeden en Gewoonten | Der Inwooneren aan de West-Zijde bij de | Straate Davis ; | 's Lands alonde en nieuwe Geschiedenisse ; | en in't bijzonder | de Verrichtingen der Mission arissen | van de | Broeder-Kerk, | door welken | Twee Gemeenten van bekeerde Heidenen aldaar gesticht zijn. | Alles in eigen Perzoon onderzocht en opgesteld | door | David Cranz. | Met Plaaten versierd, in III Deelen | uit het Hoogduitsch vertaald. |

Te Haarleem bij C. H. Bohn Amsterdam bij H. de Wit Boekverkoopers. | 1767.

3 vols. 8°.—Linguistics, vol. 1, pp. 243–256; vol. 3, pp. 236–238, 352–357.

Copies seen: Brown.

—— The | history | of | Greenland : | containing | a description | of | the country, | and | its inhabitants : | and particularly, | A Relation of the Mission, | carried on for above | these Thirty Years by the Unitas Fratrum, | at | New Herrnhuth and Lichtenfels, in that Country. | By David Crantz. | Translated from the High-Dutch, and illustrated with | Maps and other Copperplates. | In two Volumes. | Vol. I [–II]. |

London, | Printed for the Brethren's Society for the Furtherance of the | Gospel among the Heathen : | And sold by J. Dodsley, in Pall-mall ; T. Becket and | P. A. de Hondt ; and T. Cadell, Successor to | A. Millar, in the Strand ; W. Sandby, in | Fleet-street ; S. Bladon, in Pater-noster-row ; | E. and C. Dilly, in the Poultry ; and at | all the Brethren's Chapels. | MDCCLXVII [1767].

2 vols.: 2 p. ll. pp. i–lix, 1–405; 1 l. pp. 1–498. 8°.—Linguistics, vol. 1, pp. 217–220; vol. 2, pp. 350–352, 446–451.

Copies seen: Brown, Congress.

A copy at the Field sale, No. 462, brought $4.50; priced by Quaritch, Nos. 11648 and 28569, at 7s. At the Pinart sale, No. 267, a copy brought 15 fr.

—— Historia | om | Grönland, | deruti | Landet och desz Inbyg gare &c. | synnerhet | Evangeliska Brödra Forsamlingens | der warands | Mission, | och Desz Förrättninger | 1 | Ny-Herrnhut och Lichtenfels, | beskrifwas; |

Cranz (D.)—Continued.

Af | David Crantz | på Tyska författad, Men | för desz märkwärdiga Innehåll på Swensta öfwersatt, ' och | med fullst ändigt Register förstedd. | Förra Delen, | Om | Landet, Inbyggarne och Missionerne, intil År 1740. | Stockholm, | Tryckd, och uplagd af Johan Georg Lange, | År 1769.

2 vols.: 1 p. l. pp. 1-526; 520-1216, 12°. Vol. 2 has different title.—Linguistics, vol. 1, pp. 279-294; vol. 2, pp. 1011-1013, 1142-1147.

*Copies seen:* Brown.

—— The | history of Greenland: | including | an account of the mission | carried on by the | United Brethren | in that country. | From the German of David Crantz. | With | a continuation to the present time; | illustrative notes; | and an appendix, containing a sketch of the mission | of the brethren in Labrador. | [19 lines quotation.] | In two volumes. | Vol. 1[-II]. | London: | Printed for Longman, Hurst, Rees, Orme, and Brown, | Paternoster-row. | 1820.

2 vols.: pp. i-xi, 1-359; i-vi, 1-323, 8°.—Linguistics, vol. 1, pp. 201-209, 345-346; vol. 2, pp. 225-229, 293-294, 320.

The quotations from Cranz appearing in this bibliography are taken from this edition.

*Copies seen:* Boston Athenæum, British Museum, Brown, Congress, Watkinson.

A copy at the Field sale, catalogue No. 463, brought $1.75; priced by Quaritch, No. 11649, at 9s. and 10s. and in No. 28570 at 7s.

Reprinted, according to Ludewig, p. 72, in Bibliothek der neuesten Reisebeschreibungen, vol. 20, Frankfurt und Leipzig, 1779-1797, 21 vols. 8°.

Cranz (D.)—Continued.

I have seen the following editions, which contain no linguistics: Barby, 1770, 12°; Fraukfurt und Leipzig, 1779, 8°; Nürnberg und Leipzig, 1782, 12°.

Crespieul ( *R. P.* François - Xavier ). Prières | en | Algonkin | Montagnaix | Abanaki | Æsquimaux | 1676 | par le Révérend Père de Crespieul. *

Manuscript, 30 ll. 8°. Preserved in the Archbishopric of Quebec. The pagination is confused. The text commences on the verso of the leaf which bears the title, and is divided into four columns, two on the verso and two on the recto, having for headings, from left to right: Algonkin, Montagnaix, Abanaki, Æsquimaux. The first two columns only are in the handwriting of Father Crespieul. The text of the column devoted to the language of the Eskimos disappears on the recto of leaf 3, but appears again on pages 4 and 5, not being a translation of the same prayers as contained in the other columns, however. The Eskimo column is blank throughout the remainder of the manuscript.

Description furnished me by Rev. Louis Beaudet, librarian of Laval University, Quebec.

Cull (Richard). A Description of Three Esquimaux from Kinnooksook, Hogarth Sound, Cumberland Strait. By Richard Cull.

In Ethnological Society of London, Jour. vol. 4, 1856, pp. 215-225, London, [n. d.], 8°.

Numerals 1-30 of the Esquimaux of Labrador and of Cumberland Strait (from Sutherland), p. 221.

Cumberland Strait:

| | |
|---|---|
| Numerals | See Cull (R.). |
| Vocabulary. | Gilder (W. H.), |
| | Kumlien (L.). |

# D.

Dall (William Healey). Alaska | and | its resources. | By | William H. Dall, | director of the scientific corps of the late Western Union | telegraph expedition. | [Design.] | Boston: | Lee and Shepard. | 1870.

Pp. i-xii, 1-628, map, plates, 8°. Appendix F, Vocabularies, pp. 547-575, contain vocabularies of the following Eskimo dialects:

Unaláskan from Sauer.
Atkan from Sauer.
Ugalákmūt from Gibbs.
Chugátchigmūt from Wrangell.
Koniágmūt from Sauer.
Nushorgágmūt from Gibbs.
Kuskwógmūt from Baer.
Ekógmūt (Dall).
Unalígmūt (Dall).

Dall (W. H.)—Continued.

Máhlemūt (Dall).
Kaviágmūt (Dall).
Greenlandic from Egede.
Chu'klūkmūt from Hall (in part).

*Copies seen:* Boston Athenæum, British Museum, Congress, Eames, Powell, Trumbull, Watkinson.

A copy at the Field sale, catalogue No. 480, brought $1.50.

Some copies have the imprint: London: | Sampson Low, Son, and Marston, | Crown Buildings, 188, Fleet Street. | 1870. (British Museum.)

—— On the Distribution of the Native Tribes of Alaska and the adjacent territory. By W. H. Dall.

**Dall (W. H.)—Continued.**

In American Ass. Adv. Sci. Proc. vol. 18, pp. 263–273, and 2 folding sheets, Cambridge, 1870, 8°.

Contains a vocabulary of 27 words, and the numerals 1–10, of the tribes of which vocabularies are given in the same author's Alaska and its Resources.

—— On Some Peculiarities of the Eskimo Dialect. By William H. Dall.

In American Ass. Adv. Sci. Proc. vol. 19, pp. 332–349, Cambridge, 1871, 8°.

Conjugation of the affirmative form of the indicative mode of the verb *ermityŭk*, to wash, pp. 335–349.

—— Tribes of the Extreme Northwest. By W. H. Dall.

In Powell (J. W.), Contributions to N. A. Ethnology, vol. 1, pp. 1–156, Washington, 1877, 4°.

Terms of Relationship used by the Innuit, Appendix, pp. 117–119.

—— and **Baker** (Marcus). Partial list of books, pamphlets, papers in serial journals, and other publications on Alaska and adjacent regions. By W. H. Dall and Marcus Baker.

In Coast and Geodetic Survey, Pacific Coast Pilot * * second series, pp. 225–375, Washington, 1879, 4°.

While not referring directly to linguistics, this work contains titles of many works, voyages, travels, etc. which contain linguistic material.

*Copies seen:* Congress, Pilling, Powell.

**Dalton (H.).** See **Gebet des Herrn.**

**Davidib | assingitalo tuksiarutsiningit nertordlerutingillo | imgerusertaggit. |** The Book of Psalms | translated into the | Esquimaux Language, | by | the Missionaries | of the | Unitas Fratrum, or United Brethren. | Printed for the use of the Mission, | by | The British and Foreign Bible Society. |

London: W. M'Dowall Printer, [1830.

Pp. 1–216, 16°. Entirely in the language of Labrador. The translation of the Eskimo words of the title is: David's | his others his songs [*i. e.*, his other songs] and his means of praising | sung.

*Copies seen:* American Bible Society, British and Foreign Bible Society.

Bagster's Bible of Every Land mentions an edition of 1826. Sabin's Dictionary, No. 22868, and Trübner's Catalogue [1856], No. 669, mention an edition of 1834. The latter prices it at 3s.

**Davidoff** (Gavrila Ivanovich). Двукратное путешествие | въ Америку | морскихъ офице- ровъ | Хвостова и Давыдова, | писанное симъ послѣднимъ. | Часть первая [-вторая]. |

Въ С. Петербургѣ | Печатано въ Морской Типографіи 1810 [–1812] года.

**Davidoff (G. I.)—Continued.**

*Translation.*—Two voyages | to America | by the naval officers | Khwostoff and Davidoff, | written by the latter. | Part first[-second]. | At St. Petersburg | printed in the Naval Printing Office in the year 1810[-1812].

2 vols. 8°.—Kadiak names of stars and months, vol. 2, pp. 101–103.

*Copies seen:* British Museum, Congress.

The German edition, Berlin, 1816, 8°, contains no linguistics.

**Davidson** (George). Report of Assistant George Davidson relative to the resources and the coast features of Alaska Territory.

In Coast Survey Ann. Rept. 1867, pp. 187–329, Washington, 1869, 4°.

Vocabulary of the languages of the natives of Kadiak, Unalaska, and Kenai, pp. 293–298.

—— Report of Assistant George Davidson relative to the coast features and resources of Alaska territory.

In 40th Congress, 2d Session, House of Representatives, Ex. Doc. No. 177, Russian America, Message from the President of the United States, in answer to a resolution of the House of 19th of December last, transmitting correspondence in relation to Russian America. [No imprint.] Pp. 1–361, pt. 2, pp. 1–19, 8°.

Mr. Davidson's report occupies pp. 219–361, and contains, pp. 329–333, vocabularies of the Oonalashka, Kodiak, Kenay, and Sitka, all from Lisiansky's Voyage Round the World.

**Davis Strait, Vocabulary.** See Gibbs (G.).

    Words.        Brown (R.).

**De Schweinitz** (*Bishop* Edward). See **Reichelt** (G. T.).

**Dialogues, Greenland.** See Egede (H.), Kragh (P.).

**Dictionarium** Grönlandico-Danico-Latinum. See **Egede** (Paul).

**Dictionary:**

| | |
|---|---|
| Aleut. | See Buynitzky (S. N.), Pinart (A. L.). |
| Greenland. | Anderson (J.), Beyer (J. F.), Egede (Paul), Fabricius (O.), Kleinschmidt (S. P.). |
| Kaniagmut. | Pinart (A. L.). |
| Labrador. | Erdmann (F.). |
| Tchiglit. | Petitot (E. F. S. J.). |

**Dixon** (*Capt.* George). A | voyage round the world; | but more particularly to the | north-west coast of America: | performed in 1785, 1786, 1787, and 1788, | in | the King George and Queen Charlotte, | Captains Portlock and Dixon. | Dedicated, by permission, to | Sir Joseph Banks, Bart. | By Captain George Dixon. |

**Dixon (G.)—Continued.**

London: | Published by Geo. Gould-
ing, | Haydn's Head, No. 6, James
Street, Covent Garden. | 1789.

Pp. i-xxix, 1 1. pp. 1-352, appendix, pp. 353-
360, appendix 2, pp. 1-17, map, 4°.—Numerals,
1-10, of Prince William's Sound and Cook's
River, Norfolk Sound, and King George's
Sound, p. 241.

*Copies seen :* Astor, Bancroft, Boston Athenæum, British Museum, Congress, Harvard,
Watkinson.

At the Fischer sale, catalogue No. 2312, a copy
brought 1s. 6d. ; at the Brinley sale, No. 4678, a
fine copy, calf, gilt, $2.75. Priced by Quaritch,
Nos. 28950 and 28951, at 10s. and 12s.

—— Voyage | autour du monde, | et prin-
cipalement | a la côte nord-ouest de
l'Amérique, | Fait en 1785, 1786, 1787 et
1788, | A bord du King-George et de la
Queen- | Charlotte, par les Capitaines
Portlock | et Dixon. Dédié, par permis-
sion, à Sir Joseph | Banks, Baronet; |
Par le Capitaine George Dixon. | Tra-
duit de l'Anglois, par M. Lebas. | Tome
Premier[-Second]. |

A Paris, | Chez Maradan, Libraire,
Hôtel de Château- | Vieux, rue Saint-
André-des-Arcs. | 1789.

2 vols. 12°.—Linguistics, as in English edition, vol. 2, pp. 16-17, and sheet facing p. 21.

*Copies seen :* Bancroft, Boston Athenæum.

—— Der | Kapitaine Portlock's und Dix-
on's | Reise um die Welt | besonders
nach | der Nordwestlichen Küste von
Amerika | währends der Jahre 1785 bis
1788 | in den Schiffen King George und
Queen Charlotte, | Herausgegeben |
von dem | Kapitain Georg Dixon. | Aus
dem Englischen übersetzt und mit An-
merkungen erläutert | von | Johann
Reinhold Forster, | der Rechte, Medicin
und Weltweisheit Doktor, Professor der
Naturgeschichte und Mineralogie | auf
der Königl. Preusz. Friedrichs-Univer-
sität, Mitglied der Königl. Akademie
der höheren | und schönen Wissenschaf-
ten zu Berlin. | Mit vielen Kupfern und
einer Landkarte. |

Berlin, 1790. | Bei Christian Fried-
rich Bosz und Sohn.

4 p. ll. pp. i-xxii, 1-314, map, 4°.—Linguistics, pp. 216-218.

*Copies seen :* Brown.

See **Portlock** (N.); also **Portlock** (N.) and
.**Dixon** (G.).

**Dobbs** (Arthur). An | Account | of the
Countries adjoining to | Hudson's Bay,

**Dobbs (A.)—Continued.**

| in the | North-west Part of America:
| containing | a Description of their
Lakes and Rivers, the Nature of the |
Soil and Climates, and their Methods of
Commerce, &c. | Shewing the Benefit
to be made by settling Colonies, and |
opening a Trade in these Parts; where-
by the French will be | deprived in a
great Measure of their Traffick in Furs,
and | the Communication between Can-
ada and Mississippi be cut off. | With |
An Abstract of Captain Middleton's
Journal, and Observations upon | his
Behaviour during his Voyage, and since
his Return. | To which are added, | I.
A Letter from Bartholomew de Fonte,
| Vice-Admiral of Peru and Mexico; |
giving an Account of his Voyage from |
Lima in Peru, to prevent, or seize upon
| any Ships that should attempt to find
| a Northwest Passage to the South
Sea. | II. An Abstract of all the Discov-
eries | which have been publish'd of the
Islands | and Countries in and adjoin-
ing to the | Great Western Ocean, be-
tween Ame- | rica, India, and China, &c.
pointing | out the Advantages that may
be made, | if a Short Passage should
be found thro' | Hudson's Streight to
that Ocean. | III. The Hudson's Bay
Company's Charter. | IV. The Standard
of Trade in those | Parts of America;
with an Account | of the Exports and
Profits made an- | nually by the Hud-
son's Bay Company. | V. Vocabularies
of the Languages of se- | veral Indian
Nations adjoining to Hud- | son's Bay. |
The whole intended to shew the great
Probability of a Northwest | Passage,
so long desired; and which (if discov-
ered) would be of the | highest Advan-
tage to these Kingdoms. | By Arthur
Dobbs, Esq ; |

London : | Printed for J. Robinson, at
the Golden Lion in Ludgate-Street. |
M DCC XLIV [1744].

Pp. i-ii, 1-211, map, 4°.—Vocabulary of English and Eskimo words, pp. 203-205.

*Copies seen :* Astor, Boston Athenæum,
British Museum, Congress, Trumbull.

Stevens' Nuggets, No. 906, prices a copy at
10s. 6d. A copy at the Field sale, No. 538,
brought $2.50. Priced by Quaritch, No. 11650, at
£1 5s., large paper. At the Murphy sale, No.
801, a copy brought $3.25. Priced by Quaritch,
No. 28278, at £1 4s.

# 24 BIBLIOGRAPHY OF THE

**Drake** (Samuel Gardner). The | Book of
the Indians | of | North America: |
comprising | details in the lives of about
five hundred | chiefs and others, | the
most distinguished among them. | Also,
| a history of their wars; their manners
and customs; speeches of | orators, &c.,
from their first being known to | Euro-
peans to the present time. | Exhibiting
also an analysis of the most distin-
guished authors | who have written
upon the great question of the | first
peopling of America. | [Picture of
Indian, and six lines quotation.] | By
Samuel G. Drake, | Member of the
New-Hampshire Historical Society. |
Boston: | Published by Josiah Drake,
| at the Antiquarian Bookstore, 56
Cornhill. | 1833.

Frontispiece 1 l. title as above 1 l. 1 other p. l.
pp. 1-23 (Book I), 1-110 (Book II), 1-124 (Book
III), 1-47 (Book IV), 1-135 (Book V).—Short
vocabulary of the Kamskadale and Aléoutean
("from a French translation of Billings's voyage"), Book I, p. 15.
*Copies seen:* British Museum.
An earlier edition of this work, Indian Biography, Boston, 1832, 8°, contains no linguistics. (Astor, Congress.)

—— Biography and history | of the | In-
dians of North America; | comprising |
a general account of them, | and |
details in the lives of all the most
distinguished chiefs, and | others, who
have been noted, among the various |
Indian nations upon the continent. |
Also, | a history of their wars; | their
manners and customs; and the most
celebrated speeches | of their orators,
from their first being known to | Euro-
peans to the present time. | Likewise |
exhibiting an analysis | of the most dis-
tinguished, as well as absurd authors,
who | have written upon the great
question of the | first peopling of
America. | [Picture of an Indian; quo-
tation, six lines.] By Samuel G. Drake,
| Member of the New Hampshire His-
torical Society. | Third Edition, | With
large Additions and Corrections, and
numerous Engravings. |
Boston: | O. L. Perkins, 56 Cornhill,
and Hilliard, Gray & Co. | New York:
G. & C. & N. Carvill. | Philadelphia:
Grigg & Elliot. | 1834.

Engraved title 1 l. pp. i-viii, 1-28, 1-120,
1-132, 1-72, 1-158, 1 l. pp. 1-18, 1-12, plates. 8°.

**Drake** (S. G.) — Continued.
Some copies have the names Collins, Hannay
& Co. substituted for G. & C. & N. Carvill in
the imprint.
Short vocabulary of the Kamskadale and
Aléoutean, Book I, p. 15.
*Copies seen:* Astor, British Museum, Con-
gress, Wisconsin Historical Society.
Sabin's Dictionary, No. 20868, mentions the
fifth edition, Boston, 1833, 8°.

—— Biography and History | of the |
Indians of North America; | compris-
ing | a General Account of them, | and
| Details of the Lives of all the most
distinguished chiefs, and | others, who
have been noted, among the various |
Indian Nations upon the Continent. |
Also, | a History of their Wars; | their
Manners and Customs; and the most
celebrated Speeches | of their Orators,
from their first being known to | Euro-
peans to the Present Time. | Likewise
| exhibiting an Analysis | of the most
distinguished, as well as absurd authors,
who | have written upon the great
question of the | First Peopling of
America. | [Picture of an Indian; quo-
tation, six lines.] | By Samuel G. Drake,
| Member of the New Hampshire His-
torical Society. | Fourth Edition, |
With large Additions and Corrections,
and numerous Engravings. |
Boston: | J. Drake, 53 Cornhill, | at
the Antiquarian Institute. | 1836.

Engraved title 1 l. pp. i-vi, 1 l. pp. 1-4, 1-28
1-120, 1-132, 1-72, 1-158, 1-18, 1-12, plates, 8°.
*Copies seen:* British Museum.

—— Biography and history | of the |
Indians of North America. | From its
first discovery to the present time; |
comprising | details in the lives of all
the most distinguished chiefs and |
counsellors, exploits of warriors, and
the celebrated | speeches of their
orators; | also, a history of their wars,
| massacres and depredations, as well
as the wrongs and | sufferings which
the Europeans and their | descendants
have done them; | with an account of
their | Antiquities, Manners and Cus-
toms, | Religion and Laws; | likewise |
exhibiting an analysis of the most dis-
tinguished, as well as absurd | authors,
who have written upon the great ques-
tion of the | first peopling of America.
| [Monogram; six lines quotation.]
By Samuel G. Drake. | Fifth Edition, |

**Drake** (S. G.)—Continued.

With large Additions and Corrections, and numerous Engravings. |

Boston: | Antiquarian Institute, 56 Cornhill. | 1836.

1 p. l. pp. i-xii, 1-48, 1-120, 1-144, 1-90, 1-168, 8°.—Vocabulary of the Kamskadale and Aléoutean, Book I, p. 16.

*Copies seen:* Astor, British Museum, Congress.

Some copies are dated 1837. (Astor.)

The "Seventh edition" has title-page otherwise similar to the above, the date being changed to 1837. (Astor, Congress.)

A copy is priced by Quaritch, No. 11968, at 10s. At the Murphy sale, No. 831, one brought $3.75.

—— The | book of the Indians; | or, | biography and history | of the | Indians of North America, | from its first discovery | to the year 1841. | [Nine lines quotations.] | By Samuel G. Drake, | Fellow [&c. two lines]. | Eighth edition, | With large Additions and Corrections. |

Boston: | Antiquarian Bookstore, 56 Cornhill. | M.DCCC.XLI [1841].

Pp. i-xii, 1-48, 1-120, 1-156, 1-156, 1-200, and index, pp. 1-16, 8°.—Linguistics as in fifth edition.

*Copies seen:* Boston Athenæum, British Museum, Congress.

According to Sabin's Dictionary, No. 20688, Ninth Edition, Boston, 1845, 748 pp 8°; Tenth Edition, Boston, MDCCCXL[V]III, 8°.

—— Biography and History | of the | Indians of North America, | from its first discovery. [Quotation, nine lines.] | By Samuel G. Drake. | Eleventh edition. |

Boston: | Benjamin B. Mussey & Co. | M.DCCC.LI [1851].

Pp. 1-720, plates, 8°.—Vocabulary of the Kamskadale and Aleutian, p. 32.

*Copies seen:* British Museum, Eames, Massachusetts Historical Society, Wisconsin Historical Society.

According to Sabin's Dictionary, No. 20868, some copies have the imprint: Boston, Sanborn, Carter & Bazin, 1857. Another edition: Boston, 1858.

—— History | of the | Early Discovery of America, | and | Landing of the Pilgrims. | With a | Biography | of the | Indians of North America. | [Quotation, nine lines.] By Samuel G. Drake.

Boston: | Higgins and Bradley. | 1854.

**Drake** (S. G.)—Continued.

Pp. 1-720, plates, 8°.—Linguistics as in eleventh edition. Title from Mr. W. Eames.

—— The | Aboriginal Races | of | North America; | comprising | Biographical Sketches of Eminent Individuals, | and | an Historical Account of the Different Tribes, | from | the First Discovery of the Continent | to | the Present Period | With a Dissertation on their | Origin, Antiquities, Manners and Customs, | Illustrative Narratives and Anecdotes, | and a | copious analytical index | By Samuel G. Drake. Fifteenth Edition, | revised, with valuable additions, | by J. W. O'Neill. | Illustrated with Numerous Colored Steel-plate Engravings. | [Quotation, six lines.] |

Philadelphia: | Charles Desilver, | No. 714 Chestnut Street. | 1860.

Pp. 1-736, 8°. This is the Biography of the Indians, with a new title-page and some additions.—Linguistics, p. 32.

*Copies seen:* Astor, Bancroft.

—— The | Aboriginal Races | of | North America; | comprising | Biographical Sketches of Eminent Individuals, | and | an Historical Account of the Different Tribes, | from | the First Discovery of the Continent | to | the Present Period | With a Dissertation on their | Origin, Antiquities, Manners and Customs, | Illustrative Narratives and Anecdotes, | and a | copious analytical index | By Samuel G. Drake. | Fifteenth Edition, | revised, with valuable additions, | by Prof. H. L. Williams. | [Quotation, six lines.] |

New York. | Hurst & Company, Publishers. | 122 Nassau Street. | [n. d. copyright, 1880.]

Pp. 1-787, 8°.—Linguistics, p. 32.

*Copies seen:* Astor, Congress, Wisconsin Historical Society.

**Duncan** (David). American Races. | Compiled and abstracted by | Professor Duncan, M. A.

Forms Part 6 of Spencer (Herbert), Descriptive Sociology, New York, D. Appleton & Co. [1878], folio.

Under the heading "Language," pp. 40-42, there are given comments and extracts from various authors upon native tribes, among them the Esquimaux.

*Copies seen:* Congress, Powell.

# E.

**Egede** (Hans). Det gamle | Grønlands | Nye | Perlustration; | Eller: | En kort Beskrivelse om de gamle | Nordske Colonets Begryndelse og Under- | gang i Grønland. Gronlands Situation. | Lubt og Temperament, og dets etsige Ind- | byggeries klædedragt, Handtoering, Spise, | Sprog Ægteskab, og andre deres saavel i | Samguom som i egne Huuse nubruge- | lige Sæder først Anno 1724 forfattet af | Ilr. Hans Egede, Missionairius bed den derp | Sidst oprettede Colonie, og nu Anno 1729 | efter seet, og efter Forfarenhed nogel. | forfandret af een der paa nogen | Tiid har været 1 Grønland. |

Kiobenhavn, | Hos Hieronymus Christian Paulli. | Trykt hos Herman Henrik Rotmer, 1729.

Title 1 l. pp. 1–58, 16°.—Cap. XI. Grønlændernes Sprog og Tale, pp. 40–42.

The only copy I have seen is that in the library of the British Museum, and the only mention, that in Muller's catalogue of 1872, where a copy is priced at 10 florins (Dutch).

—— Des alten | Grönlands | Neue | Perlustration, | Oder | Eine kurtze Beschreibung | Derer | Alten Nordischen Colonien | Anfang und Untergang in Grönland, | wobey desselben Situation, Beschaffenheit der | Gewächsen, Thieren, Vögeln und Fischen, Lufft und | Temperament, des Himmels Constitution, der jetzigen Ein- | wohner Verhalten / Wohnungen / Sprache / Gestalt / Anse- | hen / Kleider-Tracht / Nahrung /Gebräuche/Haudthierung/ | Speisen / Handlung/Sprach/Ehestands-Ceremonien | und Kinder-zucht; | Nebst ihrer Religion oder Superstition | und anderer so wohl in ihren Zusammen | künfften, als auch zu Hausz gebräuchlichen Sitten. | Erstlich von Hans Egede, | Missionarius bey der [&c. five lines] / An. 1730. |

Frankfurt, bey Stocke | Leben und Schilling.

Pp. 1–47, 12°.—Cap. XI. Der Grönländer's Sprache, pp. 34–47.

*Copies seen :* British Museum, Brown.

**Egede** (H.) —Continued.

—— Det gamle | Grønlands | Nye | Perlustration, | Eller | Naturel-Historie, | Og | Beskrivelse over det gamle Grønlands Situation, | Luft, Temperament og Beskaffenhed ; | De gamle Norske Coloniers Begyndelse og Undergang der | Samme-Steds, de itzige Indbyggeres Oprindelse, Væsen, | Leve-Maade og Handtæringer, samt Hvad ellers Landet | Yder og giver af sig, saasom Dyer, Fiske og Fugle &c. med | hosføyet nyt Land-Caart og andre Kaaber-Stykker | over Landets Naturalier og Indbyggernis | Handtæringer, | Forfattet af | Hans Egede, | Forhen Missionair udi Grønland. |

Kjøbenhavn, 1741. | Trykt hos Johan Christoph Groth, boende paa Ulfeldsplatz.

6 p. ll. pp. 1–131, map, sm. 4°.—Greenland song, with interlinear translation, pp. 86–92.—Chapter XVII, pp. 94–105, is on language and customs; besides general remarks it contains a vocabulary, pp. 96–97; grammatic construction, with examples, pp. 97–103; and the creed and Lord's Prayer translated into the Greenland language, pp. 104–105. There are also scattered throughout many native terms.

*Copies seen :* Brown, Congress.

Priced by Quaritch, No. 11552, at £4 4s. and a half-calf copy, No. 28925, at £3 3s.

Sabin's Dictionary, No. 22024, titles an edition in German: Copenhagen, J. C. Grothen, 1742.

—— A | description | of | Greenland. | Shewing | The Natural History, Situation, Boundaries, | and Face of the Country ; the Nature of the | Soil; the Rise and Progress of the old Nor- | wegian Colonies; the ancient and modern | Inhabitants; their Genius and Way of Life, | and Produce of the Soil; their Plants, Beasts, | Fishes, &c. | with | A new Map of Greenland. | And | Several Copper Plates representing different Animals, | Birds and Fishes, the Greenlanders Way of Hunting | and Fishing; their Habitations, Dress, Sports | and Diversions, &c. | By Mr. Hans Egede, Missionary in that Country for twenty five Years. | Translated from the Danish. |

London: | Printed for C. Hitch in Pater-noster Row; S. Austen in | Newgate-Street; and J. Jackson near St. James's Gate. | MDCCXLV [1745].

**Egede (H.)**—Continued.

Pp. i-xvi, 2 ll. pp. 1-220, map, 12°.—Linguistics as in 1741 edition, pp. 155-159, 163-174.

*Copies seen:* British Museum, Brown, Congress, Watkinson.

A copy at the Squier sale, No. 324, brought $1.60; priced by Quaritch, No. 11653, at 10s; bought by Quaritch at the Pinart sale, No. 342, for 12 fr. and priced by him, No. 28926, at 12s.

—— Beschryving | van | Oud-Groenland, | Of eigentlyk van de zoogenaamde | Straat Davis: | Behelzende | Deszelfs Natuurlyke Historie, Standsgelegenheid, Gedaante, |* Grenscheidingen, Veld-Gewassen, Dieren, Vogelen, Visschen, enz. | Mitsgaders | Den Oirsprong en Voortgang der Aeloude | Noorweegsche Volkplantigen | in dat Gewest; | Benevens | Den Aart, Inborst, Wooningen, Levenswyze, Kleding, Spraak, | Bygelovigheid, Dichtkunst, Uitspanningen en Tydverdryven der | Hedendaagsche Inboorlingen. | Eerst in de Deensche Taal beschreven door | Mr. Hans Egede, | Van den jare 1721 tot 1736 Missionaris of Luitersch Predikant aldaar, | En nu in 't Nederduitsch overgebragt. | Met | Een Nieuwe Kaart van dat Landschap en | Aardige Printverbeeldingen verciert. |

Te Delft | By Reinier Boitet, 1746.

12 p. ll. pp. 1-192, map, sm. 4°.—Linguistics, pp. 131-134, 137-150.

*Copies seen:* Astor, Brown.

—— Description, et | Histoire Naturelle | du | Groenland, | par Mr. Eggede [sic], | Missionnaire & Evêque du Grönland. Traduite en François | par Mr. D. R. D. P. [Des Roches de Parthenay.]

à Copenhague et à Genève, | chez les Frères C. & A. Philibert. | M DCC LXIII [1763].

Pp. i-xxviii, 1-171, 12°.—Linguistics, pp. 119-122, 124-135.

*Copies seen:* Astor, British Museum, Brown, Congress, Watkinson.

Priced by Leclerc, 1878, No. 651, at 16 fr.; at the Murphy sale, No. 875, a copy brought $1.50; priced by Quaritch, No. 28928, at £1 10s.

—— Herrn Hans Egede, | Missionärs und Bischofes in Grönland, | Beschreibung | und | Natur-Geschichte | von Grönland, | übersetzet | von D. Joh. Ge. Krünitz. | [Design.] | Mit Kupfern. |

Berlin, | verlegts August Mylius. | 1763.

**Egede (H.)**—Continued.

Pp. i-xii, 1-237, maps, 8°.—Linguistics, pp. 173-176, 180-193.

*Copies seen:* British Museum, Congress.

—— A | Description of Greenland. | By Hans Egede, | who was a missionary in that country | for | twenty-five years. | A new edition. | With an | Historical Introduction and a life of the author. | Illustrated | with a map of Greenland, and numerous engravings on wood. | [Picture.] |

London : | Printed for T. and J. Allman, / Princes Street, Hanover Square; W. H. Reid, Charing Cross; and Baldwin, Cradock, and Joy, | Paternoster Row. | 1818.

Pp. i-cxviii, 1-225, map, 8°.—Linguistics, pp. 158-161, 165-178.

*Copies seen:* Astor, Boston Athenæum, British Museum

At the Field sale, catalogue No. 614, a copy brought $2; at the Murphy sale, No. 876, $3. Priced by Quaritch, No. 28927, at 6s.

—— [Elementa fidei Christianae, in qvibus in Grönlandorum vernacula proponuntur. 1) Ordo Salutis, 2) Catechismus Lutheri, 3) Praetinnculae qvædam et Psalmi, item 4) Formula baptizandi Infantes & Adultos.

Hafn. 1742.]

8°. Title from Giessing's Nye Samling af Danske- Norske- og Islandske- Jubel-Lærere, vol. 1, p. 68, Kiöbenhavn, 1779.

—— See **Kragh** (P.).

Hans Egede was born Jan. 31, 1686, at Trondenaes, Norway, where his father was sheriff. He was missionary in Greenland for 15 years, beginning in 1721. In 1736 he returned to Copenhagen, where for several years he instructed missionary candidates in the language of Greenland. According to Reichelt he began the translation into Eskimo of the New Testament, a work finished by his son; and according to Bagster, the elder Egede translated the Psalms and the Epistles of Paul. In 1740 he was made bishop. He died at Stub bekjöbing, Denmark, in 1758.

"The language gave Mr. [Hans] Egede infinite trouble; * * * his children learned it more easily. With their assistance he proceeded so far as to begin a Greenlandic grammar and to translate some Sunday lessons out of the gospels, together with a few short questions and illustrations. * * * Egede wrote down some of these sentiments in a Greenland dialogue between Pok and his countrymen, and another between a missionary and an angekok, at the end of his Greenland grammar."—*Cranz.*

See **Pok.**

**28** BIBLIOGRAPHY OF THE

**Egede (Paul).** Evangolium | Okausek tussarnersok | Gub Niarnanik Innuugortomik, | okausianiglo, Usornartulcniglo, tokomel- | lo umarmelo, Killaliarmello, Innuin | aunauniartlugit, aggerromartomiglo, tokorsnt tomasa umartitsar- tortlugit. | Karalit okansiet attuattlugo aglokpaka | Paul Egede. | Kongib Iglorperksoarnc, Kiobenhavuime, | 1744.

*Literal translation:* The Gospel | the word pleasant-to-hoar | concorning God's his Son become-a-man, | and his word, and his miracles, and his death | and his rosurrection, and his ascent to Heaven, Men | to strive to save them, and his coming [again ?], the dead thus to bring them to life. | Greenlanders the word that they may read it I wrote these things | Paul Egede. | At the King's city [great collection of houses], at Copenhagen, | 1744.

4 p. ll. pp. 1-392, 8°. The Four Gospels in the Eskimo language of Greenland: Matthew, pp. 3-113; Mark, pp. 113-182; Luke, pp. 182-302; John, pp. 302-392.

*Copies seen:* British Museum.

Priced by Trübner, 1856, No. 662, at 5s. At the Pinart sale a copy, No. 354, brought 6 fr.

Nyerup's Litteraturlexicon gives the above title in brief, and says the work was subsequently issued in 1758, adding the Wanderings of the Apostles. Bagster's Bible of Every Land mentions this later edition also. The latter authority says an edition of the Acts as well as of the Gospels was issued in 1758.

—— Dictiona- | rium | Grönlandico- | Danico- | Latinum, | Complectens | Primitiva cum suis Derivatis, | qvibus | interjectae sunt voces primariae | ò | Kirendo Angekkutorum, | adornatnm | a | Paulo Egede. | Hafniae, | Anno MDCCL [1750]. Snmptibus & typis Orphan. Regii, | Excudit Gotm. Frid. Kisel, Orphanotroph. Reg. Typogr.

8 p. ll. pp. 1-312, 12°.

*Copies seen:* Astor, British Museum, Brown, Trumbull.

Priced by Leclerc, 1878, No. 2224, at 80 fr.; by Quaritch, No. 12576, at 15s. At the Brinley sale, a copy, No. 5634, brought $14. Priced by Trübner, in 1882, at 18s. At the Pinart sale, No. 344, it brought 13 fr.; at the Murphy sale, No. 878, $5. Priced by Quaritch, No. 30048, at 15s.

[——] Catechismus | Mingnek | D. M. Lutherim | Aglega | Innusninuut Innungnullo Gum | Okausianik illisimaugangitsut, | suna ope- | rekullugo, kannorlo innukullugit Tokorsub kingornano Killang- | mut pekkullugit. | [Design.] |

**Egede (P.)—Continued.**

Kiöbenhavn, | Illiarsuin Igloenne uakittet | Nakittairsomit Gottman Friderich Kisel. | 1756.

*Literal translation:* Catechism | the smaller | D.[octor] M.[artin] Luther's | his writing | to the young and people of God's | his word ignorant, | what to beliove, and how to live death after it to Heaven to attain. | At Copenhagen, | at the orphans' their house printed | from the printer Gottman Friderich Kisel.

Pp. 1-160, 12°. Luther's Catechism, with a selection of hymns, translated into the language of Greenland. Introduction signed by Paul Egede. Catechism, pp. 5-56; Hymns, pp. 57-148; Index, pp. 149-160.

*Copies seen:* Yale.

A copy at the Brinley sale, No. 5636, brought $19.

—— Grammatica | Gronlandica | Danico-Latina, | Edita | a | Paulo Egede. | Havniae | Sumptibus & typis Orphantrophii Regii | Excudit Gottman, Frid. Kisel. An. 1760.

8 p. ll. pp. 1-236, 12°.

*Copies seen:* British Museum, Brown, Watkinson.

Priced by Leclerc, 1878, No. 2225, at 50 fr. Brought at the Brinley sale, No. 5635, $8; at the Murphy sale, No. 877, $5.

—— Testamente | Nutak, | eller | Det Nye | Testamente, | oversat | i det | Grönlandske Sprog, | med | Forklaringer, Paralleler | og udförlige Summarier, | af | Paul Egede, | Professor Theol. Nat. ved Kiöbenhavns | Universitet, Inspector og Proost for | den Grönl. Mission, og Præst ved det | Kongel. Alm. Hospital i Kiöbenhavn. | Kiöbenhavn, | Trykt paa Missionens Bekostning, | af Gerhard Giese Salikath, | 1766.

12 p. ll. pp. 1-1000, 4 ll. 12°. New Testament translated into the Greenland language, with commentaries, parallels, and extensive summaries.

*Copies seen:* British Museum, Congress.

Priced by Leclerc, 1878, No. 2233, at 45 fr.; at the Pinart sale, No. 886, sold to Quaritch for 8 fr.

—— Ajokoersoirsun Atuagekseit Nalegbingue Gröndlandmc. Ritual over Kirke-Forretningerne ved den Danske Mission paa Grönland. Kiöbenhavn, H. Ch. Schröder. 1783. *

*Literal translation:* Teachers' their handbook in the church in Greenland.

63 pp. 8°, in Greenland and Danish. Ecclesiastical Ritual for the use of the Danish Missions in Greenland, translated and pub-

**Egede (P.)—Continued.**

lished by Egede (?). It is a volume heretofore almost unknown. Having been printed for distribution in Greenland, only a very few copies could have remained in Europe.—*Leclerc.*

Nyerup also gives this title in brief, under Paul Egede.

For later edition see Fabricius (O.), Arkik-sutiksak.

—— [Thomas a Kempis de imitatione Christi, overs. paa Grønl. Kiobenhavnime, 1787.] *

Title from Nyerup's Dansk-Norsk Litteraturlexicon, vol. 1, p. 145.

—— Kristusimik | Mallingnaursut | pivdlugit | Thomasib å Kempisib aglega. | Kaladliunokauzeennut nuktersimarsok Pelesiunermit | Paviamit Egedemit, | Illegeeguerublo ussoruartorsub "Det Danske Mis- | sions Selskabimik" taīutiglub ama | nakittarkomago, | narkingniarkiksarallóara | A. F. Honnib. | Kjöbenhavnime. Illiårsuïn igloœ'nne nakittarsimarsok | 1824. | C. F. Skubartimit.

*Literal translation:* Christ | the imitating concerning | Thomas à Kempis' his writing. | Greenlanders' into their speech translated | by Bishop | Paul Egede, | and when the society honorable by [the name of] "Det Danske Mis- | sions Selskab" called again | printed it, ' did his best to try to revise it | A. F. Honni. | At Copenhagen. | At the orphans' their house [Waisenhaus] printed 1824. | From C. F. Schubart.

6 p. ll. pp. 1-108, 16°. Imitation of Christ, in the Eskimo language of Greenland.

*Copies seen:* Congress.

[——] Ivngerutit | tuksiutidlo, Kalaliunnut Opertuunnut, Attuægeksæt. | [Printer's mark.] |

Kiobenhavnime, | Illiarsuin Igloœnne nakittarsimauci | Hans. Christoph. Schröderib, | 1788.

*Literal translation:* Psalms | and prayers, | for Greenlanders believing | a handbook. | At Copenhagen, | At the orphans' their house [Waisenhaus] printed them | Hans. Christoph. Schroder, | 1788.

Title 1 l. preface, signed Paul Egede and dated Kiöbenhavn, d. I May 1761, 1 l. Psalms, entirely in Eskimo, pp. 5-373; Förste Register over Psalme-Samlingerne, &c. pp. 374-375; Andet Register over Psalmerne i Alphabetik Order, &c. pp. 376-384; Prayers, entirely in Eskimo, pp. 385-526; index, 1 l. 16°.

*Copies seen:* British Museum.
For edition of 1801, see Fabricius (O.).

—— Efterretuinger om Grønland, | uddragne | af en Journal | holden | fra 1721 til 1788 | af | Paul Egede. |

**Egede (P.)—Continued.**

Kiøbenhavn, | trykt i det kougelige Vaisenhuses Bogtrykkerio | af Hans Christopher Schrøder. | [1789 ?]

Portrait of Bishop Paul Egedo 1 l. title verso blank and 5 other p. ll. pp. 1-284, plates and map, 12°.—Det almindelige Sprog [a short list of Eskimo words with Danish signification, and a corresponding column of Danish meanings headed "Angekkokernes"], pp. 97-98.—Names of the constellations in Eskimo, pp. 104-106.—Names of the various kinds of ice, snow, hail, the verbs *to run* and *to die,* pp. 227-228.
*Copies seen:* British Museum, Congress.

—— Nachrichten | von Grönland. | Aus einem Tagebuche, | geführt | von 1721 bis 1788 | vom | Bischof | Paul Egede. | Aus dem Dänischen. | Mit Kupfern. | Kopenhagen, 1790. | Bey Christian Gottlob Prost, | privilegirten Universitätsbuchhändler.

Portrait of Bishop Paul Egede 1 l. pp. i-xii, 13-333, 3 pp. n. n. plates and maps, 12°.—Linguistics as in Danish edition, pp. 122-123, 130-132, 269-270.
*Copies seen:* British Museum.

Paul Egede, a son of Bishop Hans Egede, was born in Norway, October 9, 1708. He went with his father to Greenland, and, having learned the language in a few years, he went to Copenhagen in 1728 to continue his studies. In 1734 he went to Greenland as an ordained missionary. He returned in 1741 and became parson at Vartov in Copenhagen. In 1761 he obtained the degree of professor of natural theology, and was made inspector of the Greenland mission. In 1779 he became bishop. He died in 1789.

**Egede (Peter).** [Psalms in the Greenland language.]

According to Nyerup's Dansk-Norsk Litteraturlexicon, vol. 1, p. 145, a portion of the psalms contained in Egede (Paul), Catechismus, pp. 140-146, were translated by Peter Egede (a nephew of Hans Egede, who was born in Norway and was the first missionary ordained in Greenland. He died in 1789.

**Ekógmut Vocabulary.** See Dall (W. H.).

**Elementa** Fidei Christianae. See **Egede** (H.).

**Elementarbog** i Eskimoernes Sprog. See **Janssen** (C. E.).

[**Elsner** (A. F.).] Geographie | oder | Beschreibung der Länder der Erde. | · Stolpen | Buchdruckerei von Gustav Winter. | 1880.

*Second title:* Geografi | ubvalo | Nunaksûb nunangita okautlgijauuiugit. |
Stolpeneme | G. Winterib nenilauktangit | 1880.

**Elsner (A. F.)**—Continued.

German title verso of first l. recto blank, Eskimo title recto of second l. verso blank, index, pp. v-vi, proface, signed by A. F. Elsner, Hoffenthal, 1878, pp. vii-viii; text, entirely in the Eskimo language of Labrador, pp. 1-84, 12°.

*Copies seen:* Pilling, Powell.

My copy cost 1 M. 30 pf.

**English-Aleutian Vocabulary.** See **Buynitzky (S. N.).**

**Epistles.** The Epistles | of the | Apostles, | translated into the | Esquimaux Language, | by the Missionaries | of the Protestant Church | of | the United Brethren | in | Labrador. | Printed for the British and Foreign Bible | Society; | For the Use of the Christian Esquimaux in the Mission Settlements of the United Brethren at Nain, Okkak, and Hopedale, | on the Coast of Labrador. |

London: | W. M. M'Dowall, Printer, Pemberton Row, Gough Square, | Fleet Street. | 1819.

Title verso blank 1 l. pp. 1-452, 16°. Entirely in the Eskimo of Labrador.

*Copies seen:* British and Foreign Bible Society.

**Erdmann** (Friedrich). Eskimoisches Wörterbuch, | gesammelt | von den Missionaren | in | Labrador, | revidirt und herausgegeben | von | Friedrich Erdmann. |

Budissin, | gedruckt bei Ernst Moritz Monse. | 1864.

Title verso blank 1 l. preface 1 l. pp. 1-360, double columns, 8°. Eskimo-German throughout.

Dr. Rink, in furnishing me a brief title of this work, though not giving the collation, says: "In two parts, Eskimo-German and German-Eskimo." It may be there is a German-Eskimo counterpart to the work; if so, I have seen no copy of it.

*Copies seen:* Brinton, Eames, Pilling, Powell, Watkinson, Yale.

Priced by Trübner in 1882 at 8s. 6d; by Koehler (catalogue 440), No. 954, 7 M. 50 pf. My copy, bought in 1886 of the Unitäts-Buchhandlung, Gnadau, Saxony, cost 5 M. 40 pf.

**[——] Testamentetotak;** | Josuab aglanginit, Esterib | aglaugit tikkilugit. | Printed for | The British and Foreign Bible Society in London, | for the use of the Moravian Mission in Labrador. |

Stolpen: | Gustav Winterib Nêuerlauktaugit. | 1869.

**Erdmann** (F.) — Continued.

*Literal translation:* Old Testament; | from Joshua's his book, Esther's | her book coming to. | Stolpen: | Gustav Winter's his printings. 2 p. ll. pp. 1-527, 8°. Joshua to Esther in the language of Labrador.

*Copies seen:* British and Foreign Bible Society, Pilling, Powell.

My copy, bought of first hands and in cheap binding, cost 8 M.

**[——]** Testamentetokak | Hiobib aglangit, | Salomoblo | Imgerusersoauga tikkilugit. | Printed for | The British and Foreign Bible Society in London, | for the use of the Moravian Mission in Labrador. |

Stolpen: | Gustav Winterib Nêuerlauktaugit. | 1871.

*Literal translation:* Old Testament | Job's his book, | and Solomon's | his great songs coming to. | Stolpen: | Gustav Winter's his printings.

2 p. ll. pp. 1-274, 8°. Job to Song of Solomon.

*Copies seen:* British and Foreign Bible Society, Church Missionary Society, Pilling, Powell.

My copy cost 4 M.

These two works are attributed to Erdmann on the authority of Dr. Rink, who informs me that this author also rewrote the translation of Proverbs and Psalms, added many notes and emendations to the new edition of the five books of Moses and to the New Testament, and assisted the Unitas Fratrum generally in their literary labors.

**[——] Ajokertutsit** | pijarialiksuit tellimat. | I. Gûdib perkojanginik hailiginik telli- | maujortuuik. | II. Kristusemiut okperijaksanginik pinga-|sunik. | III. Nâlekab tuksiarutauukojanganik. | IV. Baptijumik hailiginik. | V. Komunionimik hailigimik. |

Stolpen | Gustav Winterib nêuilauktangit | 1883.

*Literal translation:* Instructions | very needful five. | I. About God's his commandments holy ten. | II. About the Christians' their subjects of belief three. | III. About the Lord's his prayer. | IV. About baptism holy. | V. About communion holy. | Stolpen | Gustav Winter's his printings.

Catechism in the Eskimo language of Labrador. Title verso preface 1 l. text, entirely in the language of Labrador, pp. 3-26, 16°. Pp. 25-26 contain the multiplication table.

In the preface it is stated that the translations are by Erdmann, and that an edition of the catechism, not so full as the present, appeared in 1865.

*Copies seen:* Pilling, Powell.

My copy cost 35 pf.

**Erdmann** (F.)—Continued.

Friedrich Erdmann was born at Iserlohn, Prussia, February 25, 1810, and died at Königsfeld September 15, 1873. He lived in Labrador 38 years, 1834-1872.

**erĭnĭugkat** nûtigdlit | 105, | tamalâuik imagdlit, | ilĭuiarûngno igdlunilo | atortŋgssat. | Druck von Gustav Winter in Stolpen. | 1876.

*Literal translation:* Songs having-notes | 105, | variously having contents, | in schools and in houses | things-to-be-used.

Title verso blank 1 l. text pp. 1-157, index pp. 158-160, 16°. Song book, with music, for school and private use, entirely in the language of Greenland.

*Copies seen:* Pilling, Powell.

My copy, bought of the Unitäts-Buchhandlung, Gnadau, Saxony, cost 1 M. 50 pf.

**Erkærsautiksæt** udlut. See **Kragh** (P.).

**Erkarsàutigirseksæt** sillársoarmik. See **Kragh** (P.).

**Erman** (Georg Adolph). Ethnographische Wahrnehmungen und Erfahrungen an den Küsten des Berings-Meeres von A. Erman.

In Zeitschrift für Ethnologie, vol. 2 (1870), pp. 295-307, 309-393; vol. 3 (1871), pp. 149-175, 205-219, Berlin [n. d.], 8°.

Numerals of the Aleuten, Kadjaker Insulaner, Namolli, Kángjulit, and Ttynai oder Kenaïza, vol. 3, p. 216.

**Erslew** (Thomas Hansen). Almindeligt | Forfatter-Lexicon | for | Kongeriget Danmark med tilhørende Bilande, | fra 1814 til 1840, | eller | Forteguelse | over | de sammesteds fødte Forfattere og Forfatterinder, som levede ved Begyndelsen af Aaret 1814, eller siden ere fødte, med Anførelse af deres | vigtigste Levnets-Omstaendigheder og af deres trykte Arbejder; | samt over | de i Hertugdømmerne og i Udlandet fødte Forfattere, som i bemeldte | Tidsrum have opholdt sig i Danmark og der udgivet Skrifter. | Ved | Thomas Hansen Erslew. | Første [-Tredie] Bind. | A — J [-S — Ø]. |

Kjøbenhavn. | Forlagsforeningens Forlag. | Trykt i Bianco Lunos Bogtrykkeri. | 1843 [-1853].

3 vols. 8°. General author's dictionary for the kingdom of Denmark and adjacent countries from 1814 to 1840; it contains biographies of authors who have written in the Eskimo and lists of their works.

*Copies seen:* Congress.

**Eskimaux** and English Vocabulary. See **Washington** (J.).

Eskimo:

| | |
|---|---|
| Bible, John (in part). | See Church. |
| Grammatic comments. | Adelung (J. C.) |
| | and Vater (J. S.), |
| | Dall (W. H.), |
| | Parry (W. E.), |
| | Richardson (J.), |
| | Shea (J. G.). |
| Grammatic treatise. | Adam (L.), |
| | Bancroft (H. H.), |
| | Hayes (I. I.). |
| Letters V and L. | Gallatin (A.). |
| Lord's Prayer. | Atkinson (C.), |
| | Hall (C. F.), |
| | Hössler (—). |
| Numerals. | Haldeman (S. S.), · |
| | Latham (R. G.), |
| | Pott (A. F.), |
| | Sutherland (P. C.). |
| Prayers. | Crespieul (F.X.). |
| Primer. | Abecedarium, |
| | Bompas (W. C.). |
| Remarks. | Jefferys (T.), |
| | Morillot (—), |
| | Nouvelle, |
| | Rosse (I. C.), |
| | Scherer (J. B.), |
| | Schott (W.), |
| | Seeman (B.). |
| Vocabulary. | Adelung (J. C.) and Vater (J. S.), |
| | Beechey (F.W.), |
| | Bryant (—), |
| | Buschmann (J. C. E.), |
| | Chappell (E.), |
| | Dobbs (A.), |
| | Herzog (W.), |
| | Indrenius(A.A.), |
| | Jóhan (L. F.), |
| | Kahn (P.), |
| | Latham (R. G.), |
| | Long (J.), |
| | M'Keevor (T.), |
| | Murdoch (J.), |
| | Nelson (E. W.), |
| | Newton (A.), |
| | Parry (W. E.), |
| | Petroff (I.), |
| | Rand (J.), |
| | Ross (J.), |
| | Scherer (J. B.), |
| | Schubert (—), |
| | Tomlin (J.), |
| | Washington (J.). |
| Words. | Balbi (A.), |
| | Buschmann (J. C. E.), |
| | Duncan (D.), |

**Eskimo**—Continued.

**Words.**          See **Hooper** (W. H.),
                     Latham (R. G.),
                     Pinart (A. L.),
                     Yankiewitch
                     (T.).

**Eskimoisches** Wörterbuch.  See **Erdmann** (F.).

**Esquisse** d'une Grammaire * * * Aléoute.
See **Henry** (V.).

**Ethics, Greenland.** See **Steenholdt** (W. F.).

**Evangelium** Okansok. See **Egede** (Paul).

**Everette** (Willis Eugene). Comparative vocabulary of the Chilcat or Ko-
losh with the Yukon River Eskimo.  *
Manuscript, 17 pp. folio.

—— Comparative vocabulary of the Chil-
cat, the Yukon River Indian, and the
Yukon River Eskimo.              *
Manuscript, 10 pp. folio.

**Everette** (W. E.)—Continued.

—— Comparative vocabulary of the St.
Michael's and the Aliyut or Aleut or
Onnalaska Eskimo.                *
Manuscript, 7 pp. folio.

—— Comparative vocabulary of the St.
Michael's and the Yukon River Eski-
mo.                              *
Manuscript, 7 pp. folio.

—— Comparative vocabulary of the Yukon River Eskimo, St. Michael's and
Arctic Ocean Eskimo, and the Aleut or
Onnalaska Eskimo.                *
Manuscript, 15 pp. folio.
The five vocabularies above, comprising 250
words each, are in the possession of Mr. Everette, who has furnished me the above titles, the
material having been collected during 1884-'85.

**Expositio** catechismi grönlaudici. See
**Thorhallesen** (E.).

# F.

**Fabricius** (Otho). Forsog | til | en for-
bedret | Grønlandsk Grammatica | ved
| Otho Fabricius, | Sognepræst ved Vor
Frelseres Kirke paa Christianshavn. |
Kiobenhavn, 1791. | Trykt udi det
Kongelige Vaysenhuses Bogtrykkerie,
| af Carl Frederich Schubart.
Title verso blank 1 l. pp. iii–viii, 1–322, 4
folding ll. "Om Suffixa Verborum," 12°. Gram-
mar of the language of Greenland.
Copies seen : Quaritch.
Priced by Trübner, in 1856, No. 661, at 6s.;
by Quaritch, No. 12577, at £1 10s.; No. 30050,
at £1 5s.
A later edition as follows :

—— Forsøg | til | en forbedret | Grøn-
landsk Grammatica | ved | Otho Fabri-
cius, | Sognepræst ved Vor Frelseres
Kirke paa Christianshavn. | Andet Op-
lag. |
Kiôbenhavn, 1801. | Trykt udi det
Kongelige Vaysenhuses Bogtrykkerie,
| af C. F. Schubart.
Pp. i–viii, 9–388, 12°.
Copies seen : Astor, Congress, Trumbull.
Priced by Leclerc, 1878, No. 2227, at 40 fr.; by
Quaritch, No. 12578, at 18s. Sold at the Brinley
sale, No. 5637, for $14; at the Pinart sale, No.
361, to Leclerc for 3 fr. Priced by Trübner, in
1882 (p. 53), at £1 1s.,and by Quaritch, No. 30031,
at 12s. and 14s.

[——] Testamente | Nutak | Kaladlin
okauzeennut nuktersimarsok, nar'kiu-
tingoæn- | niglo suknîarsimarsok. |
Kiôbenhavnime, | Illiarsuîn igloænne

**Fabricius** (O.)—Continued.
piugajucksânik    nakittarsimarsok |
1799. | C. F. Shubartimit.
Literal translation : Testament | New |
Greenlanders' into their speech | fully trans-
lated, and with explanations thoroughly ex-
pounded. | At Copenhagen, | at the orphans'
their house [Waisenhaus] a third time printed |
1799. | From C. F. Schubart.
Pp. i–viii, 9–1072, 16°. New Testament in
the Eskimo language of Greenland. Preface
signed Otho Fabricius and dated Kiöbenhav-
nime, 1794. Matthew, pp. 1–150; Mark, 151–
231; Luke, 232–369; John, 370–472; Acts, 473–
602; Epistles, &c. 603–1070; index, 1071–1072.
Copies seen : Brown, Congress, Watkinson.
Priced in Trübner's catalogue, 1856, No. 663,
at 7s. 6d. and by Leclerc, 1878, No. 2234, at 30 fr.
Erslew's Forfatter-Lexikon mentions an edition of 1794.

[——] Testamente | Nutak | Kaladlin
okauzeennut nuktersimarsok, nar'kiu-
tingoæn- | niglo sukuîarsimarsok. |
Kiöbenhavnime, | Illiârsuîn igloænne
sissamcksâuik nakkitarsimarsok | 1827
| C. F. Skubartimit.
Literal translation of imprint : At Copen-
hagen, | at the orphans' their house [Waisen-
haus] a fourth time printed | 1827 | From C.
F. Schubart.
Pp. i–viii, 9–1072, 12°. New Testament in
the Eskimo language of Greenland. Revised
by N. G. Wolf.
Copies seen : British Museum, Powell, Trumbull, Watkinson.
Priced by Quaritch, Nos. 12581 and 30056, at
7s. 6d.

**Fabricius (O.) — Continued.**

[——] Ivugerutit | Tuksintidlo, | Kaladlinnut Opertunnut. | Attuægeksæt. | Kiobenhavnime. | Illiarsuïu igloænune aipoksánik nakittarsimarsut | C. F. Skubartimit. | 1801.

*Literal translation:* Psalms | and prayers, | for Greenlanders believing. | A handbook. | At Copenhagen. | At the orphans' their house [Waisenhaus] a second time printed | From C. F. Schubart.

Pp. 1-528, sm. 12°. Psalms in meter. Prayers, pp. 386-528. Preface signed Otto Fabricius, 11 Jun., 1800.

*Copies seen:* British Museum, Harvard, Watkinson.

Priced by Trübner, 1856, No. 664, at 5s.; by Leclerc, 1878, No. 2228 at 25 fr.

For an edition of 1788 see **Egede** (Paul), Ivugerutit.

—— Den | Grønlandske Ordbog, | forbedret og forøget, | udgivet | ved | Otho Fabricius, | Sognepræst ved vor Frelsers Kirke paa Christianshavn. | Kjobenhavn, 1804. | Trykt i det Kongel. Vaisenhuses Bogtrykkerie | af Carl Frid. Schubart.

Pp. i-viii, 1-795, 12°. Greenland-Danish, pp. 1-544; Register, in Danish, pp. 545-795.

*Copies seen:* Astor, Bancroft, Boston Athenæum, British Museum, Congress, Trumbull, Watkinson.

Priced by Leclerc, 1878, No. 2226, at 40 fr.; by Quaritch, No. 12579, at £1 10s. Bought at the Brinley sale, No. 5638, for $20; at the Pinart sale, No. 360, by Quaritch, for 15 fr. Priced by Trübner, 1882 (p. 53), at £1 16s., and by Quaritch, No. 30052, at £1.

—— Arkiksutiksak | Pellesinnut Ajokærsóïrsunnudlo, | Kaunong-illivdlutik pirsaromarput Nâlegiartorbingne, Kâladlit Nunäénne. | Ritual | over | Kirke-Forretningerne | ved | den Danske Mission i Grønland. |

Omarbeldet og forøget | ved | Otho Fabricius, | og 2den gang trykt i det Kongelige Waysenhuses Bog- | trykkerie i Kiøbenhavn | 1819 | af Carl Friedrich Schubart.

*Literal translation:* Materials-for-rules | for priests and teachers, | how-bearing-themselves they shall act | at the time for church-going, | the Greenlanders in their country. |

Pp. 1-87, 16°, alternate pp. Eskimo and Danish. Ritual prepared for the Danish missions in Greenland.

*Copies seen:* British Museum, Harvard.

For earlier edition see **Egede** (Paul), Ajokœrsoirsun.

ESK——3

**Fabricius (O.) — Continued.**

—— Okalluktuæt Opernartut | Tersäuko | Bibelimit | Testamentitokamidlo Testamentitâmidlo | Ottob Fabriciusib | Pellesiûnernb | Kennerðj attuaegeksäukudlugit Iunungnut | koïsimarsunnut. | Kiöbenhavnime | Illiârsuïn igloæunne nakkittarsimarsut. | 1820. | C. F. Skubartimit.

*Literal translation:* Narratives true | here are | from the Bible | both from the Old Testament and the New Testament | of Otho Fabricius | the selections he wishing-to-give-means-of-reading to people | christened. | At Copenhagen | At the orphans' their house [Waisenhaus] printed. | 1821. | From C. F. Schubart.

Pp. 1-256, 16°, in the language of Greenland.

*Copies seen:* British Museum, Congress.

—— Testamentitokamit | Mosesim aglegðj | siurdleet. | Kaladliu okauzeennut . | nuktersimarsut | narkiutingoæuniglo sukkuïarsimarsut | Pellesiûnermit | Ottomit Fabriciusimit, | Attuægeksäukudlugit innungnut koïsimarsunnut. | Kiöbenhavnime, | Illiârsuïn igloænne nakkittarsimarsut. | 1822. | C. F. Skubartimit.

*Literal translation:* From the Old Testament | Moses' his book | the first. | Greenlanders into their speech | fully-translated | and with explanations thoroughly-expounded | by Bishop | Otho Fabricius, | he wishing-to-give-means-of-reading to people christened. | At Copenhagen, | at the orphans' their house [Waisenhaus] printed. | 1822. | From C. F. Schubart.

Pp. 1-202, 16°. Genesis in the Eskimo language of Greenland. The preface is signed by N. G. Wolf, who perhaps revised it.

*Copies seen:* Astor, British Museum, Congress, Powell, Trumbull, Watkinson.

—— Bibelingoak | Mordläinnut | imaloneet : | Gudiin Okauzeesaillèjt kennikkæt, | näïtsuunik kajumiksarneruik illakartut, | merdlertunnut nalektartunnut. | Kablunäén okauzeenno agleksimagalloak, | mâua kaladlin okauzeennut nuktersimarsok | Pellesiûnermit | Ottomit Fabriciusimit. | Kiöbenhavnime, | Illiarsüin igloæunne nakkitarsimarsok | 1822. | C. F. Skubartimit.

*Literal translation:* The little Bible | for children | namely: | God's his-words-some-of-them selected, | with short exhortations joined, | for

**Fabricius (O.)** — Continued.

children obedient. White man's in their speech originally-written-indeed-but, now Greenlanders into their speech translated by | Bishop | Otho Fabricius. | At Copenhagen, | at the orphans their house [Waisenhaus] printed | 1822. | From C. F. Schubart.

Pp. 1-68, 16°. Bible teachings for children in the language of Greenland.

*Copies seen:* Congress.

[——] Bibelingoak | innalônêt: | Gudim okãusêssa illúît keñersimassut | nætunigdlo okãukiksârultingoañik. | illakardluttik.

Havniame nakittarsimassok | 1849. | J. G. Salomonimit.

*Literal translation:* The little Bible | namely: | God's his words some-of-them selected | and with short little-means-of-exhorting | joined. | At Copenhagen printed | 1849. | From J. G. Salomon.

Pp. 1-59, 1 l. 16°. The Small Bible in the Eskimo language of Greenland.

*Copies seen:* Harvard.

—— See **Ajokærsutit.**

According to Erslew, Fabricius published, with amendments, in 8°, at Copenhagen, editions of the Greenland psalm-book, with appendix of prayers, and the history of Christ's passion, in 1788 [see **Egede (Paul)**]; and the explanation of the Greenland catechism, with addition of the order of salvation, in 1790.

Fabricius was born March 6, 1744, at Rudkjobing, Langeland, where his father, Hans Fabricius, was minister and dean of the district of Norre. After receiving private instruction he was sent to the university in 1762; underwent his final examination in 1768, and in March of the same year was sent as ordained missionary to the colony of Frederikshaab, in Greenland, where he remained till 1773; in 1774 he became minister at Draugedal and Torredal, in the bishopric of Aggershus; in 1779, at Hodro and Skiellerup, in the same bishopric; in 1781, at Rüse, on the island of Aero; in 1783 he was made parson at the orphanage in Copenhagen, and teacher of the Greenland language; in 1789, parson of Our Saviour's Church at Christianshavn; in the same year he was chosen director of the Society of Natural History of Copenhagen; in 1803 he received the title of professor of theology and the rank of professor at the University of Copenhagen; in 1813 he became a member of the Mission College as far as it related to the affairs of the Greenland mission; in 1815 he became Knight of the Danebroge; on March 23, 1818, he celebrated the fifty years' jubilee of his office, and on the same day received the title and rank of bishop, together with the honorary diploma of doctor of theology. He died May 20, 1822.

**Fasting (Ludvig).** Sendebrev til alle Grönlænderne i Norden (Aglekkæt neksiutæt Kaladlinnut tamannut anangnar minunnut).

Kjöbenhavn, Fabritius de Tengnagels, 1838. *

*Literal translation:* Epistle sent to Greenlanders all dwellers-in-the-north.

23 pp. 2 ll. 8°, in Danish and Greenland. Title from Leclerc's Supplement, No. 2763, where it is priced at 6 fr.

**Fauvel-Gouraud (Francis).** Practical | Cosmophonography; | a System of Writing and Printing all | the Principal Languages, with their exact Pronunciation, | by means of an original | Universal Phonetic Alphabet, | Based upon Philological Principles, and representing Analogically all the Component Elements of the Human | Voice, as they occur in | Different Tongues and Dialects; | and applicable to daily use in all the branches of business and learning; | Illustrated by Numerous Plates, | explanatory of the | Calligraphic, Steno - Phonographic, and Typo-Phonographic | Adaptations of the System; | with specimens of | The Lord's Prayer, | in One Hundred Languages: | to which is prefixed, | a General Introduction, | elucidating the origin and progress of language, writing, stenography, phonography, | etc., etc., etc. | By | Francis Fauvel-Gouraud, D. E. S. | of the Royal University of France. |

New York: | J. S. Redfield, Clinton Hall. | 1850.

1 p. l. pp. 1-186, 1 l. plates 1-21, A-T, 8°.— The Lord's Prayer in the Greenland (from ed. London, 1822), plate 14, No. 57; in the Esquimaux of Labrador (London, 1813), plate 14, No. 58.

*Copies seen:* Astor, British Museum.

**Fisher (William James).** Words, phrases, and sentences in the language of the Ugashakmüt Indians of Ugashak River, Bristol Bay, Alaska, and of the Kägeägemüt Indians, of Kaguiak-Kadiak Island, Alaska.

Manuscript, pp. 77-228, 10 ll. 4°. In the library of the Bureau of Ethnology. Recorded in a copy of Powell's Introduction to the Study of Indian Languages, 2d edition, incomplete. The two dialects are in parallel columns.

**Formula** babtizandi Infantes & Adultos. See **Egede** (H.).

**Forsøg** til en forbedret Grønlandsk Grammatica. See **Fabricius** (O.).

**Forster** (Johann Georg Adam). Geschichte der Reisen, | die seit Cook | an der | Nordwest- und Nordost-Küste | von Amerika | und in dem | nördlichsten Amerika selbst | von | Meares, Dixon, Portlock, Coxe, Long u. a. M. | unternommen worden sind. | Mit vielen Karten und Kupfern. | Aus dem Englischen, | mit Zuziehung aller anderweitigen Hülfsquellen, ausgearbeitet | von | Georg Forster. | Erster[-Dritter] Band. |

Berlin, 1791. | In der Vossischen Buchhandlung.

3 vols.: pp. i-ix, 1 l. pp. 1-130, 1-302; 5 p. ll. pp. i-xxii, 1-314; i-xv, i-iii, 1-74, 1-380, 4°.— Comparative vocabulary, and numerals 1-10, of the languages of Prince William's Sound and Cook's River, Norfolk Sound, and King George's Sound (from Portlock and Dixon), vol. 2, pp. 216-217.—Vocabulary in language of Prince William's Sound (from Portlock), vol. 3, pp. 119-121.—Vocabulary of the language of the Northwest Coast of America (from Portlock), vol. 3, p. 145.

*Copies seen:* Astor, British Museum.

Brought at the Fischer sale, No. 1071, 2s.

**Pour.** The | Four Books of Moses, | Exodus to Deuteronomy, | translated into the | Esquimaux Language : | by | the Missionaries | of the | Unitas Fratrum, or, United Brethren. | Printed for the use of the Mission, | by | The British and Foreign Bible Society. |

London : | W. M'Dowall, Printer, Pemberton Row, Gough Square. | 1811.

Title 1 l. pp. 167-698, 16°, in the language of Labrador.

*Copies seen:* British and Foreign Bible Society.

Genesis, pp. 1-166, issued with the title Mosesib Aglangita ; the Pentateuch, pp. 1-698, with the title Mosesil Aglangit.

**Fox Channel, Vocabulary.** See Hall (C. F.).

**Franklin** (*Capt.* John). Narrative of a journey | to the shores of | the Polar Sea, | in the years | 1819, 20, 21, and 22. | By | John Franklin, Captain R. N., F. R. S., | and commander of the expedition. | With an appendix on various subjects relating to | science and natural history. | Illustrated by numerous plates and maps. | Published by authority of the right honourable the Earl Bathurst. |

**Franklin** (J. ) — Continued.

London : | John Murray, Albemarle-street. | MDCCCXXIII [1823].

2 p. ll. pp. vii-xvi, 1-768, plates and maps, 4°.—Names of animals, fishes, plants, etc. in Eskimo, with English significations, pp. 87-93.— Names of the various parts of an Eskimo house, with English significations, p. 267.

*Copies seen:* Astor, British Museum, Congress.

A copy at the Field sale, No. 740, brought $9.25. Priced by Quaritch, No. 11658, at £1.10s.

According to Sabin's Dictionary, No. 25625 : Second Edition, London, John Murray, 1824, 2 vols. 8°, brought by Quaritch, No. 11659, at 10s., and No. 28980, at 5s.

—— Narrative of a journey | to the shores of the | Polar Sea, | in | the years 1819-20-21-22. | By | John Franklin, Capt. R. N., F. R. S., M. W. S., | and commander of the expedition. | Published by authority of the Right Honourable | the Earl Bathurst. | Third Edition. | Two Vols.—Vol. I[-II]. |

London : | John Murray, Albemarle-street. | MDCCCXXIV [*sic* for 1824].

2 vols.: pp. i-xix, 1-370 ; 1 p. l. pp. i-iv, 1 l. pp. 1-399, 8°.—Linguistics as in previous edition, vol. 1, pp. 134-145 ; vol. 2, p. 267.

*Copies seen :* Bancroft, Congress.

A copy at the Field sale, catalogue No. 741, half-morocco, uncut, brought $2.50. Clarke, 1886, No. 4172, prices it at $3.50.

—— Narrative of a journey | to the shores of the Polar Sea, | in the years | 1819, 20, 21, & 22. | By | John Franklin, Captain R. N., F. R. S., | and commander of the expedition. | With an appendix containing geognostical observa- | tions, and remarks on the Aurora Borealis. | Illustrated by a frontispiece and map. | Published by authority of the Rt. Hon. the Earl Bathurst. |

Philadelphia : | H. C. Carey & I. Lea, A. Small, Edward Parker, M'Carty & | Davis, B. & T. Kite, Thomas Desilver, and E. Littell. | 1824.

Pp. i-xi, 1-482, plate and map, 8°.—Names of animals, fishes, plants, etc. in the Eskimo language, pp. 78-83.

*Copies seen :* Bancroft, Congress.

—— Journey | to the | shores of the Polar Sea, | In 1819-20-21-22 ; | with | a brief account of the second journey | In 1825-26-27. | By | John Franklin, Capt. R. N. F. R. S., | and Commander of the Expedition. | Four vols.—With plates. | Vol. I [-IV].

London : | John Murray, Albemarle Street. | MDCCCXXIX [1829].

**Franklin (J.)** — Continued.

4 vols. 24°.—Names of animals, plants, &c.
vol. 1, pp. 170-182.—Parts of an Esquimaux
house, vol. 3, p. 5.

**Freitag (A.).** Grammatik | oder | Hülfs-
Buch | zur Erlernung der Eskimo-
Sprache. Original, 1839. Umgearbei-
tet 1846. von A. Freitag

Manuscript, title 1 l. contents 1 l. text pp.
1-208, 2 folding sheets, sm. 4°. The original of
this, I understand, is in use by the missionaries
at Okok, Labrador; there is a copy in Bremen,
and one, that described above, in possession of
Dr. Boas.

**Fry (Edmund).** Pantographia; | con-
taining | accurate copies of all the
known | alphabets in the world; | to-
gether with | an English explanation
of the peculiar | force or power of each
letter: | to which are added, | speci-
mens of all well-authenticated | oral
languages; | forming | a comprehensive
digest of | phonology. | By Edmund
Fry, | Letter-Founder, Type-Street. |
London. | Printed by Cooper and
Wilson, | For John and Arthur Arch,
Gracechurch-Street; | John White,
Fleet-Street; John Edwards, Pall-Mall;
and | John Debrett, Piccadilly. | MDCC
XCIX [1799].

**Fry (E.)** — Continued.

2 p. ll. pp. i-xxxvi, 1-320, 8°.—Short vocabulary and numerals (1-10) of the Esquimaux,
p. 80; of the language of Greenland, p. 104; of
Norton Sound, p. 212; of Oonalashka, p. 214;
of Prince William Sound, p. 240.
These vocabularies are extracted from Anderson (A.) and from Bryant (—) in Cook and
King's Voyages to the Pacific Ocean.

*Copies seen:* Astor, Boston Athenæum, British Museum, Congress.
At the Squier sale, catalogue No. 385, a copy
was sold for $2.13.

**Furuhelm (Gov. Hjalmar).** Notes on the
natives of Alaska. (Communicated to
the late George Gibbs, M. D., in 1862.)
By His Excellency J. Furuhelm, Late
Governor of the Russian American Col-
onies.

In Powell (J. W.), Contributions to N. A.
Ethnology, vol. 1, pp. 111-116, 121-133, Wash-
ington, 1877, 4°.
Vocabulary and grammatic comments on the
Aleut, pp. 115-116.

—— Vocabulary of the Asiagmüt (Norton
Bay).

Manuscript 2 ll. foolscap, 50 words and numerals 1-10; in the library of the Bureau of
Ethnology.

—— Vocabulary of the Kuskokwim.

Manuscript 2 ll. foolscap, 50 words and numerals 1-10; in the library of the Bureau of
Ethnology.

# G.

**Gallatin (Albert).** A synopsis of the Indian tribes within the United States
east of the Rocky Mountains, and in
the British and Russian Possessions in
North America. By the Hon. Albert
Gallatin.

In American Antiquarian Soc. Trans. (Arch-
æologia Americana), vol. 2, pp. 1-422, Cambridge, 1836, 8°.
Grammatical notice of the Esquimaux (from
Adelung's Mithridates and Cranz), pp. 211-
214.—Vocabulary of the Esquimaux of Hudson's Bay (from Parry), of Kotzebue Sound
(from Beechey), of the Tshuktchi of Asia
(from Koscheloff), of Greenland (from Egede
and Cranz), and of the Kadiak (from Klaproth),
pp. 305-367.

—— Letter to Henry Rowe Schoolcraft
respecting the use of the letters V and
L in the Eskimau language.

In American Biblical Repository, 2d series,
vol. 1, pp. 448-449, New York, 1839, 8°.

—— Hale's Indians of northwest America,
and vocabularies of North America, with
an introduction. By Albert Gallatin.

**Gallatin (A.)** — Continued.

In American Ethnol. Soc. Trans. vol. 2; In-
troduction, pp. xxiii-clxxxviii; Part First,
Hale's Indians of North America, pp. 1-70;
Part Second, Vocabularies of North America,
pp. 71-130, New York, 1848, 8°.
Vocabulary of the Eskimaux of Hudson's
Bay, pp. 78-82; of the Eskimaux of Greenland,
Kotzebue's Sound, Tschuktchi, and Kadlac, p.
104; of the Onolastia, Aleutan Islands, and
Kamshatka, p. 130.

**Gebet.** Das | Gebet des Herrn | in den |
Sprachen Russlands. | [One line quota-
tion.] |

St. Petersburg. | Buchdruckerei der
Kaiserlichen Akademie der Wissen-
schaften. | (Was. Ostr., 9. Lin., N°
12.) | 1870.

Printed cover, title leaf, pp. iii-xii, 1-88, 4°.
Texterläuterung (von H. Dalton), pp. 1-47;
Vater-Unser-Texte, pp. 49-86.—Lord's Prayer
in Tschuktschisch and Kamtschadalisch, p. 52;
in Aleutisch, p. 51.

*Copies seen:* Dr. Edward W. Gilman, secretary American Bible Society, New York.

Geographie oder Beschreibung der Län- der der Erde. See Elsner (A. F.).

Geography:
Greenland.                     See Nnnalerutit,
                               Wandall (E. A.).
Labrador.                      Elsner (A. F.).

Gibbs (George). [Vocabularies of tribes of the extreme northwest.]
In Powell (J. W.), Contributions to North American Ethnology, vol. 1, pp. 107-156, Washington, 1877, 4°.
Vocabulary of the Kaniagmut, pp. 135-142.

—— Miscellaneous Notes on the Eskimo, Kinai, and Atna Languages.
Manuscript, 25 ll. 4° and folio, in the library of the Bureau of Ethnology.

—— Vocabulary of the Eskimo of Davis Strait.
Manuscript, 211 words, 6 ll. folio, in the library of the Bureau of Ethnology.

—— Vocabulary of the Kodiak.
Manuscript, 6 ll. foolscap, 184 words; in the library of the Bureau of Ethnology. The first page contains this memorandum: "Victoria, June, 1857, from a man and woman."

Giessing (Christopher). Nye | Samling | af | Danske= Norske= | og | Islandske= | Jubel=Lærere, | med hcsføyede | Slægt= Registere og Stam=Tavler, | samled og i Trykken udgivet | af | Christopher Giessing, | Roeskilde Domkirkes og Skoles Cantor. | Første Deel [-Tredie Deels Første Bind]. |
Kiøbenhavn, | Trykt med Brødrene Berlings Skrifter. | 1779[-1786].
3 vols. in 4 parts: vol. 1; vol. 2, parts 1, 2; vol. 3, part 1, sm. 4°.—Contains biographies, &c., of a number of writers on the Eskimo language.
Copies seen: Congress.

Gilbert (—) and Rivington (—). Specimens | of the | Languages of all Nations, | and the | oriental and foreign types | now in use in | the printing offices | of | Gilbert & Rivington, | limited. | [11 lines quotations.] |
London : | 52, St. John's Square, Clerkenwell, E. C. | 1886.
Printed cover as above, contents pp. 3-4. text pp. 5-66, 12°.—St. John iii, 16, in Eskimo [of Labrador], p. 20; Greenland, p. 25.
Copies seen: Pilling.

Gilder (William H.). Innit philology. How Esquimaux talk with white men. The old language and the new. Useful glossary of a strange tongue. Old-fashioned savages.
In New York Herald, No. 16219, Monday.

Gilder (W. H.)—Continued.
January 17, 1881.—Vocabulary of about 450 words of the Eskimo of Greenland, collected by Mr. Gilder while with the Schwatka Expedition. Reprinted, with a few additions, as follows:

—— Schwatka's Search | sledging in the Arctic in quest of | the Franklin records | By | William H. Gilder | second in command | with maps and illustrations |
New York | Charles Scribner's Sons | 743 and 745 Broadway | 1881
Pp. iii-xvi, 1-316, 8°.—Inuit Philology, pp. 299-316, contains, pp. 299-307, general remarks on the Esquimaux language, and, pp. 308-316, a glossary which "comprises all the words in general use in conversation between the natives and traders in Hudson Bay and Cumberland Sound," alphabetically arranged.
Copies seen: Boston Athenæum, British Museum, Congress, Eames.

—— The Chuckchees. Some account of the strange customs of a primitive tribe. A race without religion. Superstitions and medicine men. How babies are brought up. Rotten walrus and fish. Revolting viands which constitute their daily food. Peaceful and kindly though filthy.
In New York Herald, July 31, 1882.—Contains vocabulary, 66 words, of Chuckchee and English.

ГОЛОВНИНЪ (Василій Михайловичъ). [Golovnin (Capt. Vasili Mikhailovich).] Матеріалы | для | исторіи русскихъ заселеній | по берегамъ восточнаго океана. | (Замѣчанія В. М. Головнина о Камчаткѣ и Русской Аме- | рикѣ въ 1809, 1810 и 1811 годахъ.) Выпускъ второй. | Приложеніе къ морскому Сборнику № 2, 1861 г. |
Санктпетербургъ. | Въ типографіи морскаго министерства. | 1861.
Translation.—Material | for | the history of Russian Settlements | on the shores of the Pacific Ocean. | (Remarks of V. M. Golovnin on Kamchatka and Russian Ame- | rica in the years 1809, 1810 and 1811.) | Second Series. | Appendix to the Morskoi Sbornik, No. 2, 1861. | St. Petersburg. | In the Printing Office of the Minister of Marine. | 1861.
2 p. ll. pp. 1-130.—A list of terms and expressions adopted by Russians in Kamchatka, explanatory of many terms now found in Alaskan dialects.
Copies seen: Bancroft.

Gospels according to St. Matthew, St. Mark, St. Luke, and St. John. See Burghardt (C. F.).

[**Gospels** and Epistles in the Greenland language.
Copenhagen, 1848. ]
744 pp. 16°.—Title from Sabin's Dictionary, No. 22853 (note), and Trübner's catalogue, 1856, No. 666, where it is priced at 6s. See Kragh (P.), Attuagahtit, which probably is the work meant by the above authorities.

**Gospels** (Harmony of):
Greenland.                    See Beck (J.),
                              Naleganta.
                              Nalegauta.
Labrador.                     Nalegapta.

**Graah** (Wilhelm August). Undersögelses-Reise | til | Östkysten af Grönland. | Efter kongelig Befaling udfört | i Aarene 1828–31 | af | W. A. Graah, | Capitain-Lieutenant i Söe-Etaten. | [Design.] | Kiöbenhavn. | Trykt hos J. D. Qvist, i det Christensenske Officin. | Östergade Nr. 53. | 1832.
Pp. i-xviii, 1-216, map, 4°.—Botaniske og zoologiske Gienstande, Planter, Pattedyr, Fugle og Fiske, hvilke forekomme paa Ostkysten af Grönland, App. 2, pp. 191-195.
Copies seen: Congress.

—— Narrative of an expedition | to the | east coast of Greenland, | sent by order of the king of Denmark, | in search of | the lost colonies, | under the command of | Captⁿ W. A. Graah, of the Danish royal navy, | knight of Dannebrog, &c. | Translated from the Danish, | by | the late G. Gordon Macdougall, F. R. S. N. A., | for the | Royal Geographical Society of London. | With the | original Danish chart completed by the expedition. |
London: | John W. Parker, West Strand. | M.DCCC.XXXVII [1837].
Pp. i-xvi, 1-199, map, 8°.—Greenland names of mammalia, birds, and fishes, Appendix B, pp. 178-180.
Copies seen: Congress.
At the Field sale, No. 832, a copy brought $1.63; at the Murphy sale, No. 1078, $4.

**Grammar:**
Aleut.                  See Henry (V.),
                        Veniaminoff (J.).
Greenland.              Egede (H.),
                        Egede (Paul),
                        Fabricius (O.),
                        Henry (V.),
                        Kleinschmidt (S. P.),
                        Konigseer (C. M.).
Kadiak.                 Veniaminoff (J.).
Labrador.               Bourquin (T.),
                        Freitag (A.).
Tchiglits.              Henry (V.).

**Grammatic comments:**
Aleut.                  See Buynitzky (S. N.),
                        Furuholm (H.),
                        Pinart (A. L.),
                        Veniaminoff (J.).
Eskimo.                 Adelung (J. C.) and
                        Vater (J. S.),
                        Dall (W. H.),
                        Parry (W. E.),
                        Richardson (J.).
Greenland.              Adelung (J. C.) and
                        Vater (J. S.),
                        Bastian (A.),
                        Egede (H.),
                        Gallatin (A.),
                        Shea (J. G.).
Kaniagmut.              Pinart (A. L.).
Konægen.                Adelung (J. C.) and
                        Vater (J. S.).
Labrador.               Adelung (J. C.) and
                        Vater (J. S.).
Norton Sound.           Adelung (J. C.) and
                        Vater (J. S.).
Tschugazzen.            Adelung (J. C.) and
                        Vater (J. S.).
Ugaljachmutzi.          Adelung (J. C.) and
                        Vater (J. S.).

**Grammatic treatise:**
Aleut.                  See Henry (V.),
                        Pfizmaier (A.).
Eskimo.                 Adam (L.),
                        Bancroft (H. H.).
Greenland.              Abel (I.),
                        Anderson (J.),
                        Bock (C. W.),
                        Cranz (D.),
                        Hervas (L.),
                        Pfizmaier (A.),
                        Rink (H. J.),
                        Thorhallesen (E.).
Innok.                  Henry (V.).
Kadiak.                 Pfizmaier (A.).
Kalälek.                Pfizmaier (A.).
Tchiglit.               Petitot (E. F. S. J.).
Tschuktschi.            Radloff (L.).

**Grammatica** Groulandica Danico-Latina. See **Egede** (Paul).

**Grammatik** der grönländischen Sprache. See **Kleinschmidt** (S. P.).

**Grammatik** oder Hülfs-Buch. See **Freitag** (A.).

**Greenland:**
Abecedarium.            See A B C card,
Abecedarium.            Abecedarium,
Abecedarium.            Greenland,
Abecedarium.            Kattitsiomarsut.
Apostles' Creed.        Egede (H.).
Arithmetic.             Wandall (E. A.).
Baptismal forms.        Egede (H.).
Bible.                  Testamentetokak.
  Old Testament (in     Beck (J.),
  part).
  Old Testament (in     Brodersen (J.).
  print).

**Greenland --Continued.**

Bible:

| Genesis. | See Fabricius (O.). |
|---|---|
| Exodus. | Kragh (P.). |
| Leviticus. | Kragh (P.). |
| Joshua. | Kragh (P.). |
| Judges. | Kragh (P.). |
| Ruth. | Kragh (P.). |
| Samuel I-II. | Kragh (P.). |
| Kings I-II. | Kragh (P.). |
| Ezra. | * Kragh (P.). |
| Nehemiah. | Kragh (P.). |
| Esther. | Kragh (P.). |
| Psalms. | Brun (R.), |
| Psalms. | Egede (Paul), |
| Psalms. | Egede (Peter), |
| Psalms. | Fabricius (O.), |
| Psalms. | Jörensen (T.), |
| Psalms. | Kjer (K.), |
| Psalms. | Kristumiutut, |
| Psalms. | Muller (V.), |
| Psalms. | Wolf (N. G.). |
| Proverbs. | Wolf (N. G.). |
| Isaiah. | Brodersen (J.), |
| Isaiah. | Wolf (N. G.). |
| Daniel. | Kragh (P.). |
| Minor prophets. | Kragh (P.). |
| Apocrypha (in part). | Kragh (P.). |
| New Testament. | Beck (J.), |
| New Testament. | Egede (Paul), |
| New Testament. | Fabricius (O.), |
| New Testament. | Kleinschmidt (J.C.), |
| New Testament. | Testamentetak. |
| Four Gospels. | Egede (Paul), |
| Four Gospels. | Gospels. |
| Matthew (in part). | Warden (D. B.). |
| Luke. | Apostelit. |
| John (in part). | American Bible Society, |
| John (in part). | Apostelit (note), |
| John (in part). | Bagster (J.), |
| John (in part). | Bible Society, |
| John (in part). | British and Foreign, Warden (D. B.). |
| John (in part). | Warden (D. B.). |
| Epistles. | Apostelit (note), |
| Epistles. | Gospels. |
| Revelation. | Apostelit (note). |
| Bible (small). | Fabricius (O.). |
| Bible lessons. | Fabricius (O.), |
| Bible lessons. | Jesusib, |
| Bible lessons. | Kaumarsok, |
| Bible lessons. | Kjer (K.), |
| Bible lessons. | Kragh (P.), |
| Bible lessons. | Nalekab, |
| Bible lessons. | Tamerssa. |
| Bible quotations. | Gútip. |
| Bible stories. | Fabricius (O.), |
| Bible stories. | Kragh (P.), |
| Bible stories. | Mentzel (—), |
| Bible stories. | Okautsit, |
| Bible stories. | Senfkornesutépok, |
| Bible stories. | Steenholdt (W. F.), |
| Bible stories. | Stenberg (K. J. O.), |
| Bible stories. | Tamerssa, |
| Bible stories. | Tastamantitorkamik. |

**Greenland—Continued.**

| Calendar. | See Calendar. |
|---|---|
| Canticles. | Tuksiautit. |
| Catechism. | Ajokærsoutit, |
| Catechism. | Ajokærsutit, |
| Catechism. | aperssûtit, |
| Catechism. | Egede (H.), |
| Catechism. | Egede (Paul), |
| Catechism. | Katekismuse, |
| Catechism. | Sapâme, |
| Catechism. | Tamersa, |
| Catechism. | Thorhallesen (E.), |
| Catechism. | Tuksiautit. |
| Census. | Piniartut. |
| Christ (Imitation of). | Egede (Paul), |
| Christ (Salvation through). | Kragh (P.). |
| Christian doctrine. | Jesusib, |
| Christian doctrine. | Jesusim, |
| Christian doctrine. | Konigseer (C. M.). |
| Christian faith. | Egede (H.), |
| Christ's passion. | Nalegauta. |
| Dialogues. | Egede (H.), |
| Dialogues. | Kragh (P.). |
| Dictionary. | Anderson (J.), |
| Dictionary. | Boyer (J. F.), |
| Dictionary. | Egede (Paul), |
| Dictionary | Fabricius (O.), |
| Dictionary. | Kleinschmidt (S.P.), |
| Ethics. | Steenholdt (W. F.). |
| First inhabitants of. | Kleinschmidt (S.P.). |
| Geography. | Nunalerutit, |
| Geography. | Wandall (E. A.). |
| Gospel lessons. | Kragh (P.). |
| Gospels (Harmony of). | Beck (J.), |
| Gospels (Harmony of). | Naleganta. |
| Gospels (Harmony of). | Naleganta. |
| Grammar. | Egede (H.), |
| Grammar. | Egede (Paul), |
| Grammar. | Fabricius (O.), |
| Grammar. | Henry (V.), |
| Grammar. | Kleinschmidt (S.P.), |
| Grammar. | Konigseer (C. M.). |
| Grammatic comments. | Adelung (J. C.) and Vater (J. S.), |
| Grammatic comments. | Bastian (A.), |
| Grammatic comments. | Egede (H.), |
| Grammatic comments. | Gallatin (A.), |
| Grammatic comments. | Shea (J. G.). |
| Grammatic treatise. | Abel (I.), |
| Grammatic treatise. | Anderson (J.), |
| Grammatic treatise. | Bock (C. W.), |
| Grammatic treatise. | Cranz (D.), |
| Grammatic treatise. | Hervas (L.), |
| Grammatic treatise. | Pfizmaier (A.), |
| Grammatic treatise. | Rink (H. J.), |
| Grammatic treatise. | Thorhallesen (E.). |
| History of the world. | Jaussen (C. E.), |
| History of the world. | Kleinschmidt (S.P.), |
| Hymns. | Brodersen (J.), |
| Hymns. | Egede (Paul), |
| Hymns. | Hayes (I. I.), |
| Hymns. | Kjer (K.), |
| Hymns. | Konigseer (C. M.), |
| Hymns. | Kragh (P.), |
| Hymns. | Thorhallesen (E.), |

**Greenland**—Continued.

| Hymns. | See Tugsiantit. |
| Instructions for trad- ing posts. | Kúugip. |
| Legends. | Kaladlit, |
| Legends. | Pok. |
| Linguistic discussion. | Rink (H. J.), |
| Linguistic discussion. | Wöldike (M.). |
| Litany. | ilagigsut. |
| Liturgy. | Tuksiantit. |
| Lord's Prayer. | Adelung (J. C.) and Vater (J. S.), |
| Lord's Prayer. | Auer (A.), |
| Lord's Prayer. | Bergholtz (G. F.), |
| Lord's Prayer. | Bergmann (G. von), |
| Lord's Prayer. | Bodoni (J. B.), |
| Lord's Prayer. | Egede (H.), |
| Lord's Prayer. | Fauvel-Gouraud(F.), |
| Lord's Prayer. | Hervas (L.), |
| Lord's Prayer. | Lord's Prayer, |
| Lord's Prayer. | Marcel (J. J.), |
| Lord's Prayer. | Marietti (P.), |
| Lord's Prayer. | Naphegyi (G.), |
| Lord's Prayer. | Richard (L.), |
| Lord's Prayer. | Strale (F. A.). |
| Medical manual. | Hagen (C.), |
| Medical manual. | Kragh (P.), |
| Medical manual. | Rudolph (—). |
| Numerals. | Adelung (J. C.) and Vater (J. S.), |
| Numerals. | Antrim (B. J.). |
| Ode. | Barth (J. A.). |
| Periodical. | Atuagagdliutit, |
| Periodical. | Kaladlit. |
| Prayers. | Anderson (J.), |
| Prayers. | Egede (Paul), |
| Prayers. | Kragh (P.), |
| Prayers. | Preces. |
| Primer. | Groenlandsk, |
| Primer. | Janssen (C. E.), |
| Primer. | Kattitsiomarsut, |
| Primer. | Kleinschmidt(S.P.). |
| Relationships. | Kleinschmidt (S.P.). |
| Relationships. | Morgan (L. H.). |
| Remarks. | La Harpe (J. F. de), |
| Remarks. | O'Reilly (B.), |
| Remarks. | Rink (H. J.), |
| Remarks. | Scherer (J. B.), |
| Remarks. | Schott (W.), |
| Remarks. | Steinthal (H.). |
| Reports. | Nalunaerutit. |
| Ritual. | Egede (Paul). |
| Ritual. | Fabricius (O.). |
| Sermons. | ivangkiliunik, |
| Sermons. | Kragh (P.). |
| Songs. | Cranz (D.), |
| Songs. | erñoiugkat, |
| Songs. | Kjer (K.), |
| Songs. | Rink (H. J.). |
| Tales. | Böggild (O ), |
| Tales. | Kaladlit, |
| Tales. | Kjer (K.), |
| Tales. | Pok. |
| Ten Commandments. | Anderson (J.). |
| Thomas a Kempis, | Egede (Paul). |
| Tracts. | Kragh (P.), |

**Greenland**—Continued.

| Tracts. | See Steenholdt (W. F.). |
| Vocabulary. | Balbi (A.), |
| Vocabulary. | Bartholinus (C.), |
| Vocabulary. | Barton (B. S.), |
| Vocabulary. | Bryant (—), |
| Vocabulary. | Court de Gebelin (A. de), |
| Vocabulary. | Dall (W. H. ), |
| Vocabulary. | Egede (H.), |
| Vocabulary. | Egede (Paul), |
| Vocabulary. | Franklin (J.), |
| Vocabulary. | Fry (E.), |
| Vocabulary. | Gallatin (A.), |
| Vocabulary. | Gilder (W. H.), |
| Vocabulary. | Graah (W. A.), |
| Vocabulary. | Klaproth (J.), |
| Vocabulary. | Konigseer (C. M.), |
| Vocabulary. | Markham (C. R.), |
| Vocabulary. | Morgan (L. H.)., |
| Vocabulary. | O'Reilly (B.), |
| Vocabulary. | Olearius (A.), |
| Vocabulary. | Pfizmaier (A.), |
| Vocabulary. | Prichard (J. C.), |
| Vocabulary. | Rink (H. J.), |
| Vocabulary. | Scherer (J. B.). |
| Wanderings of the Apostles. | Egede (Paul), note. |
| Words. | Buschmann (J.C.E.), |
| Words. | Lesley (J. P.), |
| Words. | Rink (H. J.), |
| Words. | Vater (J. S.), |
| Words. | Whymper (F.), |
| Words. | Umery (J.). |

"On passing from the folk-lore, preserved merely by verbal tradition, to the printed literature of Greenland, we must mention that a few old manuscripts have been found in the possession of the natives containing stories of European origin, which they had preserved in this way by copying them, such as ' Pok: or a Greenlander's Journey to Denmark,' ' Sibylle, ' Oberon,' and 'Holger the Dane.' * * * The details of these stories in their Greenland versions of course frequently appear very curious. .

\* \* \* \* \* \* \*

" The literature of the Greenlanders, printed in the Eskimo language, amounts to about as much as might make fifty ordinary volumes. Most of it has been printed in Denmark, but, as already mentioned, a small printing-office was established at Godthaab, in Greenland, in 1862, from whence about 280 sheets have issued, besides many lithographic prints. As regards its contents the Greenlandish literature includes the following books, of which, however, many are very small, or mere pamphlets :

" The Bible, in four or five larger parts, and some smaller sections as separate parts.

" Three or four volumes, and several smaller books, containing psalms.

"About twenty books concerning religious objects.

"About ten books serving for manuals in spelling, arithmetic, geography, history, &c.

**Greenland—Continued.**

"About sixteen books, with stories or other contents, chiefly entertaining.

"About six grammars and dictionaries in the Eskimo language, for Europeans.

"A Journal: Atuagagdliutit, nalinginarmik tusaruminásassnuik univkât, i. e., 'something for reading, accounts of all sorts of ontertaining subjects,' published in Greenland since 1861. Up to 1874 it comprised 194 sheets in quarto, and about 200 leaves with illustrations.

"Official reports concerning the municipal institutions, 1862 to 1872, in Danish and Greenlandish, comprising about twenty-six sheets, besides many lithographic plates containing accounts and statistical returns."—*Rink, Danish Greenland, pp. 213, 214.*

According to Crauz, printing was introduced into Greenland at least prior to 1792, Brodersen, who died in that year, having brought a small printing-press from Europe, on which he struck off a few copies of a collection of hymns for immediate use.

[**Groenlandsk** A B D Bog.
Kjöbenhavn, 1760.]
8º. Title from Ludewig. For reprint, see Kattitsiomarsut.

**Grönlænderues første Præste.** See **Kragh** (P.).

**Grønlandske Ordbog.** See **Fabricius** (O.).

**Grönlandske Ordbog.** See **Kleinschmidt** (S. P.).

**Grønlandst Psalmebog.** See **Brun** (R.)

**Guide** to the Heavenly kingdom, Alent-Fox. See **Veniaminoff** (J.).

**Gûtip** okausîsa ilait | merdlertunnut iliniagagssat. | [Three lines quotation.] | Stolpen, | Druck von Gustav Winter. | 1880.
*Literal translation:* God | his words some of them | for children lessons.
Title verso blank 1 l. text pp. 3-63, 12º.
Bible quotations for school use, entirely in the language of Greenland.
*Copies seen:* Pilling, Powell.
My copy, bought of the Unitäts-Buchhandlung, Guadau, Saxony, cost 80 pf.

## II.

**Hagen** (Carl). Náparsimassugdlit | atuartagagssait. | nugterdlugit Kavdlunait nakorsaisa agdlagait, | maligtarineruvdlugit: | "Thornams Lægebog", | "Huslægen af Raspaïl". | agdlagkat Carl Hagenmit. |
Nunguic. | Nunap nalagata nakiteriviano nakitat, | L. Möller mit. | 1866.
*Literal translation:* Those who have the sick [to cure] | their manual. He [the writer] translating white men their doctors their books, | following-mostly: | "Thornams Lægebog [Medicine]," | "Huslægen af Raspall [The household physician by Raspaïl.]" | written by Carl Hagen. | At the Point [Godthaab] | On the land's its ruler's [the Inspector's] printing-press printed, | from L. Möller.
Pp. 1-72, 8º, in the language of Greenland.
*Copies seen:* Powell.

**Haldeman** (Samuel Stehman). Analytic orthography: | an | investigation of the sounds of the voice, | and their | alphabetic notation; | including | the mechanism of speech, | and its bearing upon | etymology. | By | S. S. Haldeman, A. M., | professor in Delaware College: | member [&c. six lines]. |
Philadelphia: | J. B. Lippincott & Co. | London: Trübner & Co. Paris:

**Haldeman** (S. S.)—Continued.
Benjamin Duprat. ' Berlin: Ferd. Dümmler. | 1860.
Pp. i-viii, 5-148, 4º.—Numerals 1-10 of the Eskimo, pp. 144-146.
*Copies seen:* Boston Athenæum, British Museum, Eames, Powell, Trumbull.

**Hall** (Charles Francis). Life with the Esquimaux: | the narrative | of | Captain Charles Francis Hall, | of the whaling barque "George Henry" | from the 29th May 1860, to the 13th September, 1862. | With the results of a long intercourse with the Innuits, and full | description of their mode of life, | the discovery of | actual relics of the expedition of Martin Frobisher of | three centuries ago, and deductions in favor of yet discovering | some of the survivors of Sir John Franklin's expedition. | With maps and one hundred illustrations. | In two volumes, | Vol. I[-II]. |
London: | Sampson Low, Son, and Marston, | 14 Ludgate Hill. | 1864.
2 vols.: pp. i-xvi, 1-324; i-xii, 1-352, 8º.—Lord's Prayer in Eskimo, vol. 1, pp. 62-63.—Numerals 1-10 of the Innuit, vol. 2, p. 324.
*Copies seen:* British Museum.

**Hall (C. F.)**—Continued.

—— Arctic researches | and | life among the Esquimaux: | being the | narrative of an expedition in search of Sir John | Franklin, | in the years 1860, 1861, and 1862. | By | Charles Francis Hall. | With Maps and One Hundred Illustrations. | New York: | Harper & Brothers, Publishers, | Franklin Square. | 1865.

Engraved title 1 l. pp. i–xxviii, 29–595, map, 8°.—Lord's Prayer in Esquimaux, p. 60.—Innuit numerals 1–10, p. 577.

*Copies seen:* Astor, Boston Athenæum, British Museum, Congress.

A copy at the Squier sale, catalogue No. 450, brought $1.25.

—— Narrative | of the | second Arctic expedition | made by | Charles F. Hall: | his voyage to Repulse Bay, sledge journeys to the Straits of Fury | and Hecla and to King William's Land, | and | residence among the Eskimos during the Years 1864–'69. | Edited under the orders of the hon. secretary of the navy, | by | Prof. J. E. Nourse, U. S. N. | U. S. Naval Observatory, | 1879. | Washington: | Government Printing Office. | 1879.

5 p. ll. pp. i–l, 1–644, maps, 4°.—Besides many Eskimo terms passim, there are also in this work four lists of names of geographic features, a few with English significations, in the following localities: Northeast coast of Fox Channel (50 names), p. 351; Too-noo-nee-noo-shuk, or Admiralty Inlet (40 names), pp. 355–356; Pond's Bay (33 names), p. 370; King William's Land, and the adjacent country (16 names), p. 398.

*Copies seen:* Astor, Powell.

This author's Deux Ans chez les Esquimaux, Paris, 1880, 8°, contains no Eskimo linguistics.

**Harvard:** This word following a title indicates that a copy of the work referred to was seen by the compiler in the library of Harvard University, Cambridge, Mass.

**Hasling (—).** Eine Probe der Esquimaux-Sprache.

In Neues Lausitzisches Magazin, herausgegeben von der Oberlausitzischen Gesellschaft der Wissenschaften, vol. 14, pp. 260–262, Görlitz, 1836, 8°.

**Hayes (*Dr.* Isaac Israel).** The | land of desolation | being a | personal narrative | of | adventure in Greenland | by | Isaac J. [*sic*] Hayes, M. D. | author of | "The Open Polar Sea" | etc. |

London | Sampson Low, Marston, Low, & Searle | Crown Buildings, 188 Fleet Street | 1871 | All rights reserved.

**Hayes (I. I.)**—Continued.

2 p. ll. pp. vii–xiv, 1 l. pp. 1–312, 8°.—One stanza of an Eskimo hymn with literal translation, and two lines of another without translation, p. 81.

*Copies seen:* British Museum.

—— The | land of desolation: | being a personal narrative of | observation and adventure in | Greenland. | By Isaac I. Hayes, M. D., | gold medalist [&c. four lines]. | Illustrated. | [Design.] | New York: | Harper & Brothers, Publishers, | Franklin Square. | 1872.

2 p. ll. pp. 7–357, 8°.—Linguistics as in 1871 edition, p. 100.

*Copies seen:* British Museum, Congress.

—— La terre | de désolation | excursion d'été | au Groënland | par | le Dr I. J. [*sic*] Hayes | Auteur de la Mer libre du Pôle | Ouvrage traduit de l'anglais | avec l'autorisation de l'auteur | par J. M. L. Reclus | et contenant 43 gravures et une carte |

Paris | Librairie Hachette et Cie | 79, Boulevard Saint-Germain, 79 | 1874 | Tous droits réservés

Title verso blank 1 l. pp. i–iv, 1 l. pp. 1–360, map, 8°.—Linguistics as in edition of 1871, p. 88.

*Copies seen:* British Museum.

**Heckewelder (John Gottlieb Ernestus).** An Account of the History, Manners, and Customs, of the Indian Nations, who once inhabited Pennsylvania and the Neighbouring States. By the Rev. John Heckewelder, of Bethlehem.

In American Philosoph. Soc. Trans. of the Hist. and Lit. Com. vol. 1, pp. 1–347, Philadelphia, 1819, 8°.

Chapter ix, Languages, pp. 104–105, contains notice of the Karalit [Eskimo] language.

Separately issued as follows:

—— An account | of the | History, Manners, and Customs, | of | the Indian Nations, | who once inhabited Pennsylvania and | the neighboring states. | Communicated to the Historical and Literary Committee of | the American Philosophical Society, held at Philadel- | phia for promoting Useful Knowledge, | by | the Rev John Heckewelder, | of Bethlehem, | and | published by order of the Committee. |

Philadelphia: | Printed and Published by Abraham Small. | no. 112, Chesnut [*sic*] Street. | 1818.

Title verso blank 1 l. copyright notice verso 2d l. recto blank, contents pp. iii–iv, text pp. 1–348, 8°.—Linguistics, pp. 101–102.

**Heckewelder** (J. G. E.)—Continued.

— Johann Heckewelder's evangelischen Predigers zu Bethlehem | Nachricht | von der | Geschichte, den Sitten und Gebräuchen | der | indianischen Völkerschaften, | welche ehemals Pennsylvanien und die benach- | barten Staaten bewohnten. Aus dem Englischen übersetzt und mit den Angaben | anderer Schriftsteller über eben dieselben Gegenstände | Carver, Loskiel, Long, Volney vermehrt | von | Fr. Hesse | evangelischen Prediger zu Nienburg. | Nebst einem die Glaubwürdigkeit und den anthropolo- | gischen Werth der Nachrichten Heckewelder's | betreffenden Zusatze | von G. E. Schulze. | Göttingen | bey Vandenhoeck und Ruprecht. | 1821.

Pp. i-xlviii, 1-582, 1 l. 8°.—Linguistics, pp. 158-159.

*Copies seen:* Astor, British Museum, Congress.

A copy at the Fischer sale, catalogue No. 787, brought 2s.

— Histoire, | mœurs et coutumes | des | nations indiennes | qui habitaient autrefois la Pensylvanie | et les états voisins; | par le révérend | Jean Heckewelder, | missionnaire morave, | traduit de l'anglais | Par le Chevalier Du Ponceau. |

A Paris, | Chez L. De Bure, Libraire, | rue Guénégaud, n° 27. | 1822.

2 p. ll. pp. i-xii, 13-571, 8°.—Des langues: le Karalit, pp. 170-171.

*Copies seen:* Congress, Trumbull.

At the Squier sale, No. 465, a copy brought $5.13. Priced by Leclerc, 1878, No. 896, 18 fr. The Brinley copy, No. 5403, brought $2.

— History, | Manners, and Customs | of | The Indian Nations | who once inhabited Pennsylvania and | the neighbouring states. | By the | Rev. John Heckewelder, | of Bethlehem, Pa. | New and Revised Edition. | With an | Introduction and Notes | by the | Rev. William C. Reichel, | of Bethlehem, Pa. | Philadelphia: | Publication Fund of | the Historical Society of Pennsylvania, | No. 820 Spruce Street. | 1876.

In Pennsylvania Hist. Soc. Memoirs, vol. xii, pp. 15-348, Philadelphia, 1876, 8°.—Comments on the Karalit language, pp. 118-120.

*Copies seen:* Eames.

**Henry** (Victor). Esquisse d'une Grammaire de la langue Innok étudiée dans

**Henry** (V.)—Continued.

le dialecte des Tchiglit du Mackenzie, d'après la Grammaire et le vocabulaire Tchiglit du R. P. Petitot.

In Revue de Linguistique, tome 10, pp. 223-260, Paris, 1877, 8°.

Separately issued, without title-page, pp. 1-38, 8°.

A copy priced in Leclerc's Supplement, No. 2798, at 2 fr.

— Esquisse d'une grammaire raisonnée de la langue aléoute d'après la grammaire et le vocabulaire de Ivan Véniaminov.

In Revue de Linguistique, vol. 11, pp. 424-457; vol. 12, pp. 1-62, Paris, 1878, 1879, 8°.

Separately issued as follows:

— Esquisse | d'une grammaire raisonnée | de la | langue aléoute | d'après la grammaire et le vocabulaire de Ivan Véniaminov | Par V. Henry | [Design] | Paris | Maisonneuve et Cⁱᵉ, libraires-éditeurs | 25, Quai Voltaire, 25 | 1879

2 p. ll. pp. 1-73, 1 l. 8°.

*Copies seen:* British Museum, Powell.

Priced in Leclerc's Supplement, No. 2797, at 3 fr. 50c.; by Trübner, 1882 (p. 48), at 3s. 6d.

— Grammaire comparée de trois langues hyperboréennes: grönlandais, tchiglerts, aléoute.

"Manuscript left, August, 1879, in the hands of M. Bamps, secretary of the Congrès des Américanistes de Bruxelles, and which will probably never appear, because the Congress does not publish its memoirs, and refuses nevertheless to return the manuscripts which have been furnished it."—*Henry.*

**Hervas** (Lorenzo). Catalogo | delle lingue conosciute | e notizia | della loro affinità e diversità. | Opera | del Signor Abbate | Don Lorenzo Hervas | [Design.] |

In Cesena MDCCLXXXIV [1784]. | Per Gregorio Biasini all' Insegna di Pallade | Con Licenza de' Superiori.

1 p. l. pp. 1-260, sm. 4°.—Gronlandese, ed Eskimese lingue affini; linguaggio Lapponico-Teutonico nella Groenlandia, p. 85.

*Copies seen:* Astor, Congress.

Enlarged and reprinted as follows.

— Catálogo de las Lenguas | de las Naciones Conocidas, | y numeracion, division, y clases de estas | segun la diversidad | de sus Idiomas y Dialectos. | Su Autor | el Abate Don Lorenzo Hervás, | Teólogo del Eminentísimo Señor Cardenal Juan Francisco | Albani [&c. three lines]. | Volúmen I[-VI]. | Len-

**Hervas (L.)**—Continued.
guas y Naciones Americanas. | Con
licencia. | En la imprenta de la admi-
nistracion del real arbitrio de benefi-
cencia. |
Madrid Año 1800[-1805]. | Se hallará
en la Librería de Ranz calle de la Cruz.
6 vols. sm. 4°.—Capitulo vii. Lenguas que
se hablan en la California * * * y Groenlandia.
Copies seen: Bancroft, British Museum, Congress, Harvard.
A copy at the Squier sale, No. 486, brought
$6. Priced by Leclerc, 1878, No. 2072, at 120 fr.
At the Ramirez sale, No. 396, bought by Quaritch for £1 15s. The Murphy copy, catalogue
No. 1215, brought $42.

—— Saggio Pratico | delle Lingue | con
prolegomeni, e una raccolta di orazioni
Dominicali in | più di trecento lingue,
e dialetti, con cui si dimostra | l' infu-
sione del primo idioma dell' uman ge-
nere, e la | confusione delle lingue in
esso poi succeduta, e si | additano la
diramazione, e dispersione della na- |
zioni con molti risultati utili alla storia.
| Oficia | dell' Abate | Don Lorenzo
Hervas | Socio della Reale Accademia
delle Scienze, ed Antichità | di Dublino,
e dell' Etrusca di Cortona. | [Figure.] |
In Cesena M DCC LXXXVII [1787]. |
Per Gregorio Biasini all' Insegna di
Pallade | Con Licenza de' Superiori.
Pp. 1-256, sm. 4°.—Lord's Prayer in Greenland (two dialects), with comments, pp. 126-
127.
Copies seen : Astor, Congress.

**Herzog** (Wilhelm). Ueber die Verwand-
schaft des Yumasprachstammes mit
der Sprache der Aleuten und der Eski-
mostämme. Von Wilh. Herzog, Pfarrer.
In Zeitschrift für Ethnologie, vol. 10, pp. 449-
459, Berlin [1878], 8°.
Comparative vocabulary of various Yuma
dialects with the Aleut, pp. 450-452; and with
the Eskimo, pp. 453-457.
The Yuma material is compiled from Gat-
schet, Schoolcraft, Whipple, Buschmann, and
Hervas; the Aleut, from Veniaminoff; the Eskimo, from Gallatin, Dall, and Adelung.
History of the first inhabitants of Greenland.
See Kleinschmidt (S. P.).
History of the world, Greenland. See Janssen
(C. E.), Kleinschmidt (S. P.).

**Hoffman** (Dr. Walter James). Comparison of Eskimo Pictographs with those
of other American Aborigines.
In Anthropological Soc. of Washington,
Trans. vol. 2, pp. 128-146, Washington, 1883, 8°.

**Hoffman (W. J.)**—Continued.
Interpretation of picture-writings in the Ki'-
ato'χamut dialect of the Innuit, with literal English translation, pp. 133, 134, 143-144.— Same in
the Aigalúχamut dialect of the Innuit, p. 138.
Separately issued as follows :

—— Comparison of | Eskimo pictographs
| with those of | other American abo-
rigines. | By W. J. Hoffman, M. D., |
general secretary [&c. four lines]. |
(Reprinted from the Transactions of
the Anthropological Society of Wash-
ington, | Vol. II, 1883.) |
Washington : | Judd & Detweiler,
Printers. | 1883.
Printed cover as above, text pp. 1-19, 8°.
Copies seen : Brinton, Pilling, Powell.

—— Ein Beitrag zu dem Studium Bilder-
schrift. Von Dr. W. J. Hoffman in
Washington.
In Das Ausland for 1884, No. 33, pp. 646-651;
No. 34, pp. 666-669, Stuttgart und München,
1884, 4°.
Contains, besides observations on picture-
writing in general, some Innuit examples, with
interpretations into their own language and
translation therefrom into German.

—— Innuit sentences with interlinear
translation.
In Bureau of Ethnology, fourth annual report, pp. 148, 149, 193-194, 198, 215, Washington,
1886, 8°.

**Honne** (A. F.).   See **Egede** (Paul).

—— See **Kragh** (P.).

**Hooper** (Lieut. William Hulme). List of
Esquimaux Words collected between
Point Barrow and Cape Bathurst,
1849-50, by Lieut. W. H. Hooper, R. N.
In Arctic Expeditions, pp. 179-186, London,
1852, folio.
Contains vocabulary of the Eastern and
Western Esquimaux, and of the Coast and In-
land Tchouski, pp. 179-184.—List of Esquimaux
persons, p. 185.

—— Ten months | among | the tents of
the Tuski, | with incidents of an | arc-
tic boat expedition in search of | Sir
John Franklin, | as far as the Macken-
zie River, and Cape Bathurst. | By
Lieut. W. H. Hooper, R. N. | With a
map and illustrations. |
London : | John Murray, Albemarle
Street. | 1853.
Pp. i-xvi, 1-417, map, 8°.—Tuski phrase, with
translation, p. 87.—Tuski song of rejoicing
with translation, p. 181.—Many terms scattered
throughout.

**Hooper** (W. II.)—Continued.

*Copies seen:* Astor, British Museum, Congress.

Priced by Quaritch, No. 28996, at 5s.

**Hössler** (—). Eskimos.

Iu Allgemeine Encyklopädie, vol. 38, pp. 108–130, Leipzig, 1843, 4°.

Two versions of the Lord's Prayer, in Eskimo, p. 111.

**Hudson** Bay:

| | |
|---|---|
| Apostles' Creed. | See Peck (E. J.). |
| Benediction. | Peck (E. J.). |
| Bible, Luke. | Peck (E. J.). |
| John (in part). | Peck (E. J.). |
| Romans (in part). | Peck (E. J.). |
| Corinthians (in part). | Peck (E. J.). |
| Epistles of John (in part). | Peck (E. J.). |
| Revelation (in part). | Peck (E. J.). |
| Catechism. | Peck (E. J.). |
| Hymns. | Peck (E. J.). |

**Hudson Bay**—Continued.

| | |
|---|---|
| Lord's Prayer. | See Peck (E. J.). |
| Prayers. | Peck (E. J.). |
| Relationships. | Clare (J. R.), |
| | Morgan (L. H.). |
| Ten Commandments. | Peck (E. J.). |
| Vocabulary. | Gallatin (A.), |
| | Gilder (W. H.), |
| | Morgan (L. H.), |
| | Schomburgk (R. H.). |

**Hymns:**

| | |
|---|---|
| Greenland. | See Brodersen (J.), |
| | Egede (Paul), |
| | Hayes (I. I.), |
| | Kjer (K.), |
| | Kragh (P.), |
| | Konigseer (C. M.), |
| | Thorhallesen (E.), |
| | Tugsiautit. |
| Hudson Bay. | Peck (E. J.). |
| Labrador. | Imgerutit, |
| | Tuksiarutsit. |

## I.

**Igloolik** Numerals. See Baer (K. E. von).

**Ilagîgsut** tugsiússissutait sapâme | atortugssat sujugdlit.

*Colophon:* Druck von Gustav Winter in Stolpen. [1880.]

*Literal translation:* The congregation theirmeans-of-praying on Sunday | things to be used the first.

No title-page; pp. 1–9, 16°. Church litany, entirely in the Eskimo of Greenland.

*Copies seen:* Pilling, Powell.

My copy, bought of the Unitäts-Buchhandlung, Gnadau, Saxony, cost 15 pf.

**Illerkorsutit** makko aglekkæne. See **Kjer** (K.).

**Imgerutit** | attoræksat | illagôktunut | Labradoremêtunut. |

Stolpeneme, | G. Winterib Nêuilauktangit. | 1879.

Title verso blank 1 l. preface pp. iii–v, contents pp. vi–xiv, text pp. 1–391, 13 hymns set to music (lithograph), pp. i–viii, 16°. Hymn book in the Eskimo of Labrador.

*Copies seen:* Pilling, Powell.

My copy cost 5 M. 40 pf.

**Imgerutit** | attorekset | illagêktunuut | Labradoremêtunnut. |

Læbaume, | J. A. Duroldtib Nenilauktangit. [1840 ?]

*Literal translation:* Songs | a manual | for the communities [congregations] | living in Labrador. | Löbau, | J. A. Duroldt's his printings.

Pp. i–xii, 1–340, 16°. A collection of hymns.

*Copies seen:* Brinley, British Museum.

The Brinley copy, No. 5640, brought $7.

**Imgerutsit** nôtiggit | 100. | Hundert Eskimoische Lieder, | freie Übersetzungen und Nachbildungen | deutscher Volksgesänge. |

[E. Pöschelib Leipzigemêtub suleKatingitalo nênilaurtangit.] 1872.

Title 1 l. preface 2 ll. text (songs, set to music, in the language of Labrador) pp. 1–90, 16°. The songs were translated by Freitag, Erdmann, Elsner, Kretschmer, and Bourquin.

*Copies seen:* Pilling, Powell.

My copy cost 2 M.

**Indrenius** (Andreas Abraham). *A. καὶ Ω.* | Specimen academicum | De | Esquimaux, | gente | Americana, Quod | in Regio Fennorum Lycæo, | Consent. Ampliss. Facult. Philos. | Sub Umbone | Viri Ampliss. atque Celeberrini | Dn. Petri Kalm, | Oeconom. Profess. Reg. & Ord. item | Reg. Scient. Acad. Holm. Membri, | Placidæ eruditorum discussioni submittitur | Ab | Andrea Abrahami Indrenio, | Tavast. | Ad Diem XIX. Junii, Anni currentis MDCCLVI [1756]. | Loco horisque consvetis. | Aboæ, Impressit Direct. & Typogr. Reg. Magn. Duc. | Finland. Jacob Merckell.

1 p. l. pp. 1–24, sm. 4°.—Vocabula Esquimatica, 100 words, pp. 23–24.

*Copies seen:* Brown, Congress.

See Kalm (P.).

**Inkalit-Yugelmut:**

| | |
|---|---|
| Vocabulary. | See Buschmann (J. C. E.), |
| | Schott (W.), |
| | Zagoskin (L. A.). |

Inkilik:
Vocabulary.                 See Buschmann (J. C. E.),
                            Schott (W.),
                            Schwatka (F.),
                            Zagoskin (L. A.).
    The Inkalit and Inkilik tribes are not Es-
kimo; these vocabularies are inserted because
of the Eskimo words included in them.
Inkuluklates Vocabulary.    See Wrangell (F. von).
Innok Grammatic treatise.   See Henry (V.).
Innûb nangminek.            See **Steenholdt** (W.
    F.).
Innuit:
    Numerals.               See Hall (C. F.),
                            Kumlien (L.).
    Relationships.          Dall (W. H.).
    Sentences.              Hoffman (W. J.).
    Vocabulary.             Buschmann (J. C. E.),
                            Müller (F.),
                            Woolfe (H. D.).
Instructions for trading posts, Greenland.  See
    Küngip.
**Ivangkîliunik** | isumasiñtit | sapÂtine
    nagdliûssivingnilo | atugagssat. | su-
    jugdlît: | nkiñkut [-âipait: aussâkut]
    nagdliñtartune atugagssat. |

ivangkîliunik — Continued.
    Stolpen, | Druck von Gustav Winter. |
    1877[-1879].
    *Literal translation:* About the Gospels |
    means for discovering their meaning | on Sun-
    days and times-for-celebrating-festivals | to-be-
    used. | First: | in winter [-second: in summer]
    on-holidays-repeatedly-arriving to-be-used.
    2 vols. 12°: Half-title Grönländische Predig-
    ten, Erster Band, 1 l. title verso blank 1 l. con-
    tents verso blank 1 l. text pp. 1-147; Half title
    Grönländische Predigten, Zweiter Band, 1 l.
    title verso blank 1 l. contents 1 l. text pp. 1-
    224, 12°.—Sermons for Sundays and holy days,
    entirely in the language of Greenland.
    *Copies seen:* Pilling, Powell.
    My copy, procured of the Unitäts-Buch-
    handlung, Gnadau, Saxony, cost 4 M. 40 pf.

Ivngerutit kerssungme senningarsome.
    See **Kjer** (K.).

Ivngerutit Tuksiutidlo Kaladlinnut.
    See **Fabricius** (O.).

Ivngerutit tuksiutidlo Kalalinnut.  See
    **Egede** (Paul).

# J.

**Janssen** (Carl Emil). Kalatdlit Inuv-
    dluar-Kugamigit 1857.
    Nungme, 1858.                    *
    27 pp. 8°.—Printed at Godthaab on the first
    printing-press sent to Greenland, in the sum-
    mer of 1857.—*Sabin's Dictionary, No.* 35572.

—— [Silamiut ingerdlansiánik, . . . C.
    E. Janssen.
    Copenhagen, 1861.]                *
    *Literal translation:* The inhabitants-of-the-
    world about their history of progress.
    136 pp. 8°.  Title from Dr. Rink.

—— Elementarbog | i | Eskimoernes
    Sprog | til Brug for | Europæerne ved
    Colonierne i Grønland. | Ved | C. E.
    Janssen. |
    Kjøbenhavn. | Louis Kleins Bogtryk-
    keri. | 1862.
    Pp. 1-92, index 1 l. 12°.
    *Copies seen:* British Museum, Powell.
    Priced by Trübner, 1882 (p. 53), at 3s. 6d.

—— Elementarbog i Eskimoernes sprog
    til brug for Europæerne ved colonierne
    i Grönland.
    Kjöbenhavn. 1869.                 *
    Title from Steiger's Bibliotheca Glottica.

**Jean** (Père).  [Aléoute Catechism.]   *
    Father Jean has joined to his translation of
    the Catechism some observations upon the
    language of the Aléoutes.—*Lutké.*
    Père Jean is probably the Rev. Ivan Venia.
    minoff.

**Jefferys** (Thomas).  The natural and
    civil | history | of the | French do-
    minions | in | North and South Amer-
    ica. | Giving a particular Account of
    the | Climate, | Soil, | Minerals, | Ani-
    mals, | Vegetables, | Manufactures, |
    Trade, | Commerce, | and | Languages,
    | together with | The Religion, Govern-
    ment, Genius, Character, Manners and
    | Customs of the Indians and other In-
    habitants. | Illustrated by | Maps and
    Plans of the principal Places, | Col-
    lected from the best Authorities, and
    engraved by | T. Jefferys, Geographer to
    his Royal Highness the Prince of Wales.
    | Part I. Containing | A Description of
    Canada and Louisiana. [Part II. Con-
    taining | Part of the Islands of St.
    Domingo and St. Martin, | The Islands
    of | St. Bartholomew, Guadaloupe,
    Martinico, La Grenade, | and | The
    Island and Colony of Cayenne.] |
    London, | Printed for Thomas Jefferys
    at Charing-Cross. | MDCCLX [1760].
    Part 1, 4 p. ll. pp. 1-168; Part 2, 2 p. ll. pp.
    1-246, maps, folio.—Of the origin, languages
    * * * of the different Indian nations inhab-
    iting Canada [Eskimaux, Sioux, Assiniboels,
    Algonkins, Roundheads, Saltuers, Malbom-
    mes, Hurons], part 1, pp. 42-97.
    *Copies seen:* British Museum, Congress,
    Massachusetts Historical Society.
    Sold at the Field sale, No. 1119, for $6.50.

**Jefferys** (T.)—Continued.

—— The natural and civil | history | of the | French dominions | in | North and South America. | With an Historical Detail of the Acquisitions and Conquests made by the | British arms in those Parts. Giving a particular Account of the Climate, | Soil, | Minerals, | Animals, | Vegetables, | Manufactures, | Trade, | Commerce, | and | Languages. | Together with | the Religion, Government, Genius, Character, Manners and | Customs of the Indians and other Inhabitants. | Illustrated by | Maps and Plans of the principal Places, | Collected from the best Authorities, and engraved by | T. Jefferys, Geographer to his Majesty. | Part I. Containing | A Description of Canada and Louisiana [-Part II. Containing | &c. 5 lines]. |

London: | Printed for T. Jefferys, at Charing-Cross; W. Johnston, in Ludgate-street; J. Richardson | in Paternoster-Row; and B. Law and Co. in Ave-Mary-Lane. | MDCCLXI [1761].

Part 1, 4 p. ll. pp. 1-168, maps; Part 2, 2 p. ll. pp. 1-246, maps, folio.—Contents as in edition of 1760.

Copies seen: Astor, British Museum, Congress.

**Jéhan** (L.-F.). Troisième et dernière | Encyclopédie Théologique, | [&c. twenty-four lines]. | Publiée | par M. l'Abbé Migne | [&c. six lines]. | Tome Trente-quatrième. | Dictionnaire de Linguistique. | Tome Unique. | Prix: 7 Francs. |

S'Imprime et se vend chez J.-P. Migne, Editeur, | aux Ateliers Catholiques, Rue d'Amboise, au Petit Montrouge, | Barrière d'Enfer de Paris. | 1858.

Second title: Dictionnaire | de | Linguistique | et | de | Philologie Comparée. | Histoire de toutes les Langues mortes et vivantes, | ou | Traité complet d'Idiomographie, | embrassant l'examen critique des systèmes et de toutes les questions qui se rattachent | à l'origine et à la filiation des langues, à leur essence organique | et à leurs rapports avec l'histoire des races humaines, de leurs migrations, etc. | Précédé d'un | Essai sur le rôle du langage dans l'évolution de l'intelligence humaine. | Par L.-F. Jéhan (de Saint-Clavien), | Membre de la Société géologique de France, de l'Académie royale des sciences de Turin, etc. | [Quotation, three lines.] | Publié | par M. l'Abbé

**Jéhan** (L.-F.)—Continued.

Migne, | Editeur de la Bibliothèque Universelle du Clergé, | ou | des Cours Complets sur chaque branche de la science ecclésiastique. | Tome Unique. | Prix: 7 francs. | [Imprint as in first title.]

Outside title 1 l. titles as above 2 ll. columns (two to a page) 9-1448.—The Tableau polyglotte des langues includes the Eskimaux (Famille des idiomes), columns 542-548.

Copies seen: British Museum, Shea.

There is an edition, Paris, 1864, which I have not seen, a copy of which is in the Watkinson Library, Hartford, Conn.

**Jerusalemib** asserornekarnera. | [Picture.] |

[N. p.] 1845.

Literal translation: Jerusalem to destruction.

Pp. 1-8, 16°. Bible lessons in the dialect of Labrador.

Copies seen: American Tract Society.

**Jesus**, Judit nálegannerâet. | [Picture.]

Literal translation: Jesus, the Jews their supreme ruler.

No title-page; 1 p. l. pp. 1-8, 24°. Bible lessons in the dialect of Greenland.

Copies seen: American Tract Society.

**Jesuse**, Judikut attaninget. | [Design.]

Literal translation: Jesus, the Jews their King.

No title-page; 1 p. l. pp. 1-8, sq. 24°. Bible lessons in the dialect of Labrador.

Copies seen: American Tract Society.

**Jesusib** Kristusib | ajokaersutei | pirssariakarnerit | Gudib okauseenit aglekennit Katte- | sorsimarsut attortuksello innusuit | illageeksunnôtut ajokaersorkol- | lugit. | [Design.]

Budissimo | Ernst Gottlob Monsib nakkittaegei. | 1833.

Literal translation: Jesus Christ's | his doctrines | most necessary things | from God's his word written collected | and useful things young people | in communion | that he may instruct them. At Bautzen Ernst Gottlob Mons printed them. |

Title verso blank 1 l. text pp. 3-75, 16°. Summary of Christian Doctrine, entirely in the language of Greenland.

Copies seen: Pilling, Powell.

My copy, procured of the Unitäts-Buchhandlung, Gnadau, Saxony, cost 60 pf.

Earlier and later editions as follows:

**Jesusim** Kristusim | ajokaersutei | pirssariakarnerit | Gudim okauseenit aglekennit Katte- | sorsimarsut attortuksello | innusuit illageeksunnetut ojokaer- | sorkullugit. | [Design.]

Barbyme, 1785.

Title verso blank 1 l. text pp. 3-72, 16°.

**Jesusim** —Continued.
Abstract of Christ's Doctrines, in the Eskimo language of Greenland.
*Copies seen:* British Museum.

**Jesusjb** Krjstusib | ajokertutingita | pijuriakarnerpãngõningit. | A Summary | of | Christian Doctrine, | oder: Hauptinhalt der christlichen Lehre. | *Verso of title:* E. Bastaniermullo & Dnnskymullo. | Nênertaulaukput Lœbaume. [1867.]
*Literal translation:* Jesus Christ's | his doctrines | its most important things. | * * | By E. Bastanier and Dnnsky. | Printed at Löbau.
Title 1 l. preface pp. 3–4, contents pp. 5–6, text, entirely in the language of Labrador, pp. 7–112, 12º.
*Copies seen:* Pilling, Powell.
My copy cost 1 M. 30 pf.
Dr. Rink has communicated to me a similar title, with collation as 116 pp. 8º.

**Kadlak:**

| | |
|---|---|
| Grammar. | See Veniaminoff (J.). |
| Grammatic treatise. | Pfizmaier (A.). |
| Numerals. | Adelung (J. C.) and |
| | Vater (J. S.), |
| | Baer (K. E. von), |
| | Erman (G. A.), |
| | Pott (A. F.). |
| Remarks. | Veniaminoff (J.). |
| Texts. | Veniaminoff (J.). |
| Vocabulary. • | Baer (K. E. von), |
| | Buschmann (J. C. E.), |
| | Campbell (J.), |
| | Davidoff (G. I.), |
| | Davidson (G.), |
| | Gallatin (A.), |
| | Gibbs (G.), |
| | Khromchenko (V. S.), |
| | Klaproth (J.), |
| | Latham (R. G.), |
| | Lesseps (J. B. B.), |
| | Lisiansky (U.), |
| | Petroff (I.), |
| | Robeck (—), |
| | Sauer (M.), |
| | Schott (W.), |
| | Vocabularies, |
| | Wowodsky (—), |
| | Zagoskin (L. A.), |
| | Zelenoi (S. J.). |

**Kágĕagĕmŭt** Vocabulary. See Fisher (W. J.).

**Kaladlit** assilialiat | or | woodcuts, drawn and engraved by | Greenlanders. | [Picture of a ship, followed by two lines inscription.] |
Godthaab | in South-Greenland. | Printed in the Inspectors printing office by L. Møller | and R. Berthelsen. | 1860.

**Johannesib** koĩrsirsnb nejsã. See **Kragh** (P.).

**Johnson** (J. William). [Words, phrases, and sentences in the Iuuuit or Eskimo of Bristol Bay.]
Manuscript, pp. 77–228, 4º, in the library of the Bureau of Ethnology. Recorded in a copy of Powell's Introduction to the Study of Indian Languages, second edition. Half the schedules have no entries and the others are but scantily filled. Collected at Bristol Bay, 1884–1886.

**Jörensen** (Thoger). [Nagdliutorsiutit ernaglit.
Nûngme, 1875.] *
94 pp. 12º. Psalms in Greenland Eskimo.—
*Rink.*

**Jorgensen** (H. F.) See **Kleinschmidt** (S. P.).

# K.

**Kaladlit**—Continued.
Title 1 l. text in English descriptive of the illustrations 1 l. 24 ll. containing illustrations numbered 1–39, 2 ll. colored plates, 4º.
"These wood-cuts are the results of experiments undertaken in 1858–'60, to test the natural capabilities of the Greenlanders for this branch of art. The whole have been engraved, and with the exception of Nos. 1–8, composed and drawn without assistance, by 5 or 6 natives of Greenland, the necessary wood and instruments having been lent them. The best of these wood-cuts are the production of a Greenlander named Aron living near Godthaab, who has received no better education than the generality of his countrymen."—*Extract from text.*
*Copies seen :* Congress.
An edition in Danish as follows :

**Kaladlit** Assillaliait Grønlandske Traesuit. [Picture of church with the inscription : Kirken, Seminariet og Inspekteurboligen | ved Kolonien Godthaab.] |
Godthaab. | Trykt I Inspektoratets Bogtrykkeri af L. Møller | og R: Berthelsen. | 1860.
Title verso blank 1 l. 24 engravings numbered 1–39, followed by 1 l. text in Danish, 4º.
*Copies seen:* British Museum, Congress, Powell.
The Fischer copy, No. 2342, sold for 7s. The Pinart copy, No. 503, bought by Quaritch for 10 fr.
An edition with text in French as follows :

**Kaladlit** Assillaliait | ou | quelques gravures, dessinées et gravées | sur bois | par | des Esquimaux du Gronland.

**Kaladlit**—Continued.

[Picture of a ship, with two lines explanation in French.] |

Godthaab | Imprimé chez l'Inspecteur du Groenland Meridional ' par L: Møller et R: Berthelsen. | 1860.

25 ll.—Prints with titles in the language of Greenland.

*Copies seen:* British Museum, Yale.

At the Field sale, No. 1172, a copy brought $1.75.

**Kaladlit** Okalluktual- | linit. | kalÂdlisut kablunâtudlo. | [Design.] | Attuakæt siurdliæt[-sisamai].

Nonngme. | Nunuap Nalegata Nakitteriviane Nakittat | L. Møllermit, | Irsigirsoralugo R: Berthelsen. | 1859 [-1863].

*Literal translation:* Greenlanders the stories-told-by | -them. | Greenland and Danish. | Book the first[-fourth]. | At the Point [Godthaab]. | On the Country's its Ruler's [Inspector's] printing-press printed. | From L. Müller, | overseeing it R. Berthelsen.

*Second title:* Grönlandske Folkesagn, | opskrevne og meddeelte af Indfødte, | med dansk Oversættelse. Første[-Fjerde] Bind. | Med træsnit, | tegnede og udskaarene af | en indfødt. | Godthaab. | Trykt i Inspectoratets Bogtrykkeri | af L: Møller, | under tilsyn af hjelpelærer | R. Berthelsen. | 1859[-1863].

4 vols. 8°: 1859, 4 p. ll. 137 pp. 1 l. 8 pp. music; 1860, 4 p. ll. 111 pp. charts; 1861, 4 p. ll. 136 pp. 12 pp. illustrations, numbered 1-12; 1863, 3 p. ll. 123 pp., alternate Greenland and Danish. Greenland folklore; popular tales and legends. The illustrations were made by native Greenlanders. Berthelsen, who was, I think, the inspector, aided in the translations.

*Copies seen:* Boston Athenæum, British Museum, Congress, Powell, Trumbull.

A copy at the Fischer sale, No. 2340, bought by Quaritch for £5 5s. Priced by Leclerc, 1878, No. 2229, at 140 fr. The Pinart copy, No. 504, 3 vols. 1859-1861, sold for 52 fr.

**Kaladlit** Pelleserkângoæta. See **Kragh** (P.).

**Kalâlek** Grammatic treatise. See Pfizmaier (A.).

**Kalatdlit** Inuvdluar. See **Janssen** (C. E.).

**Kalatdlit** nunata | assinga.

*Colophon:* (Nungme nakitigkat 1858.)

*Literal translation:* Greenlanders their lands | its picture. At the Point [Godthaab] printed.

No title-page; 1 l. broadside. A map of the southern end of Greenland, showing the east coast as far north as Uinanek and the west coast to Upernivik, occupies the center of the sheet; on the two sides and at the bottom is a printed description of the various Eskimo settlements.

*Copies seen:* Congress.

**Kalatdlit** turogagssait misigssiussu- | nik, | misigssugainigdlo ukiut mako mardluk ukiñ- | titdllugit, 1857-1859.

*Colophon:* Nungme 1859.

*Literal translation:* Greenlanders their things-to-be-heard about the surveyors and their surveys, in the course of these two years, 1857-1859. At the Point [Godthaab].

No title-page; caption only; pp. 1-4, 8°, in the language of Greenland.

*Copies seen:* Congress.

**Kalm** (Peter). En | Resa | Til | Norra America, | På | Kongl. Swenska Wetenskaps | Academiens befallning, | Och | Publici kostnad, | Förrättad | Af | Pehr Kalm, | Oeconomiæ Professor i Åbo, samt Ledamot af | Kongl. Swenska Wetenskaps-Academien. | Tom. I [-III]. | Med Kongl. Maj:ts Allernådigste Privilegio. | Stockholm, | Tryckt på Lars Salvii kostnad 1753[-1761].

3 vols. 12°.—Esquimaux words, vol. 3, p. 451.

*Copies seen:* Astor, British Museum, Congress.

—— Des Herren | Peter Kalms | Professors der Haushaltungskunst in Aobo, und Mitglie- | des der königlichen schwedischen Akademie der | Wissenschaften | Beschreibung | der Reise die er | nach dem | nördlichen Amerika | auf den Befehl gedachter Akademie | und öffentlichen Kosten | unternommen hat. | der erste[-dritte] Theil. | [Design.] | Eine Uebersetzung. | Unter dem Königlichen Pohlnischen und Chur- | fürstl. Sächsischen allergnädigsten Privilegio. | Göttingen | im Verlage der Wittwe Abrams Vandenhoeck, 1754[-1764].

3 vols. 8°.—Esquimaux words, vol. 3, p. 546. Some copies have the imprint of Leipzig (*), and others of Stockholm (*). A partial reprint of this work, embracing the portion relating to natural history, was published at Paris in 1768 (*). It does not, I presume, contain the linguistics.

*Copies seen:* British Museum, Congress, Harvard.

—— Travels | into | North America; | containing | Its Natural History, and | A circumstantial Account of its Plantations | and Agriculture in general, | with the | civil, ecclesiastical and commercial | state of the country, | The Manners of the inhabitants, and several curious | and important remarks on various Subjects. | By Peter Kalm, | Professor of Oeconomy in the Univer-

**Kalm (P.)—Continued.**

sity of Aobo in Swedish | Finland, and Member of the Swedish Royal Academy of | Sciences. | Translated into English | By John Reinhold Forster, F. A. S. | Enriched with a Map, several Cuts for the Illustration of | Natural History, and some additional Notes. | Vol. I[-III]. | Warrington [London]: | Printed by William Eyres. | MDCCLXX[-MDCC-LXXI] [1770-1771].

3 vols. 8°. The imprint of vol. I is " Warrington : 1770," and of vols. II and III "London : 1771," but they seemingly belong to the same edition.—Eskimo vocabulary, vol. 3, pp. 239-240.

*Copies seen:* Boston Athenæum, British Museum, Congress, Harvard.

—— Reis | door | Noord | Amerika, | gedaan door den | Heer | Pieter Kalm, | Professor in de Huishoudingskonst op de Hoge School | te Aobo, en Medelid der Koninglyke Zweedsche | Maatschappy der Wetenschappen. | Vercierd met koperen Platen. | Eerste[-Twede] deel. | Te Utrecht. | By J. van Schoonhoven en Comp. | en G. van den Brink Janz. | MDCCLXXII [1772].

2 vols.: 9 p. ll. pp. 1-223; 6 p. ll. pp. 1-240, 4 ll. map, 4°.—Taal der Eskimaus, pp. 177-178.

*Copies seen:* Congress.

—— Travels | into | North America; | containing | Its Natural History, and | A circumstantial Account of its Plantations | and Agriculture in general, | with the | civil, ecclesiastical and commercial | state of the country, | The Manners of the Inhabitants, and several curious and | important remarks on various subjects. | By Peter Kalm, | Professor of Oeconomy in the University of Aobo in Swedish Finland, | and Member of the Swedish Royal Academy of Sciences. | Translated into English | By John Reinhold Forster, F. A. S. | Enriched with a Map, several Cuts for the Illustration of Natural | History, and some additional Notes. | The second edition. | In two volumes, | Vol. I [-II]. | London, | Printed for T. Lowndes, | N° 77, in Fleet-street. 1772.

2 vols.: pp. i-xii, 1-414; i-iv, 1-423, index 4 ll. map, 8°.—Esquimaux vocabulary, vol. 2, p. 368.

*Copies seen:* Astor, British Museum, Congress, Harvard, Watkinson.

Priced by Quaritch, Nos. 28939 and 29452, at 10s.

**Kalm (P.)—Continued.**

—— Travels into North America; containing its natural history, and a circumstantial account of its plantations and agriculture in general, with the Civil, Ecclesiastical, and Commercial state of the Country, the Manners of the Inhabitants, and several curious and important Remarks on various Subjects. By Peter Kalm, Professor of Oeconomy in the University of Abo in Swedish Finland, and Member of the Swedish Royal Academy of Sciences. Translated into English by John Reinhold Forster, F. A. S. (From the Second Edition, London 1772, 2 vols. 8vo.)

In Pinkerton (John), General Collection of Voyages and Travels, vol. 13, pp. 374-700, London, 1812, 4°.—Linguistics, p. 678.

—— Voyage de Kalm en Amérique analysé et traduit par L. W. Marchand.

Forms Books 7 and 8 of the Société Historique de Montréal, Mémoire, Montreal, 1880, 8°.—Linguistics, Book 7, p. 182.

See Indrenins (A. A.).

**Kamschatka:**

| | |
|---|---|
| Numerals. | See Latham (R. G.), |
| Vocabulary. | Drake (S. G.), |
| | Gallatin (A.), |
| | Golovnin (V. M.), |
| | Klaproth (J.), |
| | Lesseps (J. B. B.), |
| | Sauer (M.). |
| **Kángjulit:** | |
| Numerals. | See Erman (G. A.). |
| Vocabulary. | Zelenoi (S. J.). |
| **Kantagmut:** | |
| Dictionary. | See Pinart (A. L.). |
| Grammatic comments. | Pinart (A. L.). |
| Songs. | Pinart (A. L.) |
| Vocabulary. | Dall (W. H.), |
| | Gibbs (G.). |

Karalit Linguistic discussion. See Heckewelder (J. G. E.).

**Katekismuse** | Luterim | Aglega | Tersa | Iliniarkáutiksæt Gudimiglo pekkorsejnig- | lo innungnut nalegeksænnik, pidlnarsin- | náungorkudlugit unnamétidlutik | tokublo kingórngagut. | Kiöbenhavnime, | Pingajueksáuik nakittarsimarsok | 1797. | I. R. Thielimit.

*Literal translation:* Catechism | Luther's | his writing | Here are | fundamental-doctrines about God and about his commands to men to be obeyed, that they may gain the blessed land | after death. | At Copenhagen, | a third time printed. | 1797. | From I. R. Thiel.

Pp. 1-22, 16°, in the language of Greenland.

*Copies seen:* Powell.

**Katekismuse** | Luterim | Aglega. Tersa | Iliniarkäntiksæt Gudimiglo pekkorsejnig- | lo innungnut palegeksænnik, pidluarsin- | näuugorkudlugit nunamētidlntik | tokublo kingórngagut. | Kiöbenhavnime, | Illiarsuïn igloænne sissameksánik nakittarsimarsok | 1816 | C. F. Schubartinit.

*Literaltranslationofimprint:* At Copenhagen | at the orphans their house [Waisenhaus] a fourth time printed 1816 from C. F. Schubart. Pp. 1-24, 16°. Luther's Catechism in the language of Greenland.

*Copies seen:* Congress.

[**Katekismuse** Luterim. Haumiame, 1849.] * 16 pp. 8°, in the Eskimo language. Title from the Pinart sale catalogue, 1883, No. 352.

**Kattængutigeek.** See **Kjer** (K.).

**Kattitsiomarsut** attuaromarsullo Malligekseit. Guadau, 1835. * *Literal translation:* Intended to be spelled and intended to be read examples. 8°. Greenland primer; reprint of Groenlandsk A B D Bog. According to Ludewig, p. 72, a new edition of this primer, by Sténberg, was published: Kjöbenhavn, Missions Collegium, 1849, 20 pp. 8°.

**Kaumajok** | nellcjunnik | kaumatsitiksak. | [Design.] *Literal translation:* A plain | by [for] the ignorant | explanation. N. p. n. d. 1 p. l. pp. 1-8, sq. 24°. Bible lessons in the dialect of Labrador. *Copies seen:* American Tract Society. Published also in the Greenland dialect, as follows:

**Kaumarsok** naellursunnut | kaumarsautiksak. | [Picture.] *Literal translation:* A plain for the ignorant ( explanation. N. p. n. d. 1 p. l. pp. 1-8, 24°. Bible lessons in the language of Greenland. *Copies seen:* American Tract Society.

**Kaviágmüt** Vocabulary. See Dall (W. H.).

**Khromchenko** (*Capt.* Vasili Stepanovich). Journal kept during a Cruise along the Coast of Russian-America. In Northern Archives for History, Statistics, and Voyages (in Russian), Nos. 11-18, St. Petersburg, 1824, 8°. (*) Contains vocabulary of the Kadjak. Reprinted in Ferrusac's Bulletin des Sciences Historiques, &c., vol. 6, pp. 412-413, Paris, 1826, 8°. (Congress.) Reprinted in German in Hertha Zeitschrift, etc., vol. 2, Stuttgart, 1825; vocabulary pp. 219-221. (*)

**Ki'ate'χamut** Vocabulary. See Hoffman (W. J).

**King William Land** Vocabulary. See Hall (C. F.).

**Kissitsisilliornermik** iliniarkantiksæt. See **Wandall** (E. A.).

**Kjer** (Knud). Tuksiantit | Julesintit | makko | nukterdlugidloneet arsillincardlugidloneet narkringniardlugidloneet kattersorei | nakrittoegaugortidlugidlo. ] K. Kjer-ib | Amertlormint maneetsormiudlo pellesiæta. Tussarnersunnik umativsignt tuksiardluse nalekkamut. | Koloss. 3. 16. | Kjöbenhavnime. | Fabritius de Tengnagelikut nakrittareit. | 1831.

*Literal translation:* Psalms | means-for-making-Christmas | these | translating them either, copying them | or trying-to-improve-them collected them also explaining them | K. Kjer | the-people-of-the-little-place and the people-of-the "rough-place" their priest. With things pleasing-to-hear in your hearts singing psalms to the Lord. | Colossians 3. 16. ' At Copenhagen. | Fabricius de Tengnagel's people printed them.

Pp. 1-34, 1 l. 16°, in the language of Greenland.

*Copies seen:* Stren.

—— Illerkorsutit | makko | aglekkæne naktikkæniloneet | ninvertni nalegejsa akkillermæne kattersorej nakrittægangortidlugidlo | K. Kjer-ib | Amertlormiut Maneetsoruiudlo | Pellesigialloaeta. | Nakrittsimaput Elmquist-ikunnit | Aarhuns-ime | 1832.

Pp. 1-31, sq. 16°. Psalms in the language ot Greenland.

*Copies seen:* British Museum.

—— Sennerutilingmik. | Tuksiautitait, | nutanngitsndlo illainangoeet | adlangortitæt | oper kutigeet Kaladlit nunæmetnn | okatarutiksejt, | K. Kjerimit. | [Engraving, and quotation one line.] | Odensime. | Nakittarsimaput Hempelikunnit. | 1834.

4 p. ll. pp. 1-237, 1 l. errata, 12°. Hymns in the language of Greenland.

*Copies seen:* Astor, British Museum, Trumbull.

—— Ivngerutit | kerssungme senningarsome Kikicktomik ajokaersutejniglo, | illejt nutanngitsnt, illejt K. Kjerimit. | [Eight line verse in Eskimo.] | Tapekarput. | Kjöbenhavnime | 1838. | Brünnichib nakitteriviane nakkittarsimarsut.

*Literal translation:* Hymns | on the wood crossed | about the nailed one | and about his teachings, | some of them old, some of them |

**Kjer** (K.) — Continued.

by K. Kjer. | They have an addition. | At Copenhagen | 1838. | Brunnich's on his printing-press printed. |

Pp. 1-xxiv, 1-490, 16°, in the language of Greenland.—Пумпя, pp. 1-360; index, pp. 361-374; Sunday lessons, pp. 375-384; Evangelistin, &c. pp. 385-411; Unnorsontiksak, &c. pp. 412-424; Kenntit, &c. pp. 425-484; Tarkoput [contents], p. 485; Nakittarnerdlukkæet [errata], pp. 487-490.

*Copies seen:* British Museum, Trumbull.

There were two copies in the Pinart sale, No. 515 bringing 1 fr. No. 516 1 fr. 50c.

—— Kattængutigeek. | K. Kjerib | nuktigej. |

Kjöbenhavnime. | Fabritius de Tengnagelib nakitteriviane | nakittarsimarsut. | 1838.

*Literal translation:* The brothers and sisters. | K. Kjer | translated them. | At Copenhagen. | On Fabricius de Tengnagel's printing-press | printed. | 1838.

Pp. 1-45, 16°. A story in the language of Greenland.

*Copies seen:* Powell.

—— Tuksiautit | Kikioktugarursomik, pellesib K. Kjerim aglegij kattersugejlo. | [Seven lines quotation.] Tape-karput. |

M. Vogelinsib Nakittmgej, Frederikshavnime, 1856.

*Literal translation:* Psalms | about him nailed, the priest K. Kjer wrote them and collected them. | They have an addition. | M. Vogelius printed them, at Frederikshavn, 1856.

Pp. i-xviii, 1-385, 2 ll. pp. 1-97, 24°, in the language of Greenland.

*Copies seen:* Harvard.

A copy was bought by Leclerc at the Pinart sale, No. 904, for 1 fr.

According to Nyerup's Dansk-Norsk Litteraturlexicon, Kjer translated into the Greenland a contribution to Ronne's Dansk-Religionsblad, in 1827, and Anderson's poem, "The Dying Child," in 1829.

Kjer was the son of Jacob Kjer, who was parson of Løsning and Korning, in the bishopric of Aarhuus. Born October 2, 1802, at the parsonage of Løsning; went to the school of Horsen in 1814, whence he proceeded to the university; after having passed his second examination, in 1821, he became private teacher in Laaland, and in the following year returned to Copenhagen, where he was received in the Greenland Seminary as alumnus; underwent the theological official examination in 1823 and was immediately after ordained missionary for the colony of Holsteinborg in Greenland in June, 1823, he became parson at Todse, in the bishopric of Aalborg, and in October, 1838, at Skjodstrup, in the same bishopric.

**Klaproth** (Julius). Asia polyglotta von | Julius Klaproth. | Zweite Auflage. |

**Klaproth** (J.) — Continued.

Paris | Verlag von Heideloff & Campe. | 1831.

Title verso blank 1 l. dedication 1 l. preface, &c. pp. vii-xvi, text pp. 1-384, Lebon des Budd'a pp. 125-144, index pp. 1-8, 4°.—Vocabulary of Kamqatka, pp. 320-322; of the Polar Amerika-Groenlaendischner in Asien, pp. 322-324; of the Polar Amerika-Kadjaknor in Asien, pp. 324-325. Atlas as follows:

—— Asia | polyglotta | von | Julius Klaproth. | Sprachatlas. | Zweite Auflage. | Paris | Verlag von Heideloff & Campe. | 1831.

Title verso blank 1 l. text pp. i-lix, map, folio.—Vocabulary of the Korjäkon (7 dialects), Kamqadalon (5 dialects), Polar Amerikaner in Asien (2 dialects), pp. xxxxix-lvii.

*Copies seen:* Congress.

The first edition was published: Paris, 1823, 4°, atlas, folio. (*)

Priced by Trübner (catalogue 1856), No. 538 (dated 1823-31), at £1 4s.

**Kleinschmidt** (John Conrad). [Translations into the language of Greenland.] *

"John Conrad Kleinschmidt left Lichtenfels [in Greenland] for Europe July 15, 1812, the day on which, nineteen years before, he had arrived in Greenland. * * * After spending the winter at Fulneck, and marrying again, Brother Kleinschmidt and his wife * * * sailed from Leith, Scotland, for Greenland, May 24th, 1813. * * * One of the first cares of the missionaries after their return was to furnish a complete translation of the New Testament into Greenlandic, the Bible Societies, both in London and Edinburgh, having kindly offered to print it for them. This important work was committed to Brother Kleinschmidt, who, from his long residence in the country, had obtained a very competent knowledge of the language. * * * We are happy to learn from the accounts of the last year, 1819, that the whole was finished and only waited another final revision before it should be transmitted to Europe."—*Cranz.*

**Kleinschmidt** (Samuel Peter). Grammatik | der | grönländischen sprache | mit theilweisem einschluss des Labradordialects | von | S. Kleinschmidt. | Berlin, 1851. | Druck und Verlag von G. Reimer.

Pp. i-x, 1-182, 8°.

*Copies seen:* Astor, British Museum, Congress, Eames, Pilling, Powell, Trumbull.

Priced by Leclerc, 1878, No. 2553, at 15 fr.; by Trübner, 1882, p. 53, at 3s. A copy at the Pinart sale, No. 517, sold to Quaritch for 4 fr., who prices it, No. 30053, at 5s., and another copy, half-calf, uncut, No. 30054, at 6s. My copy, bought of the Unitäts-Buchhandlung, Gnadau, Saxony, cost 5 M.

**Kleinschmidt (S. P.)**—Continued.

—— Silame iliornerit . . . S. Kleinschmidt.

Nungme [Godthaab], 1859. *

128 pp. 8°. History of the world in Greenland Eskimo. Title from Dr. Rink.

—— Renseignements sur les premiers habitants de la côte occidentale du Groenland. Trad. en groenlandais par S. Kleinschmidt. 1864. *

4°. Picked-up title. I have seen reference in Rink's Danish-Greenland to Kleinschmidt's Sinerissap kavdlunâkarfiligtâ, 1866, which is possibly the above work, as the map given by Rink is taken from it.

—— Den | Grønlandske Ordbog, | omarbeidet | af | Sam. Kleinschmidt; | udgiven | paa Foranstaltning af Ministeriet for Kirke- og Underviisningsvæsenet og med | det kongelige danske Videnskabernes Selskabs Understøttelse | ved | H. F. Jørgensen. | Kiøbenhavn. | Louis Kleins Bogtrykkeri. | 1871.

Title 1 l. pp. iii-x, half-title 1 l. text pp. 1-460, in double columns, arranged alphabetically by Greenland words, 8°.

*Copies seen:* British Museum, Congress, Eames.

Priced by Leclerc, Supplement, No. 2814, at 12 fr.; by Koehler, catalogue 440, No. 960, at 7 M. 50 pf.

—— Terms of Relationship of the Eskimo, Greenland, collected by Samuel Kleinschmidt, Godthaab, Greenland.

In Morgan (L. H.), Systems of Consanguinity and Affinity, pp. 293-382, Washington, 1871, 4°.

Samuel Petrus Kleinschmidt, the son of a missionary, was born at Lichtenau, Greenland, February 27, 1814, and died at Godhaven, Greenland, February 8, 1886. In 1823 he was taken to the school of Kleinwelke, Saxony. From 1828 to 1836 he served as apothecary's apprentice in Zeist, Holland, and from 1836 to 1840 as school teacher at Christiansfeld, Slesvig. In 1840 he returned to Greenland, and was appointed in the missionary service of the Moravians, acting as teacher at the seminary from 1859. Since 1860 he has had a printing-press in his house, and has printed with his own hands several books in Greenlandish, school books in history, geography, and church history, and especially a large part of the Old Testament, but only a limited number of copies, merely intended for the use of the revisers of his new translation. Finally, he has published a new edition of the New Testament, printed at Budissin, Saxony."—*Rink*.

"A new impetus was given to the study of the Greenland tongue by Conrad [*sic*] Klein-

**Kleinschmidt (S. P.)**—Continued.

schmidt, a man of varied talents. He introduced an improved system of orthography, which had regard to the derivations of the words and has been adopted by all the Greenland missionaries, including those of the Danish church, and discarded as a model the Latin grammar, which had been painfully followed by all his predecessors, treating the Greenland tongue according to its own peculiar idioms and the existing forms of its words. His grammar of the Greenland language appeared at Berlin in 1851 and his Greenland-Danish lexicon at Copenhagen at a later time. He wrote also several school books, among them a geography and a natural history, both of which gave him abundant opportunities to construct new words and formulate new terms for many things unknown to the Greenlanders. The most important of his undertakings was a version of the Old Testament, upon which he bestowed extraordinary care and which, by this time, must be nearly completed. On a press presented to the church at Zeist, in Holland, he printed with his own hands a small edition of this work, as far as completed, for the benefit merely of the missionaries. The use of this press was cheerfully granted him, even after he had joined the Danish mission and had been appointed director of the seminary at Godthaab."—*Reichelt*.

Kleinschmidt's father, also a missionary to Greenland, was named John Conrad; hence the mistake probably in the above quotation.

[**Kohlmeister** (Benjamin Gottlieb).] Tamedsa | Johannesib Aglangit, | okautsiñik Tussarnertuñik, | Jesuse Kristusemik, | Gudim Erngninganik. | Printed for | the British and Foreign Bible Society ; | For the use of the Christian Esquimaux in the Mission-Settlements | of the United Brethren at Nain, Okkak, and Hopedale, | on the Coast of Labrador. |

Londouneme: | W. M'Dowallib, Nenilauktangit. | 1810.

*Literal translation:* Here are | John's his writings | about the words pleasant to hear | about Jesus Christ | about God's his Son. | At London: | W. M'Dowall's, his printings.

Title verso blank 1 l. pp. 1-124, 12°. Gospel of John in the language of Labrador.

*Copies seen:* Shea.

A copy at the Field sale, No. 643, brought $1.50; another, No. 2321, 87 cents. The Murphy copy, No. 2914, morocco, gilt edges, brought $2.25.

"After the successful establishment of a mission station in Labrador in 1771, the Moravian missionaries addressed themselves in the first instance to the preparation of a harmony of the Gospels for the Esquimaux of Labrador. Many years were spent in revising and correcting this

[**Kohlmeister** (B. G.)]—Continued..
work, and at length, in 1809, it was sent for publication to London. Mr. Kohlmeister, who had
been many years a missionary in Labrador, extracted from this manuscript an entire version
of the Gospel of St. John ; and in 1810 an edition
of 1,000 copies of that Gospel was published in
London at the expense of the British and Foreign Bible Society."—*Bagster.*
For the other three Gospels see **Burghardt**
(C. F.). For the Harmony of the Gospels see
**Nalegapta**.

**Koikhpagmiut** Vocabulary. See Zagoskin (L. A.).

**Konægen :**
Grammatic-comments. See Adelung (J. C.) and
Vater (J. S.).
Vocabulary.            Bancroft (II. H.).

**Konigseer**(Christopher Michael).[Green-
land Grammar and Vocabularies.]         *
"Konigseer, about 1780, wrote a Greenland
grammar and compiled various vocabularies.
These works remained in manuscript, each
newly arrived missionary making a copy of
them for his own use. In course of time they
were enlarged and improved."—*Reichelt.*

—— [Greenland Hymn Book and Summary of the Christian Doctrine.]         *
"Having received a liberal education, an ad-
vantage which none of his predecessors had
enjoyed, he [Konigseer] was enabled to correct
their translations, and also added several new
versions of useful works. Among these were
a Greenlandic hymn book and a translation of
the Summary of Christian Doctrine, which
have been printed, besides some smaller pieces
in manuscript."—*Cranz.*

—— See **Beck** (John).
Konigseer was superintendent of the Greenland Mission from 1773 to 1786. He was born
in 1723, in Thuringia, and studied at the uni-
versities of Jena and Halle. He died in Greenland on the 30th of May, 1786.

**Kotzebue** Sound Vocabulary. See Gallatin (A.).

**Kragh** (Peter). Testamentitokab | mak-
pérsægèjsa illángocet, | profetit ming-
nerit | Danieliblo Aglegèit, | Kaládlin
okàuzeennut nuktersimarsut, | nafk'i-
gntingoænniglo sukuïársimarsut | Pel-
lesimit | Petermit Kraghmit. | Attuæ-
geksäukudlugit innúngnut koïsimar-
sunnut. |
Kjöbenhavnime. | Fabritiusib de
Tengnagelib nak'itteriviáne | nak'it-
tàrsimarsut. | 1829.
*Literal translation:* The old testament's | its
books' parts of them | the prophets minor |
and Daniel's his book the Greenlanders into
their speech translated | and with notes ex-
plained | by the priest | Peter Kragh. | To be
a manual for men christened. | At Copenha-

**Kragh** (P.)—Continued.
gen. | Fabricias de Tengnagel on his print-
ing press | printed.
Pp. i-viii, 2 ll. pp. 1-290, 1 l. 12°. Minor
prophets, Daniel, and parts of the Apocrypha
(Susanna, Bel, and the Dragon) in the lan-
guage of Greenland.
*Copies seen:* Astor, British and Foreign
Bible Society, British Museum, Eames, Powell,
Watkinson.
At the Fischer sale, No. 2339, a copy brought
9s.

—— Okallnktnàntit | sajmäubingmik
annékbingmiglo Jesuse-Kristusikut, |
makpérsekkænnit Kablunäit adlædlo |
okàuzeennne agléksimarsunnit | katter-
sórsimarsut, | Kaládlidlo okàuzeennut
nuktórsimarsut | Pellesimit Peter-
Kraghmit. | [Three lines quotation.]
Kjöbenhavnime [*sic*]. | Fabritiusib
de Tengnagelib nak'itteriviáne nakk'-
ittàrsimarsut | 1830.
*Literal translation:* Discourses | about the
time of mercy and the time of salvation !
through Jesus Christ, | from the books Euro-
peans and others | in their tongues written. |
Collected, | and Greenlanders into their lan-
guage translated | by the priest Peter Kragh. |
At Copenhagen. Fabricius de Tengnagel's on
his printing-press printed.
4 p. ll. pp. 1-292, 16°. Salvation through
the mediation of Jesus Christ in the language
of Greenland.
*Copies seen:* British Museum, Congress.

—— [Tracts in Greenlandish. (21.).
Kjöbenhavnime, 1830.]
19 sheets, 12°.
"The English consul, Mr. Brown, bore the
expense of this publication."—*Erslew.*
A copy at the Fischer sale, No. 2341, brought
3s.

—— Testamentitokab | makpérsegejsa
illangoeet, | Mosesim Aglegèjsa | ardlejt
tedlimejdlo, | Jobib, Esrab, Nehemiab,
Esterib | Ratiblo aglegejt, | Kaládlin
okàuzeennut nuktórsimarsut, | nafk'i-
gntingoænniglo sukuïársimarsut |
Gjerleviminut Enslevimindlo Pellesiáen-
nit | Peter-Kraghmit. | Attnægeksäu-
kudlugit innúngnut koïsimarsunnut. |
Kjöbenhavnime. | Fabritiusib de Ten-
gnagelib nak'itteriviáne nak'it- | tàrsi-
marsut. | 1832.
*Literal translation:* The old testament's | its
books' parts of them | Moses' his books the
second and the fifth, Job's, Ezra's, Nehemiah's,
Esther's and Ruth's their books, Greenlanders
into their speech translated | and with notes
explained | by the people of Gjerlev and of
Enslev their priest | Peter Kragh. | To be a

**Kragh (P.)** — Continued.

manual for people christened. | At Copenhagen. | Fabricius de Tengnagel's on his printing-press printed.

4 p. ll. pp. 1-633, 1 l. 12°. Books of Exodus, Leviticus, Job, Ezra, Nehemiah, Esther, and Ruth in the language of Greenland.

*Copies seen:* Astor, British and Foreign Bible Society, British Museum, Powell, Watkinson.

A copy at the Fischer sale, catalogue No. 2336, brought 6s.

—— Okallòutit, | Sabbátinne akkudleesiksæt, | Evangeliumit sukuiàntèjt okiokun | attnægóksæt, | kattersórsimarsut | Kalàdlidlo okàuzeennut nuktérsimarsut | Pellesimit Peter-Kraghmit. | [Five lines quotation.]

Kjöbenhavnime 1833. | Fabritiusib de Tengnagelib nak' itteriviàne nak' ittársi- | marsut.

*Literal translation:* Discourses | on the Sabbath to be preached, | from the gospel explanations in winter | to be used, | collected and Greenlanders into their speech translated | by the priest Peter Kragh. | At Copenhagen 1833. | Fabricius de Tengnagel't on his printing press print- | ed.

Pp. i-viii, 1 l. pp. 1-464, 2 ll. (one folding), 16°. Prayers and lessons on the Gospels, for Sundays and holy days, from the beginning of Advent until Easter, in the language of Greenland.

*Copies seen:* Brinley, British Museum, Trumbull.

A copy at the Brinley sale, No. 5612, brought $3; at the Pinart sale, No. 523, a copy was bought for 2 fr. by Quaritch, who prices it, No. 30055, at 5s.

—— Testamentitokab | Makpérsægèjsa Illangoeet, | Josvab eŕkartòursirsudlo aglegèjt, | Samuelim aglegéj siñrdleet ard- | lèjdlo, aglékkæt Kouginnik | siñrdleet ardlèjdlo, | Kalàdlin okàuzeennut nuktérsimarsut, nark'igu- | tingoænniglo sukniàrsimarsut | Gjerleviniut Ensleviinudlo Pellesiénnit | Peter Kraghmit. | [Two lines quotation.]

Kjöbenhavnime. | Fabritiusib de Teugnagelib nak'itteriviàne | nak'ittársimarsut. | 1836.

*Literal translation:* The old testament's | its books' parts of them, | Joshua's and the Judges' their books | Samuel's his books the first and the sec- | ond | the books about Kings first and second | Greenlanders into their speech translated, | and with notes explained | by the people of Gjerlev and Enslev their priest | Peter Kragh. | At Copenhagen. | Fabricius de Tengnagel's on his printing-press | printed.

4 p. ll. pp. 1-708, 3 unnumbered pp. 1-°, in the language of Greenland.—Joshua, pp. 3-95.—

**Kragh (P.)** — Continued.

Judges, pp. 95-194.—I Samuel, pp. 195-329.— II Samuel, pp. 329-439.—I Kings, pp. 441-577.— II Kings, pp. 578-708.

*Copies seen:* Astor, British Museum, Powell.

—— Kaladlit | Pelleserkàngoŕéta | Hans Egedib | Okallòutèi Unnukorsiutit | ajokærsukkamiunt, | agleksimagalloæt Johan Christian Mörch-mit | Kakortormiut niuvertorigalloŕénnit | mànalo titàrnekartlsimarsut | Peter Kragh-mit | Gjerleviniut Pellesiénnit. |

Kjöbenhavnime. | Fabritius de Tengnagelib nakk'itteriviàne | nakk'ittársimarsut. | 1837.

*Literal translation:* The Greenlanders | their priest's | Hans Egede's | discourses means for passing the evening | to his disciples, | written-formerly by Johan Christian Mörch | the people of Kakortok [white place—Julianehoot] their late trader, | and now arranged by Peter Kragh | the people of Gjerlev their priest. | At Copenhagen. | Fabricius de Tengnagel's on his printing-press | printed.

Pp. 1-189, 16°, in the language of Greenland.

*Copies seen:* Congress, Harvard, Pilling, Powell.

A copy at the Pinart sale, No. 505, brought 2 fr.

Also issued with Danish translation, title as above, followed by Danish title as follows:

—— Grönlændernes | fÿrste Præsts | Hans Egedes | Aften-Samtaler | med sine Diciple, | forfattede efter Campe | af | Johan Christian Mörch, | forhenværende Kjÿbmand ved Julianehaab, | og nu udgivne af | Peter Kragh, | Præst i Gjerlev. |

Kjöbenhavn : | Trykt i Fabricius de Tengnagels Bogtrykkeri : | 1837.

Pp. 1-376, 16°, alternate pages Danish and Greenland. Eskimo title verso l. 1, Danish title recto l. 2. Evening Conversations of Hans Egede with his disciples, compiled by Mörch and newly edited by P. Kragh.

*Copies seen:* Harvard, Trumbull, Watkinson.

—— Erkarsàutigirsecksæt | sillársoarmik, | agléksimarsut | G. F. Ursinimit, | nuktersimarsut | P. Kragh-mit, | Lintrupimiut Pellesiænnit. |

Kjöbenhavnime. | Fabritius de Tengnagelib nak'itteriviàne nak'ittarsimarsut. | 1839.

*Literal translation:* Things to be thought of | about the great heavens | written by | G. F. Ursini, | translated | by P. Kragh | the people of Lintrup their priest. | At Copenhagen. | Fabricius de Tengnagel's on his printing-press printed.

**Kragh (P.)** — Continued.

Pp. 1-23, 16º. Treatise on astronomy, by Ursini, translated into the Greenland by Kragh.

It is probable that this work was issued also with alternate pages, Danish and Greenland, as Erslew mentions an edition: Kjöbenhavnime, 1839, 8º, 45 pp.

*Copies seen:* Powell.

— Okalluktualiæt, | nuktórsimarsnt, | R. J. Brandt-mit, | Kârsome niiivertuk-sâugalloamit, | ark'iksórsimarsut titâr-nekartisimarsudlo | P. Kragh-mit | Lin-trupimiut Hjertiugimiudlo Pellesiénnit | Kjöbenhavnime. | Fabritius de Ten-guagolib nak'itteriviâue nak'ittársim-arsnt. | 1839.

*Literal translation:* Discourses | translated | by R. J. Brandt | at Kârsok late assistant trader | put in order and arranged | by P. Kragh | the people of Lintrup and the people of Hjerting their priest. | At Copenhagen. | Fabricius de Tengnagel's on his printing-press printed.

Pp. 1-118, 16º, in the language of Greenland.

*Copies seen:* Harvard, Powell.

A copy at the Pinart sale, No. 140, brought 1 fr.

— Attuægâutit, | Evangeliumit sukuîâ-utôjt Paaskimit | Trinitatis Sabbateesa kingardliien- | nut attuægeksæt, | kat-tersorsimarsut Kaladlidlo | okauzeen-nut nuktersimarsut | Pellisimit Peter Kraghmit, | [Three lines quotation.] | Kjöbenhavnime: | Bianco Lunob nak-k'itteriviâue nakk'ittarsimarsnt. | 1848.

*Literal translation:* Readings | from the Gos-pel explanations from Easter | to Trinitys Sunday's its next following [the Sunday after Trinity] | to be used, | collected and Green-landers | into their speech translated | by the priest Peter Kragh. | At Copenhagen: | Bianco Luno's on his printing-press printed.

Pp. i-viii, 1-731, 2 ll. 18º, in the language of Greenland.

*Copies seen:* Harvard, Trumbull.

A copy was bought by Quaritch at the Pinart sale, No. 522, for 4 fr.

— Attuækkæn illnarsautiksæt | ille-geennut opertunnut, | kattersorsimar-snt | Umiktormint pellesiænnit, W. A. Wexelsimit, | mânalo nuktersimarsnt | Oesbymiut pellesertaénnit P. Kraghmit. | [Four lines quotation.] | Kiobenhavnime 1850. | Bianco Lunob nak'itterviane nok'ittarsimarsut.

*Literal translation:* Readings means for im-provement | for congregations faithful, | col-lected | by the people of Umiktok their priest, W. A. Wexels, | but now translated | by the people of Oesby their priest P. Kragh. | Copen-

---

**Kragh (P.)** — Continued.

hagen 1850. | Bianco Luno's on his printing-press printed.

Title 1 l. preface, signed Peter Kragh, Oct, 7, 1850, pp. iii-viii, text (translation of Wilhelm Andreas Wexels' sermons, each followed by a hymn) entirely in the Greenland, pp. 1-206, 1 l. 16º. Pp. 175-206 entirely hymns.

*Copies seen:* British Museum.

[——] Erkærsautiksæt, | udlut nungud-lugit attuægæksæt. | Kattersorsimarsnt J. Panlusimit. | Nordleen illæunit. | [Two lines quotation.] | Nakittarsimarsut Pet. Chr. Kochib | nakitterivigiksoâne, | Haderslevime. | 1853.

*Literal translatio n :* Things to be though of | every day to be used. | Collected by J. Paulus. | [?] | Printed on Pet. Chr. Koch's | his great printing-press, | at Haderslev.

Picture of the crucifixion with Eskimo title 1 l. title 1 l. preface, signed P. Kragh, pp. iii-iv, verses pp. vi-viii, text pp. 1-400, 16º. Book of daily devotion entirely in the Eskimo of Greenland.

*Copies seen:* Pilling, Powell.

My copy, bought of the Unitäts-Buchhand-lung, Gnadau, Saxony, cost 2 M. 80 pf.

— Unnersòutiksak | ernisúksiortunnut | Kalâdlit nunaunnôtunnut, | Kablunäin okâuzeenne agléksimarsok | nekkur-sârsomit Lerkimit, | Kalâdlidlo okân-zeennut nuktersimarsok | Pellesimit | Peter-Kraghmit. | Kjöbenhavnime. | Louis Kleinib nak'-itt'eriviksoâne. | 1867.

*Literal translation:* Instructions | for mid-wives | Greenlanders in their land living | Eu-ropeans in their speech written | by the healer Lerch, | and Greenlanders into their speech translated | by the priest | Peter Kragh. | At Copenhagen. | On Louis Klein's his great print-ing-press.

*Second title:* Underretning | for Jordemødre | i Grønland, | skreven paa Dansk | af | Chirurg Lerch, | oversat paa Grønlandsk | af | Præsten Kragh. | Kjöbenhavn. | Louis Kleins Bogtrykkeri. | 1867.

Pp. 2-63, alternate pages Greenland and Danish. Eskimo title verso 1 l. Danish title recto l. 2, 16º.

*Copies seen:* Powell.

Erslew titles an edition: Copenhagen, 1829, 4 sheets [64 pp.?], 8º.

— Johannesib koïrsirsnb nejsâ innuka-juîtsame . . . . nuktersimarsok P. Kragh-mit.

Haderslevime, 1871.

*Literal translation:* John's the Baptist's his warning in the wilderness . . . . trans-lated by P. Kragh. At Haderslev.

**Kragh (P.)** — Continued.

98 pp. 8°, in the Greenland language. Title from Dr. Rink.

—— Greenland Sermons. (27.) *

27 sheets, 8°, printed at the expense of the Danish Missionary Society. Title from Dr. Rink.

"Peder Kragh, the son of Michael Kragh and Kirstine Jensen, was born at Gimming, then annexed to Randers, November 20, 1794. In 1804 he entered the school at Randers, in 1806 the Latin school at the same place, and thence, in 1813, to the university. He entered the Greenland seminary in April, 1817; passed his final examination in theology in October of the same year, and in January, 1818, was sent as missionary to Egedesminde and annexed districts, in Disco Bay, in North Greenland, whither he set out in May, arriving in August, and before the end of the same month gave his first sermon in the Greenland. He remained in that office for ten years. In 1825 he established the mission of Upernivik, abandoned forty years afterward. He left Greenland in July, 1828, and arrived at Copenhagen about the end of August of the same year. In January, 1829, he became parson at Gjerlev and Enslev, in the bishopric of Aarhuus, and in October, 1838, at Lintrup and Hjerting, in the bishopric of Ribe.

"There are in circulation in Greenland by this author various translations, namely, Ingemann's Voices in the Wilderness, and The High Game, Krummacher's Parables and Feast Book, Hans Egede's Life, and some cradle songs and other songs, for the publication of which no money could be obtained."—*Erslew.*

**Krause** (Aurel). Verzeichniss einiger Tschuktschischer- und Eskimo-Wörter von der Tschukschen Halbinsel.

In Deutsche geographische Blätter, herausgegeben von der Geographischen Gesellschaft in Bremen, vol. 6, Heft 3, pp. 266-278, Bremen, 1883, 8°.

**Kristumiutut tugsiautit.**

Kjöbenhavnime, 1876.

*Literal translation:* In the Christian manner psalms. At Copenhagen.

115 pp. 8°. Psalm book in the Eskimo language of Greenland. Title from Dr. Rink.

**Kristusimik** Mallingnaursut * ʼ * Thomasib â Kempisib. See **Egede** (P.).

**Kumlien** (Ludwig). Contributions | to the | natural history | of | Arctic America, | made in connection with | the Howgate polar expedition, 1877-78, | by | Ludwig Kumlien, | naturalist of the expedition. |

**Kumlien (L.)** — Continued.

Washington: | Government Printing Office. | 1879.

Printed cover 1 l. pp. 1-179, 8°. Forms Bulletin 15 of the National Museum.

Mr. Kumlien's contributions to this pamphlet are as follows: Ethnology, pp. 11-46; Mammals, pp. 47-67; Birds, pp. 69-105. The first contains a few Innuit terms passim, and numerals 1-10, pp. 26-27; the last two contain many names of animals and birds in the Cumberland Eskimo.

*Copies seen:* Congress, Powell.

Reprinted, in part, as follows:

—— Ethnology. Fragmentary Notes on the Eskimo of Cumberland Sound. By Ludwig Kumlien.

In Science, vol. 1, pp. 85-88, 100-101, 214-218, New York, 1880, 4°.—Innuit numerals, 1-10, p. 216.

**Kúngip** tugdliata perkússutai | Kalâtdlit nisigssuissortait piv- | dlugit nunâtalo akigssautai pivdlugit, | Kungip tugdliata sulivfiane agdlagsimassut 1872 me | Januarip 31 ane.

*Literal translation:* The king's his nearest [ministers] things that he gives commands about | in reference to the Greenlanders their governors | and in reference to the land's its wealth, | at the minister's his working place [office] written in 1872 | on January 31.

No title-page; pp. 1-18, 8°. Instructions for the trading posts in Greenland, in the Eskimo language.

*Copies seen:* Powell.

**Kúpernerit** nápantânput. See **Sørensen** (B. F.).

**Kuskokwim.** [Note book with various vocabularies, notes on the dialects of Koskokwim, Nunivak, &c.]

Manuscript in possession of M. Alph. L. Pinart.

Kuskokwim:
Vocabulary.   See Baer (K. E. von), Furuhelm (H.), Kuskokwim, Vocabularies, Wrangell (F. von).

Kuskutchewak:
Vocabulary.   See Baer (K. E. von), Latham (R. G.), Morgan (L. H.), Richardson (J.).

Kuskwógmüt:
Vocabulary.   See Dall (W. H.), Schott (W.), Zagoskin (L. A.).

Kwigpak:
Vocabulary.   See Schott (W.).

# L.

**Labrador:**
　Bible:

| | |
|---|---|
| Pentateuch. | See Moselil. |
| Genesis. | Moscaib. |
| Exodus. | Four Books. |
| Leviticus. | Four Books. |
| Numbers. | Four Books. |
| Deuteronomy. | Four Books. |
| Joshua. | Erdmann (F.). |
| Judges. | Erdmann (F.). |
| Ruth. | Erdmann (F.). |
| Samuel I-II. | Erdmann (F.). |
| Kings I-II. | Erdmann (F.). |
| Chronicles I-II. | Erdmann (F.). |
| Ezra. | Erdmann (F.). |
| Nehemiah. | Erdmann (F.). |
| Esther. | Erdmann (F.). |
| Job. | Erdmann (F.). |
| Psalms. | Davidib. |
| Psalms. | Erdmann (F.). |
| Proverbs. | Erdmann (F.), |
| Proverbs. | Salomonib. |
| Ecclesiastes. | Erdmann (F.). |
| Song of Solomon. | Erdmann (F.). |
| Isaiah. | Prophetib. |
| Jeremiah. | Salomonib. |
| Ezekiel. | Salomonib. |
| Daniel. | Salomonib. |
| Minor prophets. | Salomonib. |
| New Testament. | Testamentetak ta-medsa, |
| New Testament. | Testamentitak ta-medsa. |
| Four Gospels. | Burghardt (C. F.), |
| Four Gospels. | Tamedsa Matthæusib, |
| Four Gospels. | Testamentitak ta-medsa. |
| Matthew (in part). | Warden (D. B.). |
| John (in part). | American Bible Society, |
| John (in part). | Bagster (J.), |
| John (in part). | Bible Society, |
| John (in part). | British and Foreign Bible Society, |
| John (in part). | Church, |
| John (in part). | Kohlmeister (B. G.), |
| John (in part). | Warden (D. B.). |
| Acts. | Acts, |
| Acts. | Apostelit, |
| Acts. | Testamentitak ta-medsa. |
| Epistles. | Apostelit (note), |
| Epistles. | Epistles. |
| Revelation. | Apostelit (note). |
| Bible lessons. | Jerusalemib, |
| Bible lessons. | Jesuse, |
| Bible lessons. | Kaunajok, |
| Bible lessons. | Nâlekam, |
| Bible lessons. | Nalungiak, |
| Bible lessons. | Naughtawkkoa, |
| Bible lessons. | Nauk taipkoa, |
| Bible lessons. | Nukakpiak, |
| Bible lessons. | Nukakpiarkœk, |
| Bible lessons. | Nukapiak, |

**Labrador—Continued.**

| | |
|---|---|
| Bible lessons. | See Senfkornetun-ipok, |
| Bible lessons. | Tamedsa, |
| Bible lessons. | Tussajungnik, |
| Bible lessons. | Ussornakaut. |
| Bible stories. | Okpernernik, |
| Bible stories. | Pillitikset, |
| Bible stories. | Pingortitsinermik, |
| Bible stories. | Senfkornesutépok, |
| Bible stories. | Unipkautsit. |
| Catechism. | Bourquin (T.), |
| Catechism. | Erdmann (F.). |
| Christian doctrine. | Jesuajb. |
| Chronicles. | Erdmann (F.). |
| Dictionary. | Erdmann (F.). |
| Geography. | Elsner (A. F.). |
| Gospels (Harmony of). | Nalegapta. |
| Grammar. | Bourquin (T.), |
| Grammar. | Freitag (A.). |
| Grammatic comments. | Adelung (J. C.) and Vater (J. S.). |
| Hymns. | Imgerutit, |
| Hymns. | Tukslarutsit. |
| Liturgy. | Liturgiit atoraksat, |
| Liturgy. | Liturgiit upvalo. |
| Lord's Prayer. | Bergholtz (G. F.), |
| Lord's Prayer. | Strale (F. A.). |
| Numerals. | Antrim (B. J.), |
| Numerals. | Cull (R.), |
| Numerals. | Stearns (W. A.) |
| Prayers. | Tukslarutsit |
| Primer. | Okautsit. |
| Sermons. | Okâlautsit. |
| Songs. | Imgerutsit. |
| Tract. | Bibelib. |
| Vocabulary. | Fry (E.), |
| Vocabulary. | Latrobe (P.) and Washington (J.), |
| Vocabulary. | Lesley (J. P.), |
| Vocabulary. | Lesseps (J. B. B.), |
| Vocabulary. | Morgan (L. H.), |
| Vocabulary. | Richardson (J.), |
| Vocabulary. | Stearns (W. A.). |

**La Harpe** (Jean François de). Abrégé |
de | l'histoire générale | des voyages, |
| contenant | Ce qu'il y a de plus re-
marquable, de plus utile & | de mieux
avéré dans les Pays où les Voyageurs |
ont pénétré; les mœurs des Habitans,
la Religion, | les Usages, Arts & Sci-
ences, Commerce, | Manufactures; en-
richie de Cartes géographiques | & de
figures. | Par M. De La Harpe, de
l'Académie Française. | Tome premier
[-trente-deux]. | [Design.] |
　A Paris, | Hôtel de Thou, rue des
Poitevins. | M. DCC. LXXX[-An IX.—
1801] [1780-1801]. | Avec Approbation,
& Privilége du Roi.

32 vols. 8°, and atlas, 1801, 4°.—Remarks on
the Greenland language, with examples (from

**La Harpe** (J. F. de) — Continued.
Anderson, in Cook and King's Voyages), vol. 18, pp. 369-377.
*Copies seen:* Astor, Congress.

—— Abrégé | de | l'Histoire Générale | des voyages, | contenant | ce qu'il y a de plus remarquable, de plus utile et de | mieux avéré dans les pays où les voyageurs ont | pénétré; les mœurs des habitans, la religion, les | usages; arts et sciences, commerce et manufac- | tures. | Par J. F. LaHarpe. | Tome Premier[-Vingt-quatrième]. |
A Paris, | Chez Ledoux et Tenré, Libraires, | Rue Pierre-Sarrozin, Nº 8. | 1816.
24 vols. 12º.—Linguistics, vol. 17, pp. 378-385.
*Copies seen:* British Museum.

—— Abrégé | de | l'histoire générale | des voyages, | contenant | ce qu'il y a de plus remarquable, de plus utile et de mieux | avéré dans les pays où les voyageurs ont pénétré; les | mœurs des habitans, la religion, les usages, arts et | sciences, commerce et manu- factures; | Par J. F. LaHarpe. | Nou- velle édition, | revue et corrigée avec le plus grand soin, | et accompagnée d'un bel atlas in-folio. | Tome premier [-vingt-quatrième]. |
A Paris, | chez Étienne Ledoux, li- braire, | rue Guénégand, Nº 9. | 1820.
24 vols. 8º.—Linguistics, vol. 16, pp. 217-226.
*Copies seen:* Congress.
According to Sabin's Dictionary, No. 38632, there are editions: Paris, Achille Jourdan, 1822, 30 vols. 8º; Paris, 1825, 30 vols. 8º; Lyon, Rusand, 1829-'30, 30 vols. 8º.

**Latham** (Robert Gordon). Miscellaneous Contributions to the Ethnography of North America. By R. G. Latham, M. D.
In Philological Society [of London], Proc. vol. 2, pp. 31-50, [London], 1846, 8º.
Table of words showing affinities among various American tribes, including the Eskimo, pp. 34-38.

—— On the Languages of the Oregon Territory. By R. G. Latham, M. D.
In Ethnological Soc. of London, Journal, vol. I pp 154-166, Edinburgh, [1848], 8º.
A table of ten Sussee words showing affinity with various other American tribes, among them the Eskimo, p. 161.—Short comparative vocabulary of the Sitca and Kadiack, p. 163.— Table showing miscellaneous affinities between the languages of Oregon Territory and the Es- kimo, pp. 164-165.

—— On the Ethnography of Russian America. By R. G. Latham, M. D.

**Latham** (R. G.) — Continued.
In Ethnological Soc. of London, Journal vol. I, pp. 182-191, Edinburgh, [1848], 8º.
Contains general remarks on the classifica- tion of the languages of the above region, and a very brief list of the vocabularies of the languages of that region which have been printed, including the Eskimo.

—— The | natural history | of | the varieties of man. | By | Robert Gordon Latham, M. D., F. R. S., | late Fellow of King's College, Cambridge; | one of the Vice-Presidents of the Ethnologi- cal Society, London; | Corresponding Member to the Ethnological Society, | New York, etc. | [Design.] |
London: | John Van Voorst, Pater- noster Row. | M.D.CCCL [1850].
Pp. i-xxviii, 1-574, 8º.—Remarks on the Eskimo language, pp. 288-294.
*Copies seen:* British Museum, Congress.
A presentation copy (dated 1851) at the Squier sale, catalogue No. 638, brought $2.50.

—— Opuscula. | Essays | chiefly | philo- logical and ethnographical | by | Rob- ert Gordon Latham, | M. A., M. D., F. R. S., etc. | Late Fellow of Kings Col- lege, Cambridge, late Professor of En- glish | in University College, London, late assistant physician | at the Middle- sex Hospital. | ·
Williams & Norgate, | 14 Henrietta Street, Covent Garden, London | and | 20 South Frederick Street, Edinburgh. | Leipzig, R. Hartmann. | 1860.
Pp. i-vi, 1-418, 8º. A reprint of a number of articles which appeared in the publications of the Ethnological and Philological Societies of London. Addenda and Corrigenda, pp. 379-417, contain linguistic material not appearing in any of the former articles; amongst it are the numerals, 1-5, of the Eskimo, Aleutian, and Kamskadale, p. 410.
*Copies seen:* Astor, Boston Public, Brinton, Bureau of Ethnology, Congress, Watkinson.
A presentation copy brought $2.37 at the Squier sale, catalogue No. 639. The Murphy copy, No. 1438, sold for $1.

—— Elements | of | comparative philol- ogy, | By | R. G. Latham, M. A., M. D., F. R. S., &c., | late fellow of King's College, Cambridge; and late professor of English | in University College, Lon- don. |
London: | Walton and Maberly, | Upper Gower street, and Ivy lane, Paternoster row; | Longman, Green, Longman, Roberts, and Green, | Pater-

**Latham** (R. G.) — Continued.
noster row. | 1862. | The Right of
Translation is Reserved.

Pp. i-xxxii, errata 1 l. pp. 1-774, 8°.—Comparative vocabulary of the Unalashka, Kadiak, Kuskutshewac, and Labrador, pp. 386-387.— Two Eskimo [Asiatic] vocabularies, p. 387.

*Copies seen:* Astor, British Museum, Congress, Eames, Watkinson.

**Latrobe** (*Rev.* Peter) and **Washington** (*Capt.* John). Vocabulary of the Eskimo of Labrador.

In Richardson (*Sir* John), Arctic Searching Expedition, pp. 483-496, London, 1851, 8°.

Reprinted in the New York edition of 1852, pp. 483-496.

**Leclerc** (Charles). Bibliotheca | Americana | Catalogue raisonné | d'une très-précieuse | collection de livres anciens | et modernes | sur l'Amérique et les Philippines | Classés par ordre alphabétique de noms d'Auteurs. | Rédigé par Ch. Leclerc. | [Design.] |
Paris | Maisonneuve & C^le | 15, Quai Voltaire | M.D.CCC.LXVII [1867]

Pp. i-vii, 1-407, 8°. Contains a number of Eskimo titles.

*Copies seen:* Congress, Powell.

At the Fischer sale, No. 919, a copy brought 10s.; at the Squier sale, No. 651, $1.50. Leclerc, 1878, No. 345, prices it at 4 fr. The Murphy copy, No. 1452, brought $2.75.

—— Bibliotheca | Americana | Histoire, géographie, | voyages, archéologie et linguistique | des | deux Amériques | et | des Iles Philippines | rédigée | par Ch. Leclerc | [Design.] |
Paris | Maisonneuve et C^le, libraires-éditeurs | 25, Quai Voltaire, 25. | 1878

2 p. ll. pp. i-xx, 1-737, 1 l. 8°.—The linguistic part of this volume occupies pp. 537-643, and is arranged under families, the Aléoute occurring on p. 550; the Esquiman (Greenlandals) pp. 579-581.

*Copies seen:* Boston Athenæum, Pilling.

Priced by Quaritch, No. 12172, at 12s.; another copy, No. 12173, large paper, £1 1s. Leclerc's Supplement, 1881, No. 2831, prices it at 15 fr., and No. 2832, a copy on Holland paper, at 30 fr. A large-paper copy priced by Quaritch, No. 30230, at 12s.

—— Bibliotheca Americana | Histoire, géographie, | voyages, archéologie et linguistique | des deux Amériques | Supplément | N° I. Novembre 1881 | [Design]. |
Paris | Maisonneuve & C^le, libraires-éditeurs | 25, quai Voltaire, 25 | 1881

Printed cover 1 l. title 1 l. advertisement 1 l. pp. 1-102, 1 l. 8°.

*Copies seen:* Congress, Pilling.

Legends:
Greenland.          See **Kaladlit**,
                       Pok.
Tchiglit.            Petitot (E. F. S. J.).

Lenox: This word following a title indicates that a copy of the work referred to was seen by the compiler in the Lenox Library, New York City.

**Lerch** (—). See **Kragh** (P.).

**Lesley** (Joseph Peter). On the Insensible Gradation of Words, by J. P. Lesley.

In American Philosoph. Soc. Proc. vol. 7, pp. 129-155, Philadelphia 1862, 8°.

Contains a few words on Greenland Esquimaux, Labrador, and Kadjak, pp. 136-139, 145-148, 148-152.

**Lesseps** (Jean Baptiste Barthélemy, *baron* de). Journal historique | du voyage | de M. de Lesseps, | Consul de France, employé dans l'expédition | de M. le comte de la Pérouse, en qualité | d'interprète du Roi; | Depuis l'instant où il a quitté les frégates Françoises | au port Saint-Pierre & Saint-Paul du Kamtschatka, | jusqu'à son arrivée en France, le 17 octobre 1788. | Première [-seconde] partie. | [Design.] |
A Paris, | de l'imprimerie royale. | M. DCCXC [1790].

2 vols. 8°.—Vocabulaire des langues Kamtschadale, Koriaque, Tchouktchi et Lamoute, vol. 2, pp. 355-375.—Vocabulaire de la langue Kamtschadale, vol. 2, pp. 376-380.

*Copies seen:* British Museum, Congress.

At the Fischer sale, No. 2517, a copy brought 12s.

—— Travels | in | Kamtschatka, | during the years 1787 and 1788. | Translated from the French of | M. de Lesseps, Consul of France, | and | interpreter to the Count de la Pérouse, now | engaged in a voyage round the world, by | command of His Most Christian Majesty. | In two volumes. | Volume I[-II]. |
London : | Printed for J. Johnson, St. Paul's Church-yard. | 1790.

2 vols. 8°.—Linguistics, vol. 2, pp. 384-403, 404-408.

*Copies seen:* Boston Athenæum, British Museum.

—— Voyage | de | M. De Lesseps | du Kamtschatka en France | avec | une Préface par Ferdinand de Lesseps | [Picture.] |
Paris | Maurice Dreyfours, Éditeur | 13, Rue du Faubourg-Montmartre, 13 | Tous droits réservés [n. d.]

Pp. i-xx, 1-248, table 1 l. 12°.—Vocabulaire

**Lesseps** (J. B. B.)—Continued.

des langues Kamtschadale, Koriaque, Tchouk-tchi et Lamoute, pp. 237-248.

*Copies seen:* British Museum.

The edition, Riga & Leipzig, 1791, 2 vols. 12°, contains no linguistics. (British Museum.)

Letters V and L, Eskimo. See Gallatin (A.).

Linguistic discussion:
Greenland.                  See Rink (H. J.),
                            Wöldike (M.).
Karalit.                    Heckewelder (J. G. E.).

**ЛИСЯНСКІЙ (ЮРІЙ).** [Lisiansky (*Capt.* Urey).] Путешествіе | вокругъ свѣта въ | 1803. 4. 5. и 1806 годахъ, | по повелѣнію | его императорскаго величества | Александра Перваго, | на кораблѣ | Невѣ, | подъ началь-ствомъ | флота капитанълейтенанта, нынѣ капитана | 1-го ранга и кавалера | Юрія Лисянскаго. | Часть первая[-вторая]. | Санктпетербургъ, въ типографіи Ѳ. Дрех-слера, | 1812.

*Translation.*—Voyage | around the world | in the years 1803, 4, 5 and 1806 | by order of | His Imperial Majesty | Alexander I, | on the ship | Neva, | under command | of Captain-Lieuten-ant of the Navy, now Captain | of the 1st rank | and Knight Urey Lisiansky. | Vol. I[-II]. | St. Petersburg, | in the printing-office of Th. Drechsler, | 1812.

2 vols. 8°.—Short vocabulary of the languages of the northwestern parts of America, with Russian translation; Russian-Kadiak-Kenai and Russian-Sitka-Unalaskha, vol. 2, pp. 154-181, 182-207.

*Copies seen:* British Museum, Congress.

—— A | voyage round the world, | in | the years 1803, 4, 5, & 6; | performed | by order of his imperial majesty | Alex-ander the First, emperor of Russia, | in | the ship Neva, | by | Urey Lisian-sky, | captain in the Russian navy, and | knight of the orders of St. George and St. Vladimer. ꜰ

London : | Printed for John Booth, Duke street, Portland place; and | Longman, Hurst, Rees, Orme, & Brown, Paternoster row ; | by S. Hamilton, Weybridge, Surrey. | 1814.

Pp. i-xxi, 1 l. pp. 1-388, maps, 4°.—Appendix No. 3, Vocabulary of the languages of the islands of Cadiack and Oonalashca, the bay of Kenay, and Sitca sound, pp. 329-337.

*Copies seen:* Astor, Boston Athenæum, Brit-ish Museum, Congress.

A copy at the Pinart sale, No. 1372, brought 5 fr.

These vocabularies reprinted in **Davidson** (G.), Report relative to * * * Alaska, in Coast Survey, Ann. Rept. 1867, pp. 293-298, Wash-ington, 1869, 4°; again in Davidson (G.), Report relative to * * * Alaska, in Ex. Doc. 77, 40th

**ЛИСЯНСКІЙ (ЮРІЙ)**—Continued.

Cong., 2d sess, pp. 328-333; and again in Coast Survey, Coast Pilot of Alaska, pp. 215-221, Washington, 1869, 8°. For extracts see Schott (W.), Zagoskin (L. A.), Zelenoi (S. J.).

Litany, Greenland. See ilagîgsut.

**Liturgîit** | atoraksat | Jêsusib Ânia-viane. |

London : | Printed for the Society for the | Furtherance of the Gospel among the Heathen, | 97, Hatton Garden. | By Norman & Skeen, Maiden Lane, Cov-ent Garden. | 1867.

*Literal translation:* Liturgy | to be used | at Jesus' his time of suffering.

Title verso blank 1 l. text entirely in the lan-guage of Labrador, pp. 3-48, 18°.

*Copies seen:* Pilling, Powell.

My copy, procured of the Unitäts-Buchhand-lung, Gnadau, Saxony, cost 70 pf.

**Liturgîit** | upvalo: | tuksiarutsit, im-gerutillo kujalitiksat nertordlerntik-sallo | atoraksat illagêktunut | Labra-doremêtunut. |

Stolpen. | Druck von Gustav Winter. | 1867.

*Literal translation:* Liturgy | daily ! : | psalms, and hymns of-thanksgiving and of-praise | a manual for congregations | living-in-Labrador. |

Title verso blank 1 l. contents pp. iii-iv, text entirely in the language of Labrador, pp. 1-278, 16°. Hymns sung during week day services.

*Copies seen:* Pilling, Powell.

My copy, procured of the Unitäts-Buchhand-lung, Gnadau, Saxony, cost 2 M. 80 pf.

Liturgy :
Greenland.                  See Tuksiautit.
Labrador.                   Liturglit atoraksat,
                            Liturglit upvalo.

**Long** (John). Voyages and Travels | of an | Indian Interpreter and Trader, | describing | the Manners and Customs | of the | North American Indians; | with | an Account of the Posts | sit-uated on the River Saint Laurence, Lake Ontario, &c. | To which is added, | A Vocabulary | of | the Chippeway Language. | Names of Furs and Skins, in English and French. | A list of words | in the | Iroquois, Mohegan, Shawa-nee, and Esquimeaux Tongues, | and a table, shewing | the Analogy between the Algoukin and Chippeway Lan-guages. | By J. Long. |

London : | Printed for the author; and sold by Robson, Bond-Street; De-brett, | Piccadilly; T. and J. Egerton, Charing-Cross; White and Son, Fleet-

**Long (J.)** — Continued.

| Street; Sewell, Cornhill; Edwards, Pall-Mall; and Messrs. Tay- | lors, Holborn, London; Fletcher, Oxford; and Bull, Bath. | M, DCC, XCI [1791].

1 p. l. pp. i–xi, 1–295, map, 4°.—Vocabulary of the Esquimaux (22 words), p. 183.

*Copies seen:* Astor, Boston Athenæum, British Museum, Congress, Trumbull, Watkinson. The copy at the Field sale, No. 1379, brought $5.50. Priced by Leclerc, 1878, No. 942, at 60 fr., an uncut copy. The Brinley copy, No. 5661, sold for $5.50, "tree-calf, yellow edges, a large and exceptionally fine copy." At the Pinart sale, No. 558, it brought 20 fr. and at the Murphy sale, No. 1518, $5.50.

—— J. Long's | westindischen Dolmetschers und Kaufmanns | See- und Land-Reisen, | enthaltend: | eine Beschreibung der Sitten und Gewohnheiten | der | nordamerikanischen Wilden; | der | englischen Fortes oder Schanzen längs dem St. Lorenz- | Flusse, dem See Ontario u. s. w.; | ferner | ein umständliches Wörterbuch der Chippewäischen und anderer | nordamerikanischen Sprachen. | Aus dem Englischen. | Herausgegeben | und mit einer kurzen Einleitung über Kanada und einer erbesserten | Karte versehen | von | E. A. W. Zimmermann, | Hofrath und Professor in Braunschweig. | Mit allergnädigsten Freiheiten. |

Hamburg, 1791. | bei Benjamin Gottlob Hoffmann.

Pp. i–xxiv, 1 l. pp. 1–334, map, 8°.—Linguistics, p. 217.

*Copies seen:* Brown.

At the Fischer sale, No. 969, a copy brought 1s. I have seen a German edition: Berlin, 1792, 8°, and a French one: Paris, an II [1794], 8°, neither of which contains the linguistic material. I have also seen mention of an edition: Paris, 1810.

**Lord's.** The Lord's Prayer | In One Hundred and Thirty-One Tongues. | Containing all the principal languages | spoken | in Europe, Asia, Africa, and America. |

London: | St. Paul's Publishing Company, | 12, Paternoster Square. | [n. d.]

Title verso blank 1 l. preface, signed F. Pincott, fellow of the Royal Asiatic Society, pp. 1–2, contents pp. 3–4, text pp. 5–62, 12°.—Lord's Prayer in the Greenland, p. 58.

*Copies seen:* Church Missionary Society.

Lord's Prayer:

| | |
|---|---|
| Aleut. | See Gebet. |
| Eskimo. | Atkinson (C.), |
| | Hall (C. F.), |
| | Hössler (—). |

**Lord's Prayer** — Continued.

| Greenland. | Adelung (J. C.) and Vater (J. S.), |
|---|---|
| | Auer (A.), |
| | Bergholtz (G. F.), |
| | Borgmann (G. von), |
| | Bodoni (J. B.), |
| | Egede (H.), |
| | Fauvel-Gouraud (F.), |
| | Hervas (L.), |
| | Lord's Prayer, |
| | Marcel (J. J.), |
| | Naphegyi (G.), |
| | Richard (L.), |
| | Strale (F. A.), |
| Hudson Bay. | Peck (E. J.). |
| Labrador. | Bergholtz (G. F.), |
| | Strale (F. A.). |

**Lowe (F.)** Wenjaminow über die aleutischen Inseln und deren Bewohner Von Herrn F. Lowe. ·

In Erman (A.), Archiv für wissenschaftliche Kunde von Russland, vol. 2, pp. 459–495, Berlin, 1842, 8°.

Brief remarks on the Aleut language, pp. 486–487.

Reprinted as follows:

—— Les Isles Aléoutes et leurs habitants. Par M. Venjaminov. Article de M. Erman [F. Lowe]. Traduit de l'allemand.

In Nouvelles Annales des Voyages, vol. 2, 1849 (vol. 122 of the collection), pp. 66–82, Paris, n. d. 8°, and vol. 4, 1849 (vol. 124 of the collection), pp. 112–148, Paris, n. d. 8°.

**Ludewig (Hermann E.).** The | literature | of | American aboriginal languages. | By | Hermann E. Ludewig. | With additions and corrections | by Professor Wm. W. Turner. | Edited by Nicolas Trübner. |

London: | Trübner and Co., 60, Paternoster row. | MDCCCLVIII [1858].

Pp. i–viii, 1 l. pp. ix–xxiv, 1–258, 8°. Arranged alphabetically by families. Addenda by Wm. W. Turner and Nicolas Trübner, pp. 210–246, index pp. 247–256, errata pp. 257–258.

Contains a list of grammars and vocabularies of the following peoples: Aglegmutes, pp. 3–4; Aleutans, p. 4; Eskimo, pp. 69–72, 220–221; Fox Islands, pp. 74, 221; Inkülürchliüate or Kangjulit, pp. 86, 223; Kadjak, pp. 90–91; Kuskokwimes, Tchwagmjutes, Kuskutschewak, or Kushkukchwakmutes, pp. 98, 226; Norton Sound, p. 134; Prince William's Sound, p. 154; Tschugatschi, p. 191; Tschuktchi, pp. 191, 242; Ugalenzi, pp. 194, 243; Unalashka, pp. 195, 244.

*Copies seen:* Congress, Eames, Pilling.

A copy at the Fischer sale, No. 990, brought 5s. 6d.; at the Field sale, No. 1403, $2.63; at the Squier sale, No. 699, $2 62; another copy, 1906, $2.38. Priced by Leclerc, 1878, No. 2073, at 15 fr. The Pinart copy, No. 505, sold for 25 fr. and the Murphy copy, No. 1540, for $2.50.

66

**Luther's Catechism:**
Greenland. See Ajokærsoutit.
Egede (H.),
Egede (Paul),
Katekismuse.

**Lutké** (Frédéric). Voyage | autour du monde, | exécuté par ordre | de sa majesté l'empereur Nicolas I<sup>er</sup>, | Sur la Corvette Le Séniavine, | Dans les années 1826, 1827, 1828 et 1829, | par Frédéric Lutké, | capitaine de vaisseau, aide-de-camp de S. M. l'empereur, | commandant de l'expédition. | Partie Historique, | avec un atlas, lithographié d'après les dessins originaux | d'Alexandre Postels et du

**Lutké** (F.) — Continued.
Baron Kittlitz. | Traduit du russe sur le manuscrit original, sous les yeux | de l'auteur, | par le conseiller d'état F. Boyé. | Tome premier[-troisième]. |

Paris, | typographie de Firmin Didot Frères, | imprimeurs de l'institut, rue Jacob, N° 24. | 1835[-1836].
3 vols. maps, 8°, and atlas, folio.—Remarks upon the language and a vocabulary of the Ounalachka, vol. 1, pp. 236-247.
*Copies seen:* Congress.
Dall and Baker's Bibliography of Alaska gives a brief title of an edition: Paris, Engelman & Cie. 1835-1836.

# M.

**M'Keevor** (Thomas). A | voyage | to | Hudson's Bay, | during the summer | of 1812. | Containing | a particular account of the icebergs and other | phenomena which present themselves | in those regions; | also, | a description of the Esquimeaux and North American Indians; their manners, customs, | dress, language, &c. &c. &c. | By | Thomas M'Keevor, M. D. | of the Dublin Lying-in Hospital. | [Six lines.] |
London: | Printed for Sir Richard Phillips and Co. | Bride-Court, Bridge-Street. | 1819.
2 p. ll. pp. 1-76, 8°. Appended, with full title-page, is: Voyage to the North Pole, by the Chevalier de la Poix de Freminville, pp. 77-96.
Forms portion of vol. 2 of New Voyages and Travels, London, Printed for Sir Richard Phillips & Co.—Vocabulary (27 words) of the Esquimaux, pp. 29-30.
*Copies seen:* British Museum, Congress.

**Mahlemût:**
Vocabulary. See Bannister (H. M.),
Dall (W. H.),
Pinart (A. L.),
Smith (E. E.),
Whymper (F.).

**Maisonneuve:** This word following a title indicates that a copy of the work referred to was seen by the compiler in the publishing house of Maisonneuve Frères et Ch. Leclerc, Paris, France.

**Marcel** (Jean Jacques). Oratio dominica | CL linguis versa, | et propriis cujusque linguæ | characteribus | plerumque expressa; | Edente J. J. Marcel, | typographeii imperialis administro generali. | [Design.] |
Parisiis, | typis imperialibus. | Anno repar. sal. 1805, | imperiique Napoleonis primo.

**Marcel** (J. J.) — Continued.
Half-title reverse blank 1 l. title reverse Lord's Prayer in Hebrew (version No. 1) 1 l. text 80 unnumbered ll. index 4 ll. dedication 1 l. large 8°. The versions are numbered 1-150.—Lord's Prayer in Groenlandice (ex Evang. groenlandico Hafniæ edito), No. 132.
*Copies seen:* British Museum, Congress.
Some copies printed on large paper, with the 5 ll. dedication and index immediately following the title leaf; the versos of most of the leaves are blank, and the whole work is divided by half-titles into four parts: Asia, Europe, Africa, America; 161 ll. 4°. (Congress.)

**Marietti** (Pietro), *editor.* Oratio Dominica | in CCL. lingvas versa | et | CLXXX. charactervm formis | vel nostratibvs vel peregrinis expressa | evrante | Petro Marietti | Eqvite Typographo Pontificio | Socio Administro | Typographei | S. Consilii de Propaganda Fide | [Printer's device.] |
Romae | Anno M. DCCC. LXX [1870].
5 p. ll. (half-title, title, and dedication) pp. xi-xxvii, 1-319, 4 ll. indexes, 4°.—Lord's Prayer in the Greenland, p. 309. Title furnished by Dr. J. H. Trumbull from copy in his possession.

**Markham** (Clements Robert). The Arctic Highlanders. By C. R. Markham, Esq.
In Ethnological Soc. of London Trans. vol. 4, pp. 125-137, London, 1866, 8°.
A short comparative vocabulary of the Greenlanders and Siberian, p. 133.
Reprinted in Royal Geographical Society of London's Arctic Geography and Ethnology, pp. 175-189, London, 1875, 8°. The vocabulary occurs on p. 183 names of Arctic Highlanders, pp. 188-189.

**Markham** (C. R.)—Continued.

—— Language of the Eskimo of Greenland.

In Royal Geog. Soc. of London, Arctic Geography and Ethnology, pp. 189-229, London, 1875, 8°.

In addition to a lengthy vocabulary Mr. Markham gives the Eskimo names of many geographic features, with English significations. The above is the third of a series of "Papers on the Greenland Eskimo," by Mr. Markham, in this volume.

**Massachusetts** Historical Society: These words following a title indicate that a copy of the work referred to was seen by the compiler in the library of that society, Boston, Mass.

**Medical Manual:**
Greenland. See Hagen (C.),
Kragh (P.),
Rudolph (—).

**Mednovskio** Vocabulary. See Wrangell (F. von).

**Mentzel** (—). [Jesus the Friend of Children, in the language of Greenland.] *

"Brother Mentzel translated a small duodecimo book entitled 'Jesus the Friend of Children,' being a short compendium of the Bible, written for children and recommended by a society of pious ministers in Denmark for distribution among the Greenlanders of both missions."—*Cranz.*

**Mirlewo** (T. Y. de). See **Yankiewitch** (T.).

**Mörch** (Johan Christian). See **Kragh** (P.).

**Morgan** (Lewis Henry). Smithsonian Contributions to Knowledge. | 218 Systems | of | consanguinity and affinity | of the | human family. | By | Lewis H. Morgan. |

Washington City: | Published by the Smithsonian Institution. | 1871.

Outside title 1 l. pp. i-xiv, i-xii, 1-590, 4°. Forms vol. 17 Smithsonian Contributions to Knowledge.—Comparative vocabulary of the Eskimo of Behring's Sea (Kuskutchewak) from Richardson; of Hudson's Bay, from Gallatin; of Labrador, from Latrobe; of Northumberland Inlet; of Greenland, from Cranz and Egede, p. 268.—List of relationships of the Eskimo west of Hudson's Bay, by Clare; of Greenland, by Kleinschmidt; and of Northumberland Inlet, lines 78-80, pp. 293-382.

*Copies seen:* Congress, Eames, Powell.

At the Squier sale, catalogue No. 889, a copy brought $5.50. Priced by Quaritch, No. 12425*, at £4.

**Morillot** (*Abbé*). Mythologie et Légendes des Esquimaux du Groenland.

In Société Philologique, Actes, vol. 4, 215-268, Paris, 1875, 8°. Contains remarks on the Eskimo language.

**Morillot** (*Abbé*) —Continued.

Separately issued as follows:

—— Actes | de la | Société Philologique | Tome IV.—No. 7.—Juillet 1874. | Mythologie & Légendes | des | Esquimaux | du Groenland |

Paris | Maisonneuve & Cie, Libraires-Editeurs | 15, Quai Voltaire, 15 | 1874.

Printed title on cover, pp. 215-288, 8°.

*Copies seen:* Astor, Trumbull.

**Moselil** Aglangit. | The | Five Books of Moses| translated into the | Esquimaux Language. | By the Missionaries | of the | Unitas Fratrum, | or, | United Brethren. | Printed for the use of the Missions by | The British and Foreign Bible Society. |

London. | W. M'Dowall, Printer, Pemberton Row, | Gough Square. | 1841.

Pp. 1-690, 16°, entirely in the language of Labrador. A portion of the work (Genesis), pp. 1-166, was issued in 1834 with the title: Mosesib Aglangita; and the remainder, pp. 167-698, in 1841 with the title: Four Books of Moses.

*Copies seen:* British and Foreign Bible Society, British Museum.

Bagster's Bible of Every Land mentions an edition of 1847—probably a typographic error.

**Mosesib** Aglangita | Sivorlingit | Assingitalo tuksiarutsiningit nertordlerutingillo | imgerusertaggit. | The book of Genesis | translated into the | Esquimaux language, | by the missionaries | of the | Unitas fratrum, or, United brethren. | Printed for the use of the mission, | by the British and Foreign Bible Society. |

London: | W. M'Dowall, Printer, Pemberton Row, Gough Square. | 1834.

*Literal translation:* Moses his books | their first | and the others their hymns and means-of-praising | in song.

Title 1 l. pp. 3-166, 1 l. 16°, entirely in the Eskimo language of Labrador. See **Moselil** Aglangit.

*Copies seen:* British and Foreign Bible Society.

Priced by Trübner [1856], No. 667, at 5s., and in Leclerc's Supplement, No. 2671, at 5 fr.

**Müller** (*Dr.* Friedrich). Grundriss | der | Sprachwissenschaft | von | Dr. Friedrich Müller | Professor [&c. five lines]. | I. Band. | Einleitung in die Sprachwissenschaft.—Die Sprachen der wollhaarigen Rassen[-II. Band]. |

**Müller** (F.) — Continued.

Wien 1877[-1882]. | Alfred Hölder | K. K. Hof- und Universitäts-Buchhändler. | Rothenthurmstrasse 15.

2 vols. in four parts, 8°, each volume with an outside title and each part with a double title. Vol. 2, part 1, which includes the American languages, has the following special title: Die Sprachen | der | schlichthaarigen Rassen | von | Dr. Friedrich Müller | Professor [&c. eight lines]. | I. Abtheilung. | Die Sprachen der australischen, der hyperboreischen | und der amerikanischen Rassen. | Wien 1882 | Alfred Hölder | K. K. Hof- und Universitäts - Buchhändler | Rothenthurmstrasse 15. Pp. l-x, 1-440, 8°.—Die Sprache der Aleuten, pp. 146-161; Innuit (Eskimo), pp. 162-180.

*Copies seen:* Astor, British Museum, Powell, Watkinson.

[**Muller** (*Rev.* Valentine).] Tuksiautit | erinaglit | Testamentitokame aglek- | simarsut. | [Design.] |

Budissime | nakkitarsimarsut Ernst Moritz Monsibme. | 1842.

*Literal translation:* Psalms | having a tune | in the Old Testament written. | At Bautzen | printed at Ernst Moritz Mons's.

Title verso blank 1 l. text pp. 3-200, 12°. Psalms of David entirely in the language of Greenland. See Davidib; see also Kristumiutit.

*Copies seen:* Pilling, Powell.

My copy, bought of the Unitäts-Buchhandlung Gnadau, Saxony, cost 2 M.

"A version of the Psalms [in Greenland Eskimo], prepared by the Rev. Valentine Muller, one of the Moravian missionaries, from Luther's German version, and carefully compared with the original, was published by the British and Foreign Bible Society in 1842, the edition consisting of 1,200 copies."—*Bagster.*

A later edition as follows:

[——] Tuksiautit | erinaglit Testamenti-tokame aglek- | simarsut. | [Design.] | Budissime | nakkitarsimarsut Ernst Moritz Monsibme. | 1843.

Title verso blank 1 l. text pp. 3-200, 12°. Psalms of David in Eskimo of Greenland.

*Copies seen:* British Museum.

**Murdoch** (John). Catalogue of ethnological specimens collected by the Point Barrow Expedition. Prepared by John Murdoch, A. M., Sergeant Signal Corps, U. S. Army.

In Report of the International Polar Expedition to Point Barrow, Alaska, pp. 61-87, Washington, 1885, 4°.

Gives the Eskimo names of many of the specimens.

—— Natural history. By John Murdoch, A. M., Sergeant Signal Corps, U. S. Army.

In Report of the International Polar Expedition to Point Barrow, Alaska, pp. 89-200, Washington, 1885, 4°.

Throughout sections I-III are given many Eskimo names of mammals, birds, and fishes.

—— [Linguistic results of the Point Barrow Expedition.]

Manuscript in possession of its author. Mr. Murdoch, who is now librarian of the Smithsonian Institution, has compiled all the vocabularies and grammatic notes collected by the different members of the expedition—Lieut. Ray, Dr. Oldmixon, Capt. Herendeen, and himself—and has transliterated them into a uniform spelling, nearly the same as that adopted by the Bureau of Ethnology. The vocabulary forms 132 pp. folio, containing about 1,100 words, among which are represented at least 590 radicals. These radicals are arranged alphabetically, each followed by its own compounds after the pattern of Part I of Kleinschmidt's Gronlandsk Ordbog. Following each word is the corresponding word in the dialects of Greenland, Labrador, and the Mackenzie River District, taken from the standard dictionaries, for the purpose of comparison, and the corresponding English translation.

In addition to the vocabulary, there is a list of 90 "affixes" or inseparable words, corresponding to Part II of the Gronlandsk Ordbog. Mr. Murdoch is still engaged in working up the grammatic notes, which are quite scanty, and in comparing the material collected with the language of Greenland as represented in the standard authorities.

# N.

**Nagdliutorsiutit** ernaglit. See Jörensen (T.).

**Naitsungordlugo** nunab aglautigenera. See **Wandall** (E. A.).

**Naleganta** Jesusil Kristusim Annaurcirsiuta sullirsei, okautsiunik Tussarnersunnik, Aglegniartut sissamaet Pissitausimaput Attautsimut.

Barbine. 1804.

**Naleganta** — Continued.

*Literal translation:* Our Lord Jesus Christ the Savior's his works, in words pleasant to hear. Writings four are collected into one. At Barby.

280 pp. 12°. Harmony of the Gospels, in the Greenland language.—*Sabin's Dictionary, No.* 22861.

Priced in Trübner's catalogue, 1856, No. 665 at 5s., and in No. 671 at 7s.

**Nalegapta** | Jesusib Kristusib , Piulijipta | Pinuiarningit, Āuialervinga | Nelliutingmet | Okautsinnik Tussarnertunnik. | Aglongniartut Sittamæt | Kalissimavut at- | tautsimut. | [Design.] | Barbime, 1800.

*Literal translation:* Our Lord | Jesus Christ | the Savior's | works his suffering | when the appointed time came | in words pleasing-to-hear. | Writings four are collected | into one. | At Barby.

Pp. 1-132, 12°. Harmony of the Gospels, in the dialect of Labrador.

The only copy I have seen, that at the Brinley sale, No. 5639, brought $8.50.

**Nalegapta** Jesusib Kristusib, piulijipta pinniarningit; okautsiñik tussarnertuñik, aglangniartut sittamæt, kattisimavut attautsimut. Printed for the Brethren's Society for the furtherance of the Gospel among the Heathen; for the use of the Christian Esquimaux in the Brethren's settlements, Nain, Okkak, and Hopedale, on the Coast of Labrador.

Londonneme, W. Mᶜ. Dowallib, 1810. *

*Literal translation:* Our Lord Jesus Christ, the Savior's works; in words pleasing-to-hear, writings four are collected into one.

Title from Leclerc's Bibliotheca Americana (1867), No. 1461, where it is said to be the New Testament. The translation of the title shows it to be an edition of the Harmony of the Gospels. See note to Kohlmeister (B. G.).

**Nalegauta** | Jesusib Kristusib | aunaursirsivta | sullirsei | okautsinnik tussarnersuunik aglengni- | artut sissamaet pissitausimaput | attautsimut. | [Design.] |
Budissime | Ernst Gottlob Monsib nakkittaegei. | 1829.

*Literal translation:* Our Lord | Jesus Christ | the Savior's | his works | in words pleasing-to-hear | writings four are collected | into one. | At Bautzen Ernst Gottlob Mons printed them.

Pp. 1-280, 16°. Harmony of the four Gospels, entirely in the Greenland language.

*Copies seen:* Billing, Powell.

My copy, purchased of the Unitäts-Buch handlung, Guadau, Saxony, cost 1 M. 60 pf.

**Nalekab** okausee. | [Picture.]

*Literal translation:* The Lord's his words.

No title-page; 1 p. l. pp. 1-8, 24°. Bible lessons in the language of Greenland.—Matth. 15, 21-28; Luk. 8, 5-8; Luk. 22, 39-44; Ebr. 1218-24.
*Copies seen:* American Tract Society.

**Nâlekam** okausinga. | [Picture.]

*Literal translation:* The Lord's his words.

No title-page; 1 p. l. pp. 1-8, sq. 24°. Bible

**Nâlekam** — Continued.

lessons in the Eskimo language of Labrador.—Matth. 15, 21-28; Luk. 8, 5-18; Luk. 22, 39-44 | Ebr. 12, 18-24.
*Copies seen:* American Tract Society.

**Nalunaerutit** | sinerîssap kujatâne misigssuissut | pivdlugit. | 1862-1866 [-1867]. |
Meddelelser | vedkommende Forstanderskaberne | i Sydgrønland. | 1862 -1866[-1867].

*Literal translation:* Communications | the coast's in its southern part rules | being concerned.

3 parts: 1 p. l. pp. 1-172, 1-20, 1-4, 8°.
*Copies seen:* Powell.

**Nalunaerutit** | sinerîssap kujatâne misigssuissut pivdlugit. | 7-9. | 1868-70. |
Meddelelser | vedkommende Forstanderskaberne i Syd- | grønland. | 7-9. | 1868-70.

1 p. l. pp. 1-87, 8°.
*Copies seen:* Powell.

**Nalunaerutit** | sinerîssap kujatâne misigssuissut pivdlugit. | 10. | 1870-71. |
Meddelelser | vedkommende | Forstanderskaberne i Sydgrøuland. | 10. | 1870-71.

1 p. l. pp. 1-54, 8°.
*Copies seen:* Powell.

**Nalunaerutit** | sinerîssame kujatdlarme misigssuissut | pivdlugit. | 11. | 1871-72 |
Meddelelser, | vedkommende | Forstanderskaberne i Sydgrønland. | 11. | 1871-72.

1 p. l. pp. 1-43, 8°. Reports concerning the Municipal Council of South Greenland, and statistical tables. Printed at Godthaab, Greenland.

*Copies seen:* Powell.

**Nalungiak** Bethleheme. | [Picture.] [Stuttgart, J. F. Steinkopf.] | 1847.

*Literal translation:* The child born at Bethlehem.

1 p. l. pp. 1-8, 16°. Bible lessons in the language of Labrador.

*Copies seen:* American Tract Society.

**Namolli :**
Numerals.              See Erman (G. A.).
Vocabulary.            Schott (W.).

**Náparsimassugdlit** atuartagagssait. See **Hagen** (C.).

**Naphegyi** (Gabor). The | Album of | Language | illustrated by the | Lord's Prayer | in | One hundred Languages. | By G. Naphegyi, M. D., A. M. | Member

**Naphegyi** (G.) — Continued.

of the "Sociedad Geografica y Estadistica" of Mexico, | and "Mejoras Materiales" of Texoco. |

Lith. & Printed in colors by Edward Herline, | 630 Chestnut St. Philadelphia. | Published | by | J. B. Lippincott | & Co. | Philadelphia. |

*Printed title:* The | Album of Language. | Illustrated by | The Lord's Prayer | in | One Hundred Languages, | with | historical descriptions of the principal languages, interlinear translation and | pronunciation of each prayer, a dissertation on the languages of | the world, and tables exhibiting all known | languages, dead and living. | By | G. Naphegyi, M. D. A. M. | Member of the "Sociedad Geografica y Estadistica," of Mexico, and "Mejoras Materiales," of Texoco, of the | Numismatic and Antiquarian Society of Philadelphia, etc. | [Design.] |

Philadelphia: | J. B. Lippincott & Co. | 1869. Pp. 1-324, 4°. The Lord's Prayer in the language of Greenland, p. 305.

*Copies seen:* Boston Public, British Museum, Congress.

**Naughtawkkoa** kollin-illoaet? | [Picture.]

[N. p.] 1844.

*Literal translation:* Where are the nine? No title-page; 1 p. l. pp. 1-8, 16°. Bible stories in the language of Labrador.—Luc. 4, 24-26, p. 1; Luc. 4, 27, p. 2; Jac. 5, 16-18, pp. 3-4; Matth. 23, 34-39, pp. 5-6; 2 Timoth. 1, 1-5; 2 Timoth. 3, 15-17, pp. 7-8.

*Copies seen:* American Tract Society.

**Nauk** taipkoa neinenik? | [Picture of Eskimo.]

[N. p.] 1844.

*Literal translation:* Where are the nine? No title-page; 1 p. l. pp. 1-8, 16°. Bible stories in the language of Labrador.—Luc. 4, 24-26, p. 1; Luc. 4, 27, p. 2; Jacobi 5, 16-18, pp. 3-4; Matth. 23, 34-39, pp. 5-6; 2 Timoth. 1, 1-5; 2 Timoth. 3, 15-17, pp. 7-8.

Though this tract has the same contents as that titled **Naughtawkkoa** kollin-illoaet? it is not the same work; where the stories run through more than one page, the pages do not end alike. There are also verbal discrepancies throughout.

*Copies seen:* American Tract Society.

**Nelson** (Edward William). Eskimo-English Vocabulary.

Manuscript, pp. 1-219, folio, alphabetically arranged. Written on one side only. Phrases and sentences, English-Eskimo, alphabetically arranged, pp. 176-219. In the library of the Bureau of Ethnology.

This manuscript contains material from 12 dialects of the region visited by the author. Some of the dialects are represented by but a

**Nelson** (E. W.) — Continued.

comparatively few words, from 100 upwards, while one, the Unalit, is represented by about 2,500, in addition to numerous phrases and sentences. With the exception of the Unalit, the words of all the other dialects are preceded by a distinguishing initial letter.

Mr. Nelson is arranging the Eskimo-English portion of his work, and also his notes upon the grammar and remarks upon the geographic distribution of the dialects. These, he thinks, will occupy about 500 pages of manuscript.

**Netzvietoff** (*Rev.* Jacob). See **Veniaminoff** (J.) and **Netzvietoff** (J.).

**Newton** (Alfred). Notes on Birds which have been found in Greenland.

In Royal Society [of London], Manual of the Nat. Hist. Geol. and Physics of Greenland, &c. pp. 94-115, London, 1875, 8°.

Esquimaux names of birds passim.

**Noonatarghmeutes** Vocabulary. See Oldmixon (G. S.).

**Noowookmeutes** Vocabulary. See Oldmixon (G. S.).

**Northumberland Inlet:**

| | |
|---|---|
| Relationships. | See Morgan (L. H.). |
| Vocabulary. | Morgan (L. H.). |

**Norton Sound:**

| | |
|---|---|
| Grammatic comments. | See Adelung (J. C.) and Vater (J. S.). |
| Vocabulary. | Adelung (J. C.) and Vater (J. S.), Bryant (—), Fry (E.). |
| Words. | Yankiewitch (T.). |

**Notes on the Unalaskan Islands:**

| | |
|---|---|
| Aleut. | See Veniaminoff (J.). |
| Atka. | Veniaminoff (J.). |

**Notice** sur les mœurs et coutûmes des Indiens Esquimaux de la baie de Baffins, au pôle arctique, suivie d'un vocabulaire esquimaux-français.

Tours: Mame. 1826. *

24 pp. 12°. Title from Sabin's Dictionary, No. 22863.

**Nouvelle** Bretagne. Vicariat Apostolique d'Athabaska et Mackenzie.

In Annales de la Propag. de la Foi, vol. 43, pp. 457-478, Paris, 1871, 8°.

Contains remarks on the Esquimaux and Cris languages.

**Nukakpiak** pernertok saniarsimarsok. | [Picture.] |

[Druct von J. F. Steinkopf, in Stuttgart.] | 1849.

1 p. l. pp. 1-8, 16°. Bible lessons in the language of Labrador.

*Copies seen:* American Tract Society.

**Nukakpiarkæk,** Gudemik okau- | sœoni-
glo assœoniktuk. | [Picture of Bible.] |
[Druct von J. F. Steinkopf in Stutt-
gart.] | 1851.
*Literal translation:* The two youths | God
and his words loving.
1 p. l. pp. 1-7, 16°. Bible lessons in the
language of Labrador.
*Copies seen:* American Tract Society.

**Nukapiak** augorarviksab nelliuuingane.
| [Picture.] |
[Druct von J. F. Steinkopf in Stutt-
gart.] | 1849.
*Literal translation:* The youth his own departure's at its time.
1 p. l. pp. 1-8, 16°. Bible lessons in the language of Labrador.
*Copies seen:* American Tract Society.

**Numerals:**

| | |
|---|---|
| Alout. | See Adelung (J. C.) and Vater (J. S.), Buynitzky (S. N.), Coxe (W.), Erman (G. A.), Latham, (R. G.), Pott (A. F.). |
| Behring Strait. | Baer (K. E. von). |
| Cumberland Strait. | Cull (R.). |
| Cook River. | Dixon (G.). |
| Eskimo. | Haldeman (S. S.), Latham (R. G.), Pott (A. F.), Sutherland (P. C.). |
| Greenland. | Adelung (J. C.) and Vater (J. S.), Antrim (B. J.), |
| Igloolik. | Baer (K. E. von). |
| Innuit. | Hall (C. F.), Kumlien (L.). |
| Kadiak. | Adelung (J. C.) and Vater (J. S.), |

**Numerals** — Continued.

| | |
|---|---|
| Kadiak. | See Baer (K. E. von), Erman (G. A.), Pott (A. F.). |
| Kángjulit. | Erman (G. A.). |
| Kamskudale. | Latham (R. G.). |
| Labrador. | Antrim (B. J.), Cull (R.), Erman (G. A.), Stearns (W. A.). |
| Prince William Sound. | Buschmann (J. C. E. von), Dixon (G.), Forster (J. G. A.), Portlock (N.) and Dixon (G.). |
| Tschuktschi. | Pott (A. F.). |
| Tschugazi. | Pott (A. F.). |
| Unalaska. | Baer (K. E. von). |

**Nunalerutit.** Nungme sanat, 1858.
*Literal translation:* Means for thinking about
the earth. At the Point [Godthaab] published.
60 pp. 8°. Geography in Greenland Eskimo.
Title from Dr. Rink.

**Nunap** missigssnissok. See **Rink** (H. J.).

**Nuniwok Island** Vocabulary. See Buschmann
(J. C. E.).

**Nushergágmūt** Vocabulary. See Dall (W. H.).

**[Nyerup** (Rasmus)]. Dansk-norsk | Lit-
teraturlexicon. | Første[-Anden] Halv-
del. | A—L [-M—Ø]. |
Kjøbenhavn. | Trykt, paa den Gyl-
dendalske Boghandlings Forlag, i det
Schultziske Officin. | 1818[-1819].
2 vols. sm. 4°, arranged alphabetically by
authors. Contains biographies of a number of
authors who have written in the Eskimo and
lists of their works.
*Copies seen:* Congress.

## O.

Ode, Greenland. See Brodersen (J.).

**Okâlautsit** | attoraksat | kattimajunut
Sontagine, |·piluartomik | kattimav-
ingmit apsimanerme. | Sermons |
printed for the S. F. G. in London, |
for the use of the Moravian Mission in |
Labrador. |
Stolpen: | Gustav Winterib nêner-
lauktangit, | 1870.
*Literal translation:* Discourses | things to be
used | for congregations on Sundays | espe-
cially | by the church on (?) | Stolpen: | Gustav
Winter's his printings.
Title verso blank 1 l. contents verso blank
1 l. text (sermons 1-18) entirely in the language
of Labrador, pp. 1-140, 16°.
*Copies seen:* Pilling, Powell.

**Okâlautsit** — Continued.
My copy, from the Unitäts-Buchhandlung,
Gnadau, Saxony, cost 2 M.
A second series as follows:

**Okâlautsit** | attoraksat | kattimajunut
Sontagine, | piluartomik kattimaving-
mit | apsimanerme. | Sermons and
addresses | printed for the S. F. G. in
London, | for the use of the Moravian
Mission in | Labrador. |
Stolpen: | Gustav Winterib nêner-
lauktangit. | 1871.
Title verso blank 1 l. contents verso blank
1 l. text (sermons 19-35) entirely in the language
of Labrador, pp. 1-127, 16°. Followed by:

**Okâlautsit** | attoraksat | kattimajunut
Sontagine, | uvloksiorvinguelo, ania-

**Okâlautsit — Continued.**

vianelo. | Sermons and addresses | printed for the S. F. G. in London, | for the use of the Moravian Mission in | Labrador. | Stolpen: | Gustav Winterib nĕnerlanktangit. | 1871.

*Literal translation:* Discourses | things to bo used | for congregations on Sundays, | and on festivals, and at the time of suffering. | Stolpen: | Gustav Winter's his printings.

Title verso blank 1·l. contents verso blank 1 l. text (sermons 36–51 and a portion of the liturgy) entirely in the language of Labrador, pp. 131–271, 16°.

*Copies seen:* Pilling, Powell.

My copy (3 parts), bought at the Unitäts-Buchhandlung, Gnadau, Saxony, cost 4 M.

**Okallòutit** Sabbátine akkudlcesiksæt. See **Kragh** (P.).

**Okalluktuæt** Bibelimit pisimasut. See **Steenholdt** (W. F.).

**Okalluktuæt** Opernartut Tersäuko. See **Fabricius** (O.).

**Okalluktualiæt,** nnktórsimarsut. See **Kragh** (P.).

**Okalluktuàutit** sajmäubingmik. See **Kragh** (P.).

**Okautsit** | illiniaraksat | Sorrutsinut. | Budisinemo: | E. M. Monsib, nĕnilaulktangit. | 1867.

*Literal translation:* Words | instruction | for children. | At Bautzen: | E. M. Mons', his printings.

Title verso blank 1 1. text pp. 3–11, 16°. Primer in the Eskimo language of Labrador.

*Copies seen:* Pilling, Powell.

My copy cost 35 pf.

**Okautsit** | Testamentitokamo agleksimarsut illeit.

*Literal translation:* Words | in the old testament written part of them.

No title-page; 1 p. l. pp. 1–8, 18°. Bible stories in the language of Greenland.

*Copies seen:* American Tract Society, Powell.

**Okomiut:**

Songs. See **Boas** (F.).
Tales. **Boas** (F.).

**Okpernermik** mallingninganiglo. | [Picture.]

*Literal translation:* About faith and about obedience.

No title-page; 1 p. l. pp. 1–8, 16°. Bible stories in the language of Labrador.

*Copies seen:* American Tract Society, Powell.

**Oldmixon** ( George Scott ). [Words, phrases, and sentences in the languages of the Noowookmentes and Noonatarghmentes.]

Manuscript, pp. 77–135, sparsely filled, 4°. Collected by Dr. G. S. Oldmixon, Act. Asst. Surgeon, U. S. A. at Point Barrow, Arctic Alaska, during 1882 and 1883, and recorded in a copy of Powell's Introduction to the Study of Indian Languages, 2d edition. Transliterated into the alphabet adopted by the Bureau of Ethnology by Rev. J. Owen Dorsey as far as p. 127. In the library of the Bureau of Ethnology.

**Olearius** (Adam). Relation | dv | Voyage | d'Adam Olearivs | en Moscovie, | Tartarie | et Perse. | Avgmentée en cette novvelle édition | de plus d'vn tiers, & particulièrement d'vne seconde Partie | contenant le Voyage de | Iean Albert de Mandelslo | avx Indes Orientales. | Traduit de l'Allemand par A. de Wicqvefort, | Résident de Brandebourg. | Tome Premier [-Second]. | [Device.] | A Paris, | Chez Iean dv Pvis, ruë Saint Iacques, à la Couronne d'or. | M. DC. LVI [1656]. | Avec privilège dv Roy.

2 vols. maps, plates, 4°.—Greenland vocabulary, 106 words, vol. 1, pp. 133–134. The earliest account of the Eskimo language.

*Copies seen:* British Museum.

"The author, who hath here made one digression, to speak of the Samojedes, * * * thinks he may make another to say somewhat of Groenland, * * * as for that he hath seen, and discoursed with, some inhabitants of Groenland. * * * In the spring of 1654 a ship was set out, which going from Copenhagen in the beginning of the spring, arriv'd not on the coasts of Groenland, till the 23 of July. * * * As soon as this ship appear'd upon the coasts of Groenland, the inhabitants set out above a hundred boats. * * * The Danes thought this freedom of the Groenlanders a good opportunity to carry away some of them. * * * They also sent back one of the women, as being too old to be transported; so that they had but four persons, one man, two women, and a girl. * * * The plague, then very rife all over Denmark, had oblig'd the king to retire to Flensbourg, in the Dutchy of Holstein, where these Groenlanders were presented to him. * * * The king honour'd the duke, my master, so far as to send them to him to Gottorp, where they were lodg'd in my house for some days, which I spent in sifting out their humour and manner of life."—*Olearius.*

—— Vermehrte | Newe Beschreibung | der | Muscowitischen und Persischen |

**Olearius (A.) — Continued.**

Reyse | so durch gelegenheit einer Hol-
steinischen Gesandschafft an | den Rus-
sischen Zaar und König in Persien ge-
schehen. | Worinnen die Gelegenheit
derer Orter und Länder/durch | welche
die Reyse gangen/ als Liffland/ Russ-
land/ Tartarien/ Meden und | Persien/
sampt dero Einwohner Natur/ Leben/
Sitten/ Haus= Welt= und Geistlichen |
Stand mit fleiss auffgezeichnet/ und mit
vielen meist nach dem Leben | gestel-
leten Figuren gezieret/ zu befinden. |
Welche | zum andern mahl heraus
gibt | Adam Olearius Ascanius/ der
Fürstlichen Regierenden | Herrschafft
zu Schleswig Holstein Bibliothecarius
und Hoff Mathematicus. | [Design.] |
Mit Röm: Kayserl. Mayest. Privilegio
nicht nachzudrucken. |
Schleswig/ | Gedruckt in der Fürstl.
Druckerey/durch Johan Holwein/ | Im
Jahr MDCLVI [1656].

10 p. ll. pp. 1-778, 17 ll. maps, plates, folio.
Engraved title recto 1. 1.—Greenland vocabu-
lary, 106 words, p. 171.
*Copies seen :* Boston Public, British Museum.

—— Relation | dv | Voyage | d'Adam
Olearivs | en Moscovie, Tartarie | et
Perse. | Avgmentée en cette novvelle
édition | de plus d'vn tiers, & particu-
lierement d'vne seconde Partie | conte-
nant le Voyage de | Ioan Albert de Man-
delslo | avx Indes Orientales. | Traduit
de l'Allemand par A. de Wicqvefort, |
Resident de Brandebourg. | Tome Pre-
mier[-Second]. | [Device.] |
A Paris, | Chez Ioan dv Pvis, ruö
Saint Iacqnes, à la Couronne d'or. |
M. DC. LIX [1659]. | Avec privilège dv
Roy.

2 vols. maps, plates, 4°.—Greenland vocabulary, 106 words, vol. 1, pp. 133-134.
*Copies seen :* Boston Athenæum.

—— The | Voyages & Travels | of the |
Ambassadors | from the | Duke of Hol-
stein, to the Great Duke | of Muscovy,
and the King of Persia. | Begun in the
year M. DC. XXXIII and finish'd in
M. DC. XXXIX. | Containing a com-
pleat History of | Muscovy, Tartary, |
Persia, | And other adjacent Countries, |
with several Public Transactions reach-
ing neer [*sic*] the Present Times; | In
Seven Books. | Illustrated with diverse
accurate Mapps and Figures. | By Adam

**Olearius (A.) — Continued.**

Olearius, Secretary of the Embassy. |
Rendered into English, by John Davies
of Kidwelly. | [Design.] |
London | Printed for Thomas Dring,
and John Starkey, and are to be sold at
their Shops, at the George | in Fleet-
street, near Clifford's-Inn, and the Mi-
tre, between the Middle-Temple-Gate |
and Temple Barr. M. DC. LXII [1662].

12 p. ll. pp. 1-424, frontispiece, maps, plates,
folio.—Greenland vocabulary, pp. 71-72.
Mandelslo's Voyages is appended with separate title, same imprint, pp. 1-187, 5 ll.
*Copies seen :* British Museum, Harvard.

—— The | Voyages and Travels | of the |
ambassadors | Sent by Frederick Duke
of Holstein, | to the Great Duke of Mus-
covy, and the King of Persia. | Begun
in the year M. DC. XXXIII. and finish'd
in M. DC. XXXIX. | Containing a Com-
pleat | history | of | Muscovy, Tartary,
Persia. | And other adjacent Countries.
| With several Publick Transactions
reaching near the Present Times; | In
VII. Books. | Whereto are added | The
Travels of John Albert de Mandelslo, |
(a Gentleman belonging to the Em-
bassy) from Persia, into the | East-
Indies. | Containing | A particular De-
scription of Indosthan, the Mogul's Em-
pire, the | Oriental Ilands, Japan,
China, &c. and the Revo- | lutions
which happened in those Countries,
within these few years. | In III. Books. |
The whole Work illustrated with divers
accurate Mapps, and Figures. | Written
originally by Adam Olearius, Secretary
to the Embassy. | Faithfully rendred
into English, by John Davies of Kid-
welly. | The Second Edition Corrected. |
London, | Printed for John Starkey,
and Thomas Basset, at the Mitre near
Temple-Barr, and at the George near |
St. Dunstans Church in Fleet-street.
1669.

10 p. ll. pp. 1-316, folio. Greenland vocabulary, pp. 53-54.
Mandelslo's Travels is appended with separate title, 3 p. ll. pp. 1-232, 5 ll.
*Copies seen :* Astor, Congress.

—— Relation | du | Voyage | d'Adam Ole-
arius | en Moscovie, | Tartarie, | et
Perse, | Augmentée en cette nouvelle
édition | de plus d'un tiers, & particu-
lierement d'une seconde Partie ; | coute-

**Olearius (A.)** — Continued.

nant le voyage de | Iean Albert de Man-
delslo | aux Indes Orientales. | Traduit
de l'Allemand par A. de Wicqvefort, |
Resident de Brandebourg. | Tome Pre-
mier[-Second]. | Seconde édition. |
[Device.] |
A Paris, | Chez Antoine Dezallier, ruë
Saint Jacques, | à la Couronne d'or. |
M. DC. LXXIX [1679] | Avec privilège
du Roy.

2 vols. maps, 4°.—Greenland vocabulary,
106 words, vol. 1, pp. 133–134.

*Copies seen :* Boston Athenæum.

—— Voyages | très curieux & très renom-
mez, | faits en | Moscovie, | Tartarie,
et Perse, | par | le S$^r$. Adam Olearius, |
Bibliothecaire du Duc de Holstein, &
Mathematicien de sa Cour. | Dans les-
quels on trouve une Description curi-
euse & la Situation | exacte des Pays &
Etats, par où il a passé, tels que sont la |
Livonie, la Moscovie, la Tartarie, la
Medie, & la Perse; | Et où il est parlé
du Naturel, des Manieres de vivre, des
Mœurs, & des Coutumes | de leurs Ha-
bitans; du Gouvernement Politique &
Ecclesiastique; des Raretez | qui se
trouvent dans ce Pays; & des Ceremo-
nies qui s'y observent. | Traduits de
l'Original & augmentez | par le S$^r$. De
Wicquefort. | Conseiller aux Conseils
d'Estat & Privé du Duc de Brunswic |
& Lunebourg Zell &c. | Auteur de
l'Ambassadeur & de ses fonctions. |
Divisez en deux parties. | Nouvelle Edi-
tion revûe & corrigée exactement, aug-
mentée considerablement, tant | dans
les corps de l'Ouvrage, que dans les
Marginales, & surpassant en bonté | &
en beauté les précedentes Editions. |
A quoi on a joint des Cartes Geographiques, des Représentations des Villes,
& autres | Tailles-douces très belles &
très exactes. | Tome Premier[-Second].
| [Design.] |
A Leide, | Chez Pierre Vander Aa,
Marchand Libraire, | Imprimeur ordi-
naire de l'Université & de la Ville, de-
meurant dans l'Academie. | Chez qui
l'on trouve toutes sortes de Livres eu-
rieux, comme aussi de Cartes Geo-
graphiques, des Villes, | tant en plan
qu'en profil, des Portraits des Hommes

**Olearius (A.)** — Continued.

Illustres, & autres Tailles-douces. |
MDCCXVIIII [1719]. | Avec Privilege.

2 vols. maps, plates, folio.— Greenland vo-
cabulary, vol. 1, columns 187–188.
*Copies seen :* Astor, British Museum.
Quaritch, No. 28862*, prices a copy at 7*s.* 6*d.*

—— Voyages Très-curieux & très-renom-
mez | faits en | Moscovie, | Tartarie et
Perse, | par le Sr. | Adam Olearius, |
Bibliothecaire du Duc de Holstein, &
Mathematicien de sa Cour. | Dans les-
quels on trouve une Description curi-
euse & la Situation exacte des | Pays &
Etats, par où il a passé, tels que sont
la Livonie, | la Moscovie, la Tartarie,
la Medie, & la Perse; | et où il est parlé
du Naturel, des Manieres de vivre, des
Mœurs, & des Coutumes de | leurs Ha-
bitans; du Gouvernement Politique &
Ecclesiastique, des Raretez qui | se trou-
vent dans ce Pays; & des Ceremonies
qui s'y observent. | Traduits de l'Origi-
nal & Augmentez | par le Sr. De Wic-
quefort, | Conseiller aux Conseils d'Etat
& Privé du Duc de Brunswick & Lune-
bourg, Zell, &c. | Auteur de l'Ambas-
sadeur & de ses Fonctions | Divisez en
Deux Parties. | Nouvelle Edition revûe
& corrigée exactement, augmentée con-
siderablement, tant dans le Corps de |
l'Ouvrage, que dans les Marginales, &
surpassant en bonté & en beauté les |
précedentes Editions. | A quoi on a joint
des Cartes Geographiques, des Représentations des Villes, & autres Taille-
douces | très-belles & très-exactes. |
Tome Premier [-Second]. | [Design.] |
A Amsterdam, | Chez Michael Charles
Le Céne, Libraire, | Chez qui l'on trouve
un assortiment general de Musique. |
MDCCXXVII [1727]. | Avec Privilege.

2 vols. maps, plates, folio. No page numbering; columns, two on a page, numbered.—
Greenland vocabulary, about 100 words, vol.
1, columns 187–188.
*Copies seen :* Boston Public, British Museum, Congress.
I have seen in the British Museum Library
the following editions of Olearius, none of
which contains the Greenland vocabulary: Amsterdam, 1651; Utrecht, 1651; Paris, 1656;
Viterbo, 1658; Amsterdam, 1670.
I have also seen mention of the following
editions; in German: Sleswig, 1647; +1663;
+1669; +1671; Hamburg, 1696; in Dutch: Amsterdam, 1691; Amsterdam, 1728.

**Oppert** (Gustav).] On the Classification of Languages. A Contribution to Comparative Philology.

In Madras Journal of Literature and Science for the year 1879, pp. 1–137, London, 1879, 8°.

In addition to frequent allusions to American languages, there is, on pp. 110–112, a table of relationships of different American "nations," among them the Arctic family.

**Ordo Salutis.** See **Egede** (H.).

**O'Reilly** (Bernard). Greenland, | the | adjacent seas, | and | the north-west passage | to | The Pacific Ocean, | illustrated in a voyage to Davis's strait, | during the summer of 1817. | With charts and numerous plates, | from drawings of the author taken on the spot. | By | Bernard O'Reilly, Esq. |

London: | printed for Baldwin, Cradock, and Joy, | 47, Paternoster-Row. | 1818.

Pp. i–viii, 1–293, maps, plates, 4°.—Remarks

**O'Reilly** (B.)—Continued.

on the language of Greenland, pp. 60–61, 83–84; "Brief list of words [27] from the language of the Greenlander," pp. 84–85.

*Copies seen:* Astor, British Museum, Congress, Harvard, Watkinson.

A copy at the Field sale, No. 1734, brought $3. Priced by Quaritch, No. 28973, at 7s. 6d.

—— Greenland, | the | adjacent seas, | and | the north-west passage | to the | Pacific Ocean, | illustrated in a | voyage to Davis's strait, | During the Summer of 1817. | By Bernard O'Reilly, Esq. |

New-York: | published by James Eastburn and Co. | at the literary rooms, Broadway. | Clayton & Kingsland, Printers. | 1818.

Pp. i–viii, 1–251, maps, 8°.—Linguistics, pp. 73–74.

*Copies seen:* Boston Athenæum, Bureau of Ethnology, Congress.

**Osmer** (—). See **Beechey** (F. W.).

# P.

**Parry** (*Admiral* William Edward). Journal | of a | Second Voyage for the Discovery of a | North-west Passage | from the Atlantic to the Pacific; | performed in the years 1821-22-23, | in His Majesty's Ships | Fury and Hecla, | under the orders of | Captain William Edward Parry, R. N., F. R. S., | and Commander of the Expedition. | Illustrated by numerous plates. Published by Authority of the Lords Commissioners | of the Admiralty. |

London: | John Murray, | Publisher to the Admiralty, and Board of Longitude. | M DCCC XXIV [1824].

4 p. ll. pp. i–xxxii, 1–571, maps, plates, 4°.—Grammatic remarks and a few examples of the Esquimaux language, pp. 551–558. —Vocabulary of Esquimaux words and sentences, pp. 559–569.—Esquimaux names of places, pp. 570–571.

*Copies seen:* Boston Athenæum, Boston Public, British Museum, Congress.

—— Journal | of a | second voyage for the discovery | of a | north-west passage | from | the Atlantic to the Pacific; | performed in the years 1821-22-23, | in his majesty's ships | Fury and Hecla, | under the orders of | Captain William Edward Parry, R. N., F. R. S., | and commander of the expedition. |

**Parry** (W. E.)—Continued.

New-York: | published by E. Duyckinck, G. Long, Collins & Co., Collins & Hannay, | W. B. Gilley, and Henry I. Megarey. | W. E. Dean, Printer, 90 William-Street: | 1824.

Pp. i–vii, 1–xx, 1–464, 8°.—Linguistics as in English edition, pp. 451–457, 459–464.

*Copies seen:* Boston Athenæum, British Museum, Bureau of Ethnology, Congress.

According to Sabin's Dictionary, No. 58866, a German translation was published at Jena, 1824, 8°.

A copy at the Field sale, No. 1768, brought $8.

**Paulus** (J.) See **Kragh** (P.).

**Peck** (*Rev.* Edmund J.). Portions of the Holy Scripture, | for the | use of the Esquimaux | on the | northern and eastern shores of Hudson's Bay, | edited by | Edmund Peck, | C. M. S. Missionary to the Esquimaux. |

Printed for the | Society for Promoting Christian Knowledge. | 77, Great Queen Street, Lincoln's-Inn-Fields. | 1878.

2 p. ll. pp. 1–93, appendix pp. 1–8, 16°.—Portions of the Gospel of John, pp. 1–45.—Romans, pp. 45–46. —Corinthians, pp. 57–66.—Epistles of John, pp. 66–71.—Revelation, pp. 71–75.—Scattered verses, pp. 75–88.—Creed, Ten Commandments, Lord's Prayer, Benediction,

FAC-SIMILE OF FIRST SYLLABARY USED IN PRINTING ESKIMO TEXTS
(The explanations are in manuscript.)

**Peck** (E. J.)—Continued.

pp. 89-93.—"Appendix. (Printed for the Church Missionary Society.) Watts's First Catechism, in Esquimaux," pp. 1-8.

The first publication in the Eskimo language in which the syllabic characters were used. See accompanying fac-simile of the syllabary, the explanations of which are in manuscript.

*Copies seen:* Church Missionary Society, Pilling, Powell.

—— Portions | of the | book of common prayer; | together with | hymns, addresses, etc., | for the use of | the Eskimo of Hudson's Bay. | By the | Rev. E. J. Peck, | missionary of the Church Missionary Society. | [Design.] | Society for Promoting Christian Knowledge, | Northumberland Avenue, Charing Cross, London. | 1881.

Pp. 1-90, 16°. Title 1 l. syllabarium p. 3.— Hymns, pp. 5-22.—Portions of the Book of Common Prayer, pp. 23-56.—Prayer for each day in the week, pp. 57-66.—Catechism and short addresses, pp. 67-90. In syllabic characters, with a number of changes in the characters from the foregoing.

*Copies seen:* Church Missionary Society, Pilling, Powell, Society for Promoting Christian Knowledge.

—— St. Luke's Gospel. | Translated into the language | of the | Eskimo of Hudson's Bay | by the | Rev. E. J. Peck. | London : | printed for the British and Foreign Bible Society, | Queen Victoria street. | 1881.

Title 1 l. syllabarium 1 l. text, in syllabic characters and entirely in Eskimo, pp. 1-116, 16°.

*Copies seen:* British and Foreign Bible Society, Pilling, Powell.

[——] Watts's | First Catechism, | in Esquimaux.

*Colophon:* F. Arnold, Printer, 86, Fleet Street, E. C. [n. d.]

Five unnumbered ll. 16°, syllabic characters. Half-title as above, on the verso of which begins the text in syllabic characters, with heading in English, Gothic characters: "Watts's First Catechism in Esquimanx." This extends to bottom of recto of 3d l. the verso containing the Creed and the Commandments, the latter ending on verso of 4th l. which also contains the Lord's Prayer, baptismal sentence, marriage sentences, the latter ending on recto of 5th l. which also contains a prayer. Verso of 5th l. a hymn, the benediction.

This is the best example of printing in the syllabic characters I have seen. I am inclined to think it is from engraved plates.

*Copies seen:* Church Missionary Society, Pilling, Powell.

Periodical :
Greenland. See Atuagagdliutit, Kaladlit.

**Petitot** (*Père* Émile Fortuné Stanislas Joseph). Les Esquimaux.

In Congrès Int. des Américanistes, Compte-rendu, first session, vol. 1, pp. 329-339, Nancy and Paris, 1875, 8°.

Comparative Vocabulary of the Esquimaux of Bathurst with various foreign languages, pp. 333-334.—Myths (The Deluge and Origin of the Human Family) in Eskimo, with French translation, pp. 336-337.

—— Monographie | des | Esquimaux Tchiglit | du Mackenzie | et de l'Anderson | par | Le R. P. E. Petitot | Missionnaire Oblat de Marie-Immaculée, Officier d'Académie, Membre correspondant de l'Académie de Nancy | et des Sociétés d'Anthropologie et de Philologie de Paris | [Vignette.] | Paris | Ernest Leroux, Éditeur | Libraire de la Société Asiatique | de l'École des Langues Orientales Vivantes, de la Société Philologique | des Sociétés Asiatiques de Calcutta, de Shanghaï, de New-Haven, etc. | 28, rue Bonaparte, 28 | 1876

2 p. ll. pp. 1-28, 4°.—Esquimaux traditions in the original, with French translations, pp. 16, 26; and scattered terms and phrases.

*Copies seen:* Astor.

Priced by Leclerc, 1878, No. 2231, at 4 fr.

—— Vocabulaire | français-esquimau | Dialecte des Tchiglit | des bouches du Mackenzie et de l'Anderson | précédé d'une | monographie de cette tribu | et de notes grammaticales | par | le R. P. E. Petitot | Missionnaire Oblat de Marie-Immaculée, Officier d'Académie, Membre-correspondant de l'Académie de Nancy | et des Sociétés d'Anthropologie et de Philologie de Paris | [Design.] | Paris | Ernest Leroux, Éditeur | libraire de la Société Asiatique | de l'École des Langues Orientales Vivantes, de la Société Philologique | des sociétés de Calcutta, de New-Haven (États-Unis), de Shanghaï, etc. | 28, Rue Bonaparte, 28 | Maisonneuve, 15, quai Voltaire | San Francisco.—A. L. Bancroft and Cº | 1876

3 p. ll. pp. i-lxiv, 1-78, 4°. Forms vol. 3 of Pinart (Alph. L.), Bibliothèque de Linguistique et d'Ethnographie Américaines.

Introduction, pp. iii-viii.—Monographie des Esquimaux Tchiglit du Mackenzie et de

**Petitot** (É. F. S. J.)—Continued.

l'Anderson, pp. ix-xxxvi.—Précis de Grammaire Esquimaude, &c. pp. xxxix-lxiv.—Dictionnaire Français-Esquimau, pp. 1-75.

*Copies seen:* Astor, Boston Public, Congress, Powell.

Published at 50 fr. Priced by Leclerc, 1878, No. 2230, at 50 fr.; by Trübner, 1882 (p. 53), at £2; by Quaritch, No. 30059, at £1 12s.

—— De l'origine asiatique des Indiens de l'Amérique arctique. Par le R. P. Émile Petitot, O. M. I. Missionnaire au Mackenzie, officier d'Académie, etc.

In Les Missions Catholiques, onzième année, Nos. 543-550, pp. 529-532, 540-544, 550-553, 564-566, 576-578, 589-591, 600-604, 609-611, Paris, Oct. to Dec. 1879, 4°.

List of stone implements, in the Eskimo language, p. 350.

—— Traditions indiennes | du | Canada nord-ouest | par | Émile Petitot | ancien missionnaire | [Design.] |

Paris | Maisonneuve Frères et Ch. Leclerc | 25, quai Voltaire, 2[5] | 1886 | Tous droits réservés

5 p. ll. pp. i-xvii, 1-521, 24°. Forms vol. 23 of Les Littératures Populaires.—Première Partie, Traditions des Esquimaux Tchiglit, pp. 1-10, contains on p. 9 a tradition in Esquimaux with interlinear French translation, and on p. 10 the names with definitions of the Tchiglit deities and heroes.

*Copies seen:* Bureau of Ethnology.

**Petroff** (Ivan). Report on the population, industries, and resources of Alaska. By Ivan Petroff, special agent.

In Census Reports of 1880, vol. 8, 2d paper; title, 2 p. ll. pp. iii-vi, text pp. 1-189, 4°.

A few remarks on the spelling of Russian and native [Eskimo] names, p. 46.—Derivation and meaning of the words Innuit and Tinneh, p. 124.—List of local Kadiak names, from Shelikhof, compared with those of the present; also names of the months, with meanings, p. 145.—Aleut names of seasons and months, with meanings, p. 160.

Under date of Dec. 12, 1886, Mr. Petroff writes the Bureau of Ethnology from Kadiak, Alaska: "I should have forwarded another vocabulary—an Eskimo dialect—from the Aliaskan Peninsula before this, but for the illness of my assistant. I hope to forward it in the spring."

In his present work Mr. Petroff is using the forms and alphabet adopted by the Bureau.

**Pfizmaier** (Dr. A.). Die Sprache der Aleuten und Fuchsinseln.

In Kaiserliche Akademie der Wissenschaften, Philosophisch-Historische Classe, Sitzungsberichte, vol. 105, pp. 801-830; vol. 106, pp. 237-316, Wien, 1884, 8°.

**Pfizmaier** (A.)—Continued.

Die Redetheile, vol. 105, pp. 811-875; vol. 106, pp. 238-261.—Erklärung der Zählungen, vol. 105, pp. 875-879.—Die Wortfügung, vol. 106, pp. 261-266.—Die Wortfolge, vol. 106, pp. 266.—Der Ton, vol. 106, pp. 266-270.—Ein Aleutischer Anfsatz, vol. 106, pp. 270-275.—Ergänzung der Zählungen, vol. 106, pp. 275-276.—Zehn aleutische Lieder, vol. 106, pp. 276-307.—Aleutische Ableitungen, vol. 106, pp. 307-316.

—— Die Abarten der grönländischen Sprache.

In Kaiserliche Akademie der Wissenschaften, Philosophisch-Historische Classe, Sitzungsberichte, vol. 107, pp. 803-882, Wien, 1884, 8°.

Allgemeines über das Kadiakische, pp. 804-833.—Die grönländischen Wörter der eskimotschukschischen Sprache, pp. 833-842.—Grönländische Ergänzungen, pp. 842-876.—Beispiele von grönländischer Apposition, pp. 876-882.

—— Kennzeichnungen des kalâlekischen Sprachstammes.

In Kaiserliche Akademie der Wissenschaften, Philosophisch-Historische Classe, Sitzungsberichte, vol. 108, pp. 87-166, Wien, 1885, 8°.

Bildung der Duale und Plurale, pp. 88-103.—Die Bildung des transitiven Nominativs, pp. 103-107.—Die Nominalsuffixe, 107-133.—Die Apposition, pp. 133-150.—Von dem Adjectivum, pp. 150-155.—Von dem Adverbium, pp. 155-158.—Von dem Verbum, pp. 158-166.

—— Darlegungen grönländischer Verbalformen.

In Kaiserliche Akademie der Wissenschaften, Philosophisch-Historische Classe, Sitzungsberichte, vol. 109, pp. 401-480, Wien, 1885, 8°.

Bildung der Arten und Zeiten des Verbums, pp. 402-430.—Die Abwandlung des Verbums nach Zahlen und Personen, pp. 431-438.—Von den Verbalsuffixen, pp. 438-480.

—— Der Prophet Jesaias grönländisch.

In Kaiserliche Akademie der Wissenschaften, Philosophisch-Historische Classe, Sitzungsberichte, vol. 111, pp. 647-722, Wien, 1886, 8°.

Preface to Wolf's 1825 translation of Isaiah into Greenland, signed Niels Gjessing Wolf, Kjöbenhavnime, 1824, with German translation, pp. 647-649.—The following portions of Isaiah, from Wolf's 1825 translation, with literal German translation, verse by verse, each verse followed by detailed explanation of each word: i, 13-31; ii, 1, 2, 4, 7, 8, 20, 22; iii, 16-24; xiii, 14-22; xiv, 9, 10, 12-23; xxxiv, 9-11, 13-15.—Appendix, treating principally of verbal suffixes, pp. 713-722.

**Pick** (Rev. B.). The Bible in the languages of America. By Rev. B. Pick, Ph. D., Rochester, N. Y.

In The New-York Evangelist, No. 2518. New York, June 27, 1878.

**Pick (B.)** —Continued.

An article on twenty-four different versions of portions of the Bible extant in the languages of America, No. 1 treating of the Greenland, No. 2 of the Esquimaux [of Labrador].

Pilling: This word following a title indicates that a copy of the work referred to is in the possession of the compiler of this bibliography.

**Pillitikset** Kittornganut. | [Picture.] | [N. p.] 1845.

*Literal translation:* Things-meant-for-prosecuts for children.

1 p. l. pp. 1-8, 16°. Bible stories in the Eskimo language of Labrador.

*Copies seen:* American Tract Society.

**Pinart** (Alphonse L.). Eskimaux et Koloches | Idées religieuses et traditions des Kaniagmioutes | par M. Alphonse Pinart

*Colophon:* Paris.—Typographie A. Hennuyer, rue du Boulevard, 7.

Pp. 1-8, 8°. Extract from the Revue d'Anthropologie, 1873.—Eskimo terms passim.

*Copies seen:* British Museum, Brinton, Powell, Trumbull.

—— Les Aléoutes, leurs origines et leurs légendes.

In Société d'Ethnographie Actes, session of 1872, pp. 87-92, Paris [1873], 8°.

Aleutian terms passim.

—— [Dictionary, grammatical notes, texts, songs, and sentences in the Aleutian, Lisievsky (Fox) dialect.] *

Manuscript of about 700 pages, in Aleutian and Russian. Collected by Mr. Pinart in 1871 in Unalashka, Belkoffsky, Unga, and Kadiak.

—— [Dictionary, grammatical notes, songs, descriptions of dances and religious ceremonies, etc.] *

Manuscript of about 1,000 pages, Russian and Kaniagmiout, collected in 1871 and 1872 at Kadiak, Afognak, Katmay, Sutkhum, etc. by M. Pinart.

—— [Vocabulary and texts in the Aglegmiout dialect of Nushagak.] *

Manuscript of about 50 pages, 4°, Russian and Aglegmiout, collected by M. Pinart in 1871.

—— [Vocabulary of the Malehmiont dialect.] *

Manuscript of about 25 pages, 4°, Russian and Malehmiont, collected by M. Pinart at St. Michael in 1871.

These manuscripts are in the possession of the collector, who has kindly furnished me these titles and descriptions.

—— See **Catalogue** de livres rares.

**Pingortitsinermik.** | [Picture.] | [Druck von J. F. Steinkopf in Stuttgart.] 1848.

*Literal translation:* About the creation.

1 p. l. pp. 1-8, 16°. Bible stories in the Eskimo language of Labrador.

*Copies seen:* American Tract Society.

**Piniartut** | pissaiuut titartauvfit katiternere. | Kakortume, Pâmiune, Nûngme, Manitsume, | Amerdlnmilo. | ukiuno 1873|74-1874|76. | Sammendrag | af Fangelister for | Julianehaabs, Frederikshaabs, Godthaabs, | Sukkertoppens, og Holstensborgs Districter; | for Aarene | 1873|74-1875|76. |

Nûngme nakitigkat, | L. Møller. | 1877.

*Literal translation:* The workmen [seal hunters] | for their gains, the lists their collections. | At Kahoitok, at Pamiok, at Nuk, at Manitsok | and at Amudlok. In the years 1873|74-1875|76. | At the Point [Godthaab] printed, | L. Möller.

Title 1 l. pp. 1-41, 12°. Statistics of the seal fisheries of Greenland.

*Copies seen:* Powell.

Point Barrow:

Census.　　　　　　See Ray (P. H.).

Vocabulary.　　　　Ray (P. H.),

　　　　　　　　　　Simpson (J.).

**Pond Bay Vocabulary.** See Hall (C. F.).

**Pok.** | kalalek avalangnek, nunalikame nuna- | katiminut okaluktnartok. | Angakordlo | palasimik napitsivdlune agssortnissok. | agdlagkat pisorkat navssarissat nong- | miut ilanit. | Akât missigssnissut avgnasavait uvig- | dlarnernut kainakut pisut kinguainut. | [Design.] |

Nongme. 1857. | nalagkap nongmitup nakitirivsiane naki- | tigkat R: Bertelsenmit Pelivdlo ornera- | nit Lars Möllermit.

*Inside title:* Pok, | kalalek avalangnek, nunalikamo | unnakatiminut okalugtuartok. | Angakordlo, | palasimik napitsivdlune agssortui- | ssok. | agdlagkat pisorkat navssarissat | nongmiut ilanit. |

nalagkap nongmetup nakiterivsiane | nakitigkat R: Bertelsenmit Pelivdlo | erneranit Lars Möllermit. | 1857.

*Literal translation of first title:* Pok. | a Greenlander traveled when he landed to his | countrymen tells the story. | And the Angekok who | the priest meeting disputes with him. | Written things [manuscript] old discovered the people of the Point [Godthaab] by some of them. | The proceeds the authorities will distribute them to the who have lost their

**Pok**—Continued.

husbands by kayaks surviving widows. | At the Point [Godthaab]. 1857. | The ruler's who is at the Point on his printing-press printed | by R: Bertelsen and Pole's his son Lars Möller.

Printed cover as above; title as above 1 l. pp. 1-18, 4 plates on 2 ll. 2 of the plates being colored, 8°. Written, printed, and illustrated by native Eskimo of Greenland; the wood-cuts and their coloring are curious specimens of native art. On the back cover is the following in Danish:

Pok, | en Grönlænder, som har reist og ved sin | Hjemkomst fortæller derom til sine Lands- | mænd | og | Angekokken | som möder Præsten og disputerer med ham. | Efter gamle Haandskrifter, fundne hos | Grönlændere ved Godthaab. | Hele indtægten skal af forstandei-ska- | borne deles mellem onker, som have mi- | stet deres mænd ved kajakfangst. | [Do-sign.] |

Godthaab. 1857. | Trykt af R: Bertelsen og L: Möller, | Peles Sön, i Inspectourens Bog-trykkeri.

*Copies seen:* Astor, Brinley, Brinton, Congress.

At the Brinley sale, No. 5611, an uncut copy, half-calf extra, gilt top, brought $10.50. Priced in Leclerc's Supplement, No. 2906, at 10 fr.

See Egede (Hans).

**Portions** of the Book of Common Prayer. See **Peck** (E. J.).

**Portions** of the Holy Scripture. See **Peck** (E. J.).

**Portlock** (*Capt.* Nathaniel). A | voyage round the world; | but more particularly to the | north-west coast of America: | performed in 1785, 1786, 1787, and 1788, | in | the King George and Queen Charlotte, | Captains Portlock and Dixon. | Embellished with twenty copper-plates. | Dedicated, by permission, to | his majesty. | By Captain Nathaniel Portlock. |

London: | Printed for John Stockdale, opposite Burlington-House, Piccadilly; | and George Goulding, James Street, Covent Garden. | M. DCC. LXXXIX [1789].

Pp. i-xii, 1-384, appendix i-xl, maps, 4°.—Vocabulary of the language of Prince William's Sound, pp. 254-255.

*Copies seen:* Astor, Bancroft, Boston Athenæum, Congress, Harvard, Watkinson.

At the Field sale, No. 1843, a copy brought $1.25. Priced by Quaritch, No. 28949, at 14s. and a copy in russia, gilt, at £1.

—— and **Dixon** (George). Reis | naar de | nord-west kust | van | Amerika. |

**Portlock** (N.)—Continued.

Gedaan in de jaren 1785, 1786, 1787 en 1788. | Door | de Kapteins | Nathaniel Portlock | en | George Dixon. | Uit derzelver oorspronklijke reisverhalen zamengesteld en vertaald. | Met platen.

Te Amsterdam, bij | Matthijs Schalekamp. | 1795.

Pp. i-xvi, 1-265, map, sm. 4°.—Vocabulary of the natives of Prince William's Sound (from Portlock), pp. 109-110.—Numerals (1-10) of Prince William's Sound (from Dixon), p. 209.

*Copies seen:* Brown, Congress.

See Dixon (George); see also Forster (J. G. A.).

**Pott** (August Friedrich). Die | quinare und vigesimale | Zählmethode | bei Völkern aller Welttheile. | Nebst ausführlicheren Bemerkungen | über die Zahlwörter indogermanischen Stammes | und einem Anhange über Fingernamen. | Von | Dr. August Friedrich Pott, | ord. Prof. der [&c. four lines]. Halle, | C. A. Schwetschke und Sohn. | 1847.

Pp. i-viii, 1-304, 8°.—Numerals of the Tschuk-tschi, Aleut, Kadjak, Tschugazi, Koljasck and Eskimo, pp. 59-61.

*Copies seen:* Astor, British Museum, Watkinson.

**Powell:** This word following a title indicates that a copy of the work referred to was seen by the compiler in the library of Major J. W. Powell, Washington, D. C.

**Prætiunculæ** qvædam et Psalmi. See **Egede** (H.).

**Prayers:**

| | |
|---|---|
| Eskimo. | See Crespicul (F. X.). |
| Greenland. | Anderson, (J.), |
| | Egede (Paul), |
| | Kragh (P.), |
| | Proces. |
| Hudson Bay | Peck (E. J.). |
| Labrador. | Tuksiarutsit. |

**Precationes** et hymni gröulandici. See **Thorhallesen** (E.).

**Preces** | sancti | Nersetis Clajensis | Armeniorum Patriarchae | triginta tribus linguis | editae |

Venetiis | in Insula S. Lazari | 1862

Engraved title 1 l. printed title as above 1 l. dedication, &c. 7 ll. text pp. 1-562, 32°.—Prayer in the Greenland language, pp. 181-194.

*Copies seen:* Eames.

There are editions: Venetiis, 1823, 12° (Congress), and Venetiis, 1837, 12° (Congress), neither of which contains the Greenland specimen.

Prichard (James Cowles). Researches |
into the | Physical History | of Man-
kind. | By | James Cowles Prichard,
M. D. | Second Edition. | In two vol-
umes. | Vol. I[–II]. |
London: | Printed for John and Ar-
thur Arch, | Cornhill. | 1826.

2 vols.: pp. i-xxxii, 1-541; 2 p. ll. pp. 1-623,
11 plates, 8°.—Comparative vocabulary of
American and Asiatic languages, pp. 353-354,
includes a short vocabulary of the Greenland.—
Comparative vocabulary Mexican, Ugalimuch-
mutzi, and Kolusch, p. 381.
*Copies seen:* British Museum.
The first edition, London, 1813, 8°, contains
no linguistics. (British Museum.)

—— Researches | into the | physical his-
tory | of | mankind. | By | James Cowles
Prichard, M. D. F. R. S. M. R. I. A. |
Corresponding Member [&c. three
lines]. | Third edition. | Vol. I[–V]. |
London: | Sherwood, Gilbert, and
Piper, | Paternoster row; | and J. and
A. Arch, | Cornhill. | 1836[–1847].

5 vols. 8°.—Comparative vocabulary of the
Esquimaux, Kinai, and Ugaljachmutzi, vol. 5,
p. 440.
*Copies seen:* Bancroft, Boston Athenæum,
Congress, Eames.
There is a German edition: Leipzig, Leo-
pold Bosk, 1840-1848, 5 vols. in four, 12°. The
linguistics appear in vol. 4. (British Museum.)

—— Researches | into the | Physical His-
tory | of | Mankind. | By James Cowles
Prichard, M. D. F. R. S. M. R. I. A. |
Corresponding Member [&c. four
lines]. | Fourth edition. | Vol. I[–V]. |
London: | Sherwood, Gilbert, and
Piper, | Paternoster Row. | 1841[–1851].

5 vols. 8°. Paging and contents the same as
in the third edition.

Prichard (J. C.) — Continued.
*Copies seen:* Astor.
There is a copy of this work, 5 vols. in the
Library of Congress, composed of volumes from
different editions. I am inclined to think that
all issues subsequent to 1840 were made up of
volumes from the preceding editions.

Primer:

| Aleut. | See Aleutian. |
| Alout-Kadiak. | Tishnoff (E.). |
| Eskimo. | Abécédaire, |
| | Bompas (W. C.). |
| Greenland. | Groenlandsk, |
| | Janssen (C. E.), |
| | Kattitsiomàrsut. |
| Labrador. | Okautsit. |

Prince William Sound:

| Numerals. | See Buschmann (J. C. E.), |
| | Dixon (G.), |
| | Forster (J. G. A.), |
| | Portlock (N.) and |
| | Dixon (G.). |
| Vocabulary. | Anderson (W.), |
| | Buschmann (J. C. E.), |
| | Forster (J. G. A.), |
| | Fry (E.), |
| | Portlock (N.). |

Prophetib Icsaiasib | Aglangit. | The
Book of Isaiah | translated into the |
Esquimaux Language, | by | the Mis-
sionaries | of the Unitas Fratrum, or
United Brethren. | Printed for the use
of the Mission, | by | The British and
Foreign Bible Society. |
London: | W. M'Dowall, Printer,
Pemberton Row, Gough Square. | 1837.

*Literal translation:* The prophet Isaiah's |
his written things.
Pp. 1-168, 12°, entirely in the language of
Labrador. See Wolf (N. G.) for edition of 1825.
*Copies seen:* British Museum.

## Q.

Quaritch: This word following a title indicates
that a copy of the work referred to was seen by
the compiler in the possession of Mr. Bernard
Quaritch, London, Eng.

Quaritch (Bernard). A general | cata-
logue of books, | offered to the public
at the affixed prices | by | Bernard
Quaritch. |
London: | 15 Piccadilly. | 1880.

Title 1 l. preface pp. ili-iv, contents v-x,
catalogue 1-2166, index 2167-2395, 12°. Includes the parts issued with the numbers 309-
330.
Besides many scattered Eskimo titles there

Quaritch (B.) — Continued.
is a group "Arctic Explorations," pp. 1148-1152,
and one "Eskimo language," p. 1253.
Subsequent to the above there have been
printed Nos. 331-369 of the general catalogue
(1880-1886) and various miscellaneous parts
which will, I presume, form part of another
volume. Of these general parts Nos. 362 and
363 are entitled: "Catalogue of the History,
Geography, and of the Philology of America,
Australia * * *" Scattered through them
are a number of titles referring to the Eskimo,
and on pp. 3022-3023 (part 363) is a section
headed "Language of Labrador and Greenland."
*Copies seen:* Congress, Bureau of Ethnology.

# R.

**Radloff** (Léopold). Mémoires | de | l'Académie Impériale des Sciences de St.-Pétersbourg, VIIᵉ série. | Tome III, Nᵒ 10. | Über die | Sprache der Tschuktschen | und ihr | Verhältniss zum Korjakischen | von | L. Radloff. | Der Akademie vorgelegt am 9. März 1860. | St. Petersburg, 1861. | Commissionäre der Kaiserlichen Akademie der Wissenschaften: | in St. Petersburg [&c. three lines].

Printed cover as above, title as above 1 l. pp. 1-60, 4°.—Grammar, pp. 11-30.—Vocabulary, alphabetic according to German words, pp. 31-51.—Tschuktschische und Korjakische Sprachprobe, eingesandt von dem Hafen-Commandeur Capitain-Lieutenant Subow, pp. 57-59.

Copies seen: British Museum, Congress.

—— Über die Sprache der Ugalachmut.

In Académie des Sciences, Bull. de la Classe Hist.-Phil. vol. 15(*); and in the same society's Mélanges russes, vol. 3, pp. 468-524. (*)

**Rand** (Rev. Silas Tertius). About a thou- | sand Esquimaux | words, gathered | from the New- | Testament in | that Language |

Manuscript, English and Eskimo, recorded, alphabetically by English words, in a 4° book of about 35 pp., which apparently had been previously devoted to the reception of Micmac material, the Eskimo matter occupying in some cases whole pages, in others part of a page, and in still others additional sheets of note paper.

In possession of Mr. Rand, Hantsport, Nova Scotia.

**Ray** (Lieut. Patrick Henry). Ethnographic sketch of the natives of Point Barrow. By Lieut. P. H. Ray.

In Report of the International Polar Expedition to Point Barrow, Alaska, pp. 35-87, Washington, 1885, 4°.

Approximate census of Eskimos at the Cape Smythe village [a list of 137 proper names], p. 49.—Vocabulary collected among the Eskimos of Point Barrow and Cape Smythe [711 words and 307 phrases and sentences, being the schedules given in Powell's Introduction to the Study of Indian Languages], pp. 51-60.—Alphabet [used in recording the vocabulary], p. 87.

**Reichelt** (Rev. G. T.). The Literary Works of the Foreign Missionaries of the Moravian Church. By the Rev. G. Th. Reichelt, of Herrnhut, Saxony. (Translated and annotated by Bishop Edmund De Schweinitz.)

In The Moravian, vol. 31, pp. 355-356, 371-372, Bethlehem, Penn'a, 1886, 4°.

Reprinted as follows:

**Reichelt** (G. T.)—Continued.

—— The literary works of the Foreign Missionaries of the Moravian Church. By the Rev. G. Th. Reichelt, of Herrnhut, Saxony. Translated and Annotated by Bishop Edmund de Schweinitz.

In Moravian Historical Society Trans. series 2, part 8, pp. 375-395, Bethlehem, Pa. 1886, 8°.

Separately issued as follows:

—— The Literary Works | of the | Foreign Missionaries of the Moravian Church. | By | the Rev. G. Th. Reichelt of Herrnhut, Saxony. | Translated and annotated by Bishop Edmund de Schweinitz. | (Reprinted from the Transactions of the Moravian Historical Society.) | [1886.]

Printed cover as above, half-title as above 1 l. pp. 3-21, 8°. Besides translating and annotating the above, Bishop de Schweinitz added many notes, biographic and bibliographic, which will be found scattered through these pages.

Copies seen: Eames, Pilling.

Relationships:

| | |
|---|---|
| Arctic. | See Oppert (G.). |
| Greenland. | Kleinschmidt (S. P.). |
| Hudson Bay. | Clare (J. R.), |
| | Morgan (L. H.). |
| Innuit. | Dall (W. H.). |
| Northumberland Inlet. | Morgan (L. H.). |

Remarks:

| | |
|---|---|
| Aleut. | See Lowe (F.). |
| Eskimo. | Jefferys (T.), |
| | Morillot (—), |
| | Nouvelle Bretagne, |
| | Rosse (I. C.), |
| | Scherer (J. B.), |
| | Schott (W.), |
| | Seemann (B.). |
| Greenland. | La Harpe (J. F. de), |
| | O'Reilly (B.), |
| | Rink (H. J.), |
| | Scherer (J. B.), |
| | Schott (W.), |
| | Steinthal (H.). |
| Kadiak. | Veniaminoff (J.). |
| Ugalachmut. | Radloff (L.). |

Reports, Greenland. See Nalunnerutit.

**Richard** (L.). Manuel des Langues, | Mortes et vivantes. Contenant les | Alphabets, la numération, et | l'Oraison Dominicale, en 190 langues. | Par L. Richard. | Première Edition 1839. | Se trouve à Paris, | chez Mʳ. Mansut fils, Libraire, | Rue des Mathurins Sᵗ. | Jacques 17, | et chez l'auteur, Place

**Richard (L.)**—Continued.

Maubert 19. | Imprimerie Lithographe de Petit, rue de Bourgogne nᵒ. 25.

Title reverse blank 1 l. pp. 1-112, 8°.—Oratio Dominica, Groenlandice, p. 60.

Copies seen: British Museum, Congress.

Trübner's catalogue, 1856, No. 560, prices a copy at 10s. 6d.

**Richardson** (*Sir* John). Arctic | searching expedition: | a | journal of a boat-voyage | through Rupert's Land and the Arctic Sea, | in search of | the discovery ships under command of | Sir John Franklin. | With an appendix on the physical geography | of North America. | By Sir John Richardson, C. B., F. R. S. | Inspector of Naval Hospitals and Fleets, | etc. etc. etc. | In two volumes. | Vol. I[-II]. | Published by authority. |

London: | Longman, Brown, Green, and Longmans. | 1851.

2 vols. maps, plates, 8°.—Remarks on the Eskimo language, with examples of nouns declined transitively and intransitively, vol. 2, pp. 363-368.—Comparative table of the dialects spoken by the Beering's Sea and Labrador Eskimos, comprising the two following:

Baer (K. E. von). Kuskutchewak vocabulary, vol. 2, pp. 369-382.

Latrobe (P.) and **Washington** (J.). Vocabulary of the Labrador Eskimo, vol. 2, pp. 369-382.

Copies seen: Astor, Bancroft, Boston Athenæum, British Museum, Congress, Trumbull.

At the Field sale, catalogue No. 1970, a copy brought $4.50. Priced by Quaritch, No. 28995, at 15s.

—— Arctic | Searching Expedition: | a | Journal of a Boat-Voyage through Rupert's | Land and the Arctic Sea, | in search of the Discovery Ships under command of | Sir John Franklin. | With an Appendix on the Physical Geogra- | phy of North America. | By Sir John Richardson, C. B., F. R. S., | Inspector of Naval Hospitals and Fleets, | etc., etc., etc. |

New York: | Harper & Brothers, Publishers, | 82 Cliff Street. | 1852.

Pp. i-xi, 13-516, 12°.—Linguistics, pp. 235-236, 273, 479-516.

Copies seen: Harvard.

Field's sale catalogue, No. 1971, mentions an edition: New York, Harper & Brothers, 1856, 516 pp. 12°. It sold for 35 cents.

[**Rink** (Heinrik Johannes).] Nunap misigssuissok arnigssa | pivdlugo inuit tusagagssait | [Signed: H. Rink. | Nunap nalaga.]

**Rink (H. J.)**—Continued.

Colophon: Nongme 3 Sept: 1857.

Literal translation: The country's its intended survey | in reference to it people their-things-to-be-heard [things for the people to hear about it]. | [Signed: H. Rink | the country's its ruler.] | At the Point (Godthaab) 3 Sept: 1857.

No title-page; caption only; 2 ll. 8°. An announcement by the inspector, Dr. Rink, to the Greenlanders, in their own language, of the establishment of a system of surveys.

Copies seen: Congress.

—— Eskimoiske | eventyr og sagn | oversatte | efter de indfødte fortællores opskrifter | og meddelelser | af | H. Rink, | inspektør i Sydgrønland.

Kjøbenhavn. | C. A. Reitzels Boghandel. | Louis Kleins Bogtrykkeri. | 1866.

Pp. i-vi, 1 l. pp. 1-376, 8°.—Songs in Eskimo, pp. 349-350.—"Alfabetisk Folklaring over forskjellige Udtryk og Benævnelser (tildeels fastsatte blot for Afbenyttelse i dette Skrift)," pp. 369-376.

Copies seen: British Museum, Congress.

At the Pinart sale, No. 791, Quaritch bought a copy for 14 fr. He prices it, No. 30058, at £1.

A supplement to this work was published at Copenhagen in 1871, 8°. (*)

—— Tales and traditions | of the | Eskimo | with a sketch of | their habits, religion, language | and other peculiarities | by | Dr Henry Rink | knight of Dannebrog | [&c. four lines]. | Translated from the Danish by the author | Edited by | Dr Robert Brown | F. L. S., F. R. G. S. | author of 'The races of mankind', etc. | With numerous illustrations, drawn and | engraved by Eskimo |

William Blackwood and Sons | Edinburgh and London | MDCCCLXXV [1875] | All Rights reserved

Pp. i-xii, 1-473, 12°.—Language, pp. 12-22.—A myth-song, with translation, pp. 66-67.—Scattered throughout are also many Eskimo words.

Copies seen: Astor, Boston Athenæum, British Museum.

—— Danish Greenland | its people and its products | By | Dr Henry Rink | knight of the order of Dannebrog [&c. three lines]. | [Seal.] | Edited by | Dr Robert Brown, F. L. S. F. R. G. S. | author of 'The races of mankind' etc. | With illustrations by the Eskimo, and a map |

Rink (H. J.)—Continued.

Henry S. King & Co., London [ 1877
Pp. i-xvii, 1-468, maps, plates, 8°.—Remarks
on the language of the natives of Greenland,
pp. 197-198.—Vocabulary of Eskimo words and
names, pp. 394-402.—Scattered thoughout are
many Eskimo words.

*Copies seen:* Astor, British Museum, Congress, Eames, Harvard.

—— De grønlandske Stednavnes | Retskrivning og Etymologi | af | Dr. H.
Rink, | Direktør for den Kongl. grønlandske Handel. | 1877.

Forms an appendix, pp. 351-366, to Johnstrup
(F.), Gieseckes Mineralogiske Rejse i Grønland,
Kjøbenhavn, 1878, 8°.—Of letters, accents, &c.
p. 355.—Verbal affixes, p. 356.—Nominal affixes,
p. 356.—De grønlandske Stednavnes Retskrivning og Etymologi, pp. 358-366.

—— Les dialectes de la langue esquimaude, éclaircis par un tableau synoptique de mots, arrangés d'après le système du dictionnaire groenlandais.

In Congrès Int. des Américanistes, Compterendu, fifth session, pp. 328-337, Copenhague,
1884, 8°.

Issued separately as follows:

—— Dialectes de la langue esquimaude.
· | Par | H. Rink. | Extrait du Compterendu du Congrès International des
Américanistes | Copenhague 1883. |
Copenhague. Imprimerie de Thiele. |
1884.

Outside title as above, text pp. 328-337, 8°.—
Greenland and western Esquimaux words for
*fire, thou, thee*, p. 333.—Greenland alphabet, pp.
333-334.

*Copies seen:* Pilling.

—— The Eskimo Dialects as serving to
determine the Relationship between the
Eskimo Tribes. By Dr. H. Rink.

In Anthropological Institute of Great Britain and Ireland, vol. 15, pp. 239-245, London,
1885, 8°.
A general discussion, including a few Eskimo terms and a genealogical table of dialects.

Issued separately as follows:

—— The Eskimo dialects | as serving to
determine the relationship | between |
the Eskimo tribes. | By | Dr. H. Rink, |
Knight of the Order of Danneborg [*sic*],
etc. |
London: | Harrison and Sons, St.
Martin's Lane, | Printers in Ordinary
to Her Majesty. | 1885.

Title on cover as above, text pp. 239-245, 8°.
*Copies seen:* Powell.

—— Om de eskimoiske dialekter, som
bidrag til bedømmelsen af spørgsmaalet

ESK——6

Rink (H. J.)—Continued.

om eskimoernes herkomst og vandringer. Af H. Rink.

In Aarbøger for nordisk oldkyndighed og
historie, udgivne af det kongelige nordiske
oldskrift-selskab, 1885, tredie hefte, pp. 219-
260, Kjøbenhavn, 1885, 8°.
This work has the following divisions: 1.
The character of the language in general. 2.
The difference of the dialects in general. 3. The
difference of the dialects in respect of expressions for certain classes of ideas. 4. The difference of the dialects in regard to the stemwords. 5. Comparison among the dialects in
respect to grammar, comprising also construction of words. 6. Glance at the results of the
preceding. 7. List of the works employed in
writing this essay. Many words and stems
throughout.

Issued separately as follows:

—— Om de eskimoiske dialekter, som
bidrag til bedømmelsen af spørgsmaalet om | eskimoernes herkomst og
vandringer. | Af | H. Rink. | Saertryk
af Aarb. f. nord. Oldk. og Hist. 1885. |
Kjøbenhavn. |Thieles bogtrykkeri. |
1885.

Title as above on cover, no inside title, pp.
1-42, 8°, the original pagination, 219-260, being
also retained.
*Copies seen:* Powell.

—— [The linguistic results of Dr. Franz
Boas's ethnographical researches in
Baffin Land, by H. Rink.]

Manuscript, pp. 1-23, 4°, in The Bureau of
Ethnology. For a description of the material
which Dr. Rink herein reviews see Boas (F.).
Division of the Eskimo regions, pp. 1-3.—
Orthography, pp. 4-6.—Collection of words and
phrases (remarks on), pp. 6-7.—Radical and
additional words, flectional forms, pp. 8-10.—
Division of words according to classes of notions, p. 10.—List of words in the vocabulary from Baffin's Land classed according to
the notions conveyed, pp. 11-12.—Samples of
the text of songs, with explanations, pp. 13-
22.

—— [Brief catalogue of books in the
Eskimo language of Greenland.]

Manuscript slips furnished me by Dr. Rink;
in its preparation he had the assistance of "a
Greenland missionary."

Heinrik Johannes Rink was born in Copenhagen, August 26, 1819. He studied in his native town from 1840 to 1844, and then for a year
or two in Germany. In June, 1845, he left Copenhagen for a circumnavigation, as geologist
of an expedition, but remained in India as assistant to the governor of the Danish colony on
the Nicobar Islands. Considerations of health
obliged him to leave India, and after a stay in
Egypt and Naples he returned to Copenhagen

**Rink** (H. J.)—Continued.

in December, 1846. In 1848 he went to Greenland, where he spent twenty-two summers and sixteen winters. From 1853 to 1868 he served as inspector of Southern Greenland, and in 1871 was appointed director of the trade. His last visit to Greenland was made in 1872. In 1883 he settled down in Norway, and at present (1887) is spending a retired life at Christiania, Norway.

**Ritual:**

Greenland.          See Egede (Paul),
                    Fabricius (O.).

**Robeck** (*Dr.* —). [Vocabularies of Asiatic and American Eskimo.]

In Saricheff (G. A.), [Journey of Captain Billings across the Chukchi country], St. Petersburg, 1811, 4°. In Russian.

Vocabulary of the settled Tschukchi and nomadic Tschukchi, pp. 102–111.—Parallel vocabularies of about 300 words each, Russian, Andreanoffski Aleuts, Lisie Aleuts, and Kadiak Eskimo, in modern Russian type, part 4, pp. 121–129.

For partial reprints see Schott (W.); also Zagoskin (L. A.).

**Romberg** (Heinrich). Ein Tschuktschisches Wörterverzeichniss. Von Herrn Heinrich Romberg.

In Erman (A.), Archiv für wissenschaftliche Kunde von Russland, vol. 19, pp. 310–345, Berlin, 1860, 8°.

Chuckchee vocabulary and numerals 1–100.

**Ross** (*Sir* John). A | voyage of discovery, | made under the orders of the admiralty, | in | his majesty's ships | Isabella and Alexander, | for the purpose of | exploring Baffin's Bay, | and inquiring into the probability of a | north-west passage. | By John Ross, K. S. Captain Royal Navy. |

London: | John Murray, Albemarle-street. | 1819.

2 p. ll. pp. i-xl, 1–252, i-cxliv, 1 l. maps, 4°.—A comparative list of the northern and southern Eskimaux language, p. 122.—Words the same in both dialects, pp. 122–123.

*Copies seen:* Astor, British Museum, Congress, Harvard.

—— A | Voyage of Discovery, | made under the Orders of the Admiralty, | in | his Majesty's Ships | Isabella and Alexander, | for the Purpose of | exploring Baffin's Bay, | and enquiring into the Probability of a North-west Passage. | By John Ross, K. S. Captain Royal Navy. | Second Edition. | In two volumes | Vol. I[-II]. |

London: | Printed by Strahan and Spottiswoode, Printers-Street; | For

**Ross** (J.)—Continued.

Longman, Hurst, Rees, Orme, and Brown, | Paternoster-Row. | 1819.

2 vols. map, 8°.—Linguistics, as in first edition, vol. 1, pp. 167–168.

*Copies seen:* Boston Athenæum, British Museum.

—— Entdeckungsreise | der | königlichen Schiffe Isabella und Alexander | nach der Baffins-Bai, | zur Untersuchung der Möglichkeit einer Nord-West- | Durchfahrt. | Nach dem Englischen | des | Herrn John Ross, | Capitains der königlichen Marine. | (Aus dem Ethnographischen Archiv besonders abgedruckt.) |

Jena, | in der Bran'schen Buchhandlung. | 1819.

Pp. i–iv, 1–184, 8°.—Vergleichungs-Liste der nördlichen und südlichen Esquimaux-Sprache, p. 99.—Worte, die in beiden Mundarten gleich sind, p. 100.

*Copies seen:* Astor.

A Dutch translation: 's Gravenhaag, 1821, 8°, is mentioned in F. Muller's catalogue, 1872, No. 1378. An English edition: London [1834], 4°, contains no linguistics.

—— Narrative | of a | second voyage in search of | a | north-west passage, | and of a | residence in the arctic Regions | during the years 1829, 1830, 1831, 1832, 1833. | By | Sir John Ross, C. B., K. S. A., K. C. S., &c. &c. | captain in the royal navy. | Including the reports of | Commander, now Captain, James Clark Ross, R. N., F. R. S., F. L. S., &c. | and | The Discovery of the Northern Magnetic Pole. |

London: | A. W. Webster, 156, Regent Street. | 1835.

4 p. ll. pp. i-xxxiv, 1–740, maps, plates, 4°.—Hymn in the Esquimaux language, p. 76.

*Copies seen:* Astor, Boston Athenæum, British Museum, Congress.

—— Appendix | to the | narrative | of a | second voyage in search | of a | north-west passage, | and of a | residence in the arctic regions | during the years 1829, 1830, 1831, 1832, 1833. | By | Sir John Ross, C. B., K. S. A., K. C. S. &c. &c. | captain in the royal navy. | Including the reports of | Commander, now Captain, James Clark Ross, R. N., F. R. S., F. L. S., &c. | and | The Discovery of the Northern Magnetic Pole. |

London: | A. W. Webster, 156, Regent street. | 1835.

Pp. i-xii, 1–120, i-cxliv, i-cii, 4°.—Vocabulary

**Ross** (J.)—Continued.

of the English, Danish, and Esquimaux languages, pp. 61-89.—Dialogues in the English, Danish, and Esquimaux languages, pp. 91-104.

*Copies seen:* Astor, British Museum, Congress, Harvard.

—— Narrative | of a | second voyage | in search | of a northwest passage, | and of | a residence in the arctic regions, | during the years 1829, 1830, 1831, 1832, 1833; | By Sir John Ross, C. B., K. S. A., K. C. S., &c. &c. | captain in the royal navy. | Including | the reports of Commander (now Captain) J. C. Ross, R. N. F. R. S., F. L. S., &c. | and | the Discovery of the Northern Magnetic Pole.

Philadelphia: | E. L. Carey & A. Hart. | Baltimore: | Carey, Hart & Co. | 1835.

Pp. i-xxiii, 1-456, map, 8°.—Hymn in the Esquimaux language, p. 43.

*Copies seen:* Boston Athenæum.

—— Relation | du | second voyage | fait à la recherche | d'un passage au nord-ouest, | Par Sir John Ross, | capitaine de la marine royale, chevalier de l'Ordre du Bain, etc., etc. | et de sa résidence dans les régions arctiques | pendant les années 1829 à 1833 ; | contenant le rapport du capitaine de la marine royale Sir James Clarck Ross, et les | observations relatives à la découverte du pole nord; | ouvrage traduit sous les yeux de l'auteur, | par A.-J.-B. Defauconpret, | Traducteur des Œuvres de W. Scott, etc.; | Accompagné d'une Carte du Voyage et orné du portrait de l'Auteur, gravé | à Lou-

**Ross** (J.)—Continued.

dres, par Robert Hart, et des deux Vues les plus remarquables de | ces régions, gravées sur acier, d'après Finden, par Skelton. | Tome premier[-deuxième]. |

Paris, | Bellizard, Barthès, Dufour et Lowell, | libraires de la cour impériale de Russie, rue de Verneuil, 1 bis. | 1835.

2 vols. maps, 8°.—Hymn in the Eskimo language, vol. 1, p. 99.

*Copies seen:* Congress.

An edition in English, Brussels, 1835, 8°, is mentioned in F. Muller's catalogue, 1872, No. 1379.

**Rosse** (*Dr.* Irving C.). Medical and anthropological notes.

In Cruise of the Revenue-steamer Corwin, pp. 7-44 (47th Congress, 2d session, House of Representatives, Ex. Doc. No. 105), Washington, 1883, 4°.

Linguistic peculiarities, pp. 30-33, contains a few words in and general remarks upon the Eskimo language.

**Rudolph** (—). Anner' láb innungorsimasub | pârinek ' arneranik, | Rudolph-ib | Nekkursaisub ag' logèinik. | áipagssânik nakitigkat, sujugdlit ássilinardlugit. |

Kjøbenhavn. | Louis Kleins Bogtrykkeri. | 1870.

*Literal translation:* The just-come-out-one [who has] become-a-human being | about the taking care of it | Rudolph | the healer's about his writings. | A second time printed, | the first copying it.

Pp. 1-16, 16°. Manual for midwives in the Eskimo language of Greenland.

*Copies seen:* Powell.

See Kragh (P.) for an earlier treatise on this subject.

# S.

**Sabin** (Joseph). A | dictionary | of | Books relating to America, | from its discovery to the present time. | By Joseph Sabin. | Volume I[-XVI]. | [Three lines quotation.]

New-York : | Joseph Sabin, 81 Nassau street. | 1868[-1886].

16 vols. 8°, still in course of publication, and including thus far entries to "Remarks." Contains titles of many works in the Eskimo language. Now edited by Mr. Wilberforce Eames.

*Copies seen:* Congress, Eames, Powell.

Sacred history, Aleut. See Veniaminoff (J.) and Netzvietoff (J.).

**Sagoskin.** See Zagoskin.

**St. Luke's** Gospel. See **Peck** (E. J.).

St. Michael Vocabulary. See Everette (W. E.).

**Salomonib** Okâlagatäningit | Profeteniglo. | The Proverbs of Solomon and the Prophe- | cies of Jeremiah, Ezekiel, Daniel and | the Twelve Minor Prophets: | Translated into | the Esquimaux Language | by | the Missionaries | of the | Unitas Fratrum, or United Brethren. |

London: | Printed for the use of the Mission in Labrador, | by the British and Foreign Bible Society. | 1849.

*Literal translation:* Solomon's his sayings | and about the Prophets.

1 p. l. pp. 1-675, 12°.

*Copies seen:* American Bible Society, British and Foreign Bible Society, British Museum.

**Sapâme** únúkut atugagssat ardlait.

*Colophon :* Druck von Gustav Winter in Stolpen. [n. d.]

*Literal translation :* On Sunday in the even ing things to be used the second.

No title-page; pp. 1-7, 12°. Litany Cate chism, entirely in the language of Greenland. *Copies seen :* Pilling, Powell.

My copy, procured of the Unitäts-Buchhand lung, Gnadau, Saxony, cost, 20 pf.

**Sauer** (Martin). An | account | of a | geographical and astronomical | ex pedition | to the | northern parts of Russia, | for ascertaining the degrees of latitude and longitude of | the mouth of the river Kovima; | of the whole coast of the Tshutski, to East Cape; | and of the islands in the Eastern Ocean, stretching to | the American coast. | Performed, | By Command of Her Imperial Majesty Catherine the Second, | empress of all the Russias, | by Commodore Joseph Billings, | In the Years 1785, &c. to 1794. | The whole narrated from the original papers, | by Martin Sauer, | secretary to the expe dition. |

London : | Printed by A. Strahan, Printers Street; | For T. Cadell, Jun. and W. Davies, in the Strand. | 1802.

Pp. i-xxvii, 1-332, and appendix pp. 1-58, map, 4°.—Vocabulary of the languages of Kamtshatka, the Aleutan Islands, and of Kadiak, pp. 9-14 of appendix.

*Copies seen :* Astor, Bancroft, Boston Athe nœum, Boston Public, British Museum, Con gress, Watkinson.

—— Voyage | fait par ordre de l'impé ratrice de Russie | Catherine II, | dans le nord | de la Russie Asiatique, | dans la mer Glaciale, | dans la mer d'Anadyr, et sur les | côtes de l'Amérique, | depuis 1785 jusqu'en 1794, | par le commodore Billings; | rédigé par M. Sauer, | Secré taire-Interprète de l'Expédition, | et traduit de l'anglais avec des notes, | par J. Castéra. | Avec une Collection de quinze Planches, format in-4°., dessinées sur les Lieux. | Tome Premier [-Second]. |

A Paris, | chez F. Buisson, Impri meur-Libraire, rue Hautefeuille, No. 20. | an X (1802)

2 vols. 8°, atlas 4°.—Vocabulaire Kamtcha dale, vol. 2, pp. 289-295.—Vocabulaire Aléoute, vol. 2, pp. 296-303.—Vocabulaire de la langue de Kadiak, vol. 2, pp. 304-311.

*Copies seen :* Congress.

**Sauer** (M.) — Continued.

According to Ludewig, there was a German translation: Berlin, 1802, 8°, the vocabularies occurring on pp. 399-406.

—— Reise | nach | Siberien, Kam tschatka, und zur | Untersuchung | der Mündung des Kowima-Flusses, der ganzen | Küste der Tschutschen und der zwischen dem fe- | sten Lande von Asien und Amerika be- | findlichen Inseln [&c. eight lines] von | Martin Sauer, | Sekretär der Expedition. | Aus dem Englischen übersetzt. | Mit Kup fern und | Karte. |

Berlin und Hamburg. | 1803.

2 p. ll. pp. i-vii, 9-331, 8°.—Vocabularies, pp. 325-330.

*Copies seen :* British Museum.

A copy at the Fischer sale, No. 2125, brought 3s.

**Schediasma** hocce etymologico-philolo gicum * * * Grönlandicum. See **Abel** (I.).

**Schema** conjugationis Grönlandicæ. See **Thorhallesen** (E.).

**Scherer** (Johann Benedict). Recherches | Historiques | et Géographiques | sur | le Nouveau-Monde. | Par Jean-Benoît Scherer, Pensionnaire du Roi; | Em ployé aux affaires étrangères; Membre de plusieurs | Académies & Sociétés littéraires; ci-devant Juriscon- | sulte du Collége Impérial de Justice à Saint- Pétersbourg, | pour les affaires de la Livonie, d'Esthonie & de Finlande. | [Design.] |

A Paris, | Chez Brunet, Libraire, rue des Écrivains. | M. DCC. LXXVII [1777].

Pp. i-xii, 2 ll. pp. 1-352, map, plates, 8°.— Short vocabulary, 17 words, Esquimaux and Greenland, p. 19.—Essai sur les rapports des mots entre les Langues du Nouveau-Monde & celles de l'Ancien, par Court de Gebelin (A. de), pp. 302-345, contains: Langue des Esqui maux & des Groenlandois, pp. 306-312.

*Copies seen :* Astor, Boston Athenæum, Con gress.

Priced by Leclerc, 1878, No. 2087, at 20 fr. Quaritch bought a copy at the Ramirez sale, No. 772, for 3s. 6d.

**Schomburgk** (*Sir* Robert H.). Contri butions to the Philological Ethnogra phy of South America. By Sir R. H. Schomburgk.

In Philological Soc. [of London] Proc. vol. 3, pp. 228-237 London, 1848, 8°.

"Affinity of words in the Guiana with other

**Schomburgk (R. H.)**—Continued.

Languages and Dialects in America," pp. 236-237, contains among others examples in Eskimaux of Hudson's Bay.

—— A vocabulary of the Maiongkong Language [South America]. By Sir Robert Schomburgk.

In Philological Soc. [of London] Proc. vol. 4, pp. 217-222, London, 1850, 8°.

Contains the word for *sun* in Esquimaux, Tchouktche American or Aglomoute, &c.

**Schott (W.).** Ueber die Sprachen des russischen Amerika's, nach Wenjaminow.

In Erman (A ), Archiv für wissenschaftliche Kunde von Russland, vol. 7, pp. 126-143, Berlin, 1849, 8°.

—— Ueber ethnographische Ergebnisse der Sagoskinschen Reise, von W. Schott.

In Erman (A.), Archiv für wissenschaftliche Kunde von Russland, vol. 7, pp. 480-512, Berlin, 1849, 8°.

Vocabulary of the Inkilik and Inkalit-Ingelnut (from Zagoskin), pp. 481-187.—Vocabulary of the Tschnagmjute, Kwigpakjute, and Kuskowigmjute (from Zagoskin), Kadjaker (from Billings and Lisiansky), and Namoller (from Robek), pp. 488-512.

—— Die Sprache der Eskimos auf Grönland.

In Magazin für die Litteratur des Auslands, Nos. 38, 39, Berlin, 1856. Title from Ludewig, p. 221.

**Schubert** (*Hofrath* von), *editor*. Correspondenz-Nachrichten aus Labrador. Mitgetheilt von Hrn. Hofrath v. Schubert.

In Königliche Akad. der Wiss. zu München, vol. 18, columns 417-430, München [1844], 4°.

Eskimo vocabulary, columns 417-422, 425-429.

**Schwatka** (*Lieut.* Frederick). Vocabulary of the Eskimo. *

Manuscript in possession of the author. Concerning it he writes me as follows: "My linguistic material pertaining to the Eskimo is in rough manuscript form, containing probably 500 or 600 words in most common use by the Inkillik Innuits of Repulse Bay, gathered from August, 1878, to August, 1880, while sojourning with this tribe, each word being noted in a small calf-bound journal as its use made it prominent and I became assured that I had it sufficiently correct for conversational purposes."

**Seemann** (Berthold). Narrative of the voyage of H. M. S. Herald | during the years 1845-51, | under the command of | Captain Henry Kellett, R. N., C. B.; | being | A Circumnavigation of the

**Seemann (B.)**—Continued.

Globe, | and three cruizes to the arctic regions in search | of Sir John Franklin. | By | Berthold Seemann, F. L. S., | member of [&c. two lines]. | In two volumes. | Vol. I[-II]. |

London : | Reeve and Co., Henrietta Street, Covent Garden. | 1853.

2 vols. 8°.—Brief reference to the Eskimo language, vol. 2, pp. 68-69.

Copies seen : Astor, Bancroft, Boston Atheneum, British Museum, Congress.

—— Reise um die Welt | und | drei Fahrten | der Königlich Britischen Fregatte Herald | nach dem nördlichen Polarmeere | zur | Aufsuchung Sir John Franklin's | in den Jahren 1845-1851. | Von | Berthold Seemann. Erster [-Zweiter] Band. | [2 lines.] |

Hannover. | Carl Rümpler. | 1853.

2 vols. : pp. i-xi, 1-335; i-vi, 1-291, 8°.—Sprache der Eskimos, vol. 2, pp. 72-73.

Copies seen : British Museum, Congress.

**Selenie (S. J.).** See Zelenie (S. J.).

**Sendebrev** til alle Grönlænderne. See **Fasting** (L.).

**Senfkornesutépok.** [ Picture. ]

No title-page; pp. 1-8, 24°. Bible stories in the Eskimo language of Greenland.—Apost. sull. 7, 9-14, pp. 1-2.—Joh. 10, 12-18, pp. 3-4.—Matth. 20, 29-34, pp. 5-6.—Apost. sull. 8, 27-39, pp. 7-8.

Copies seen : American Tract Society, Powell.

**Senfkornetun-ípok.** [ Picture.]

No title-page; 1 p. l. pp. 1-8, sq. 24°. Bible lessons in the Eskimo language of Labrador.—Apostetit Piniarningit 7, 9-14.—Joh. 10, 12-18. Matth. 20, 29-34.—Apost. Pin. 8, 27-39.

Copies seen : American Tract Society.

**Sennerutilingmik Tuksiautitait.** See **Kjer** (K.).

Sentences :
Greenland. See Kragh (P.).
Innuit. Hoffman (W. J.).
Koksoagmyut. Turner (L. M.).
Unalashkan. Turner (L. M.).

Sermons :
Greenland. See Ivangkilinnik, Kragh (P.).
Labrador. Okálautsit.

**Shea** (John Gilmary). Languages of the American Indians.

In American Cyclopædia, vol. 1, pp. 407-414, New York, 1873, 8°.

Contains grammatical examples of a number of American languages, among them the Esquimaux.

**Silame** iliornerit. See **Kleinschmidt** (S. P.).

**Silamiut** ingordlaunsiánik. See **Janssen** (C. E.).

**Simonimik** Syrenimiumik. See **Böggild** (O.).

**Simpson** (*Dr.* John). Observations on the Western Esquimaux and the Country they inhabit; from notes taken during two years at Point Barrow, by Mr. John Simpson, R. N., Her Majesty's Discovery Ship "Plover."

In Further papers relative to the recent Arctic expeditions, pp. 917-942, London, 1855, folio.

Contains the names of the seasons and months in Esquimaux, p. 933.

Reprinted in Royal Geographical Society, Arctic Geography and Ethnology, pp. 233-275, London, 1875, 8°. (British Museum, Powell.)

**Smith** (E. Everett). [Vocabulary of the Malemute, Kotzebue Sound.]

10 pp. 4°, 190 words. In the library of the Bureau of Ethnology.

**Society for Promoting Christian Knowledge:** These words following a title indicate that a copy of the work referred to was seen by the compiler in the library of this society, London, England.

**Songs:**

| | |
|---|---|
| Akudnirmiut. | See Boas (F.). |
| Aleut. | Pinart (A. L.), |
| | Veniaminoff (J.). |
| Atka. | Veniaminoff (J.). |
| Greenland. | Cranz (D.), |
| | oriniugkat, |
| | Kjer (K.), |
| | Rink (H. J.). |
| Kaniagmiout. | Pinart (A. L.). |
| Labrador. | Imgerutit, |
| | Imgerutsit. |
| Okomiut. | Boas (F.). |
| Tuski. | Hooper (W. H.). |

**[Sørensen** (B. F.).] Kúpernerit nápautáuput tunitdlanvdlutik kisiáne tikiñtartut; [&c.] [Signed B. F. Sørensen.] [Nungme aipagssanik nakitigkat. | L. Möller. | 1874.]

*Literal translation:* The small-pox is a disease by infecting only that comes [*i. e.*, that comes only by infection). At the Point [Godthaab) a second time printed. L. Möller.

No title-page or caption; begins as above; pp. 1-6, 8°; in the Greenland language. It is an account of the symptoms etc. of small-pox, with the methods of treatment and precautions for preventing the spread of the disease.

*Copies seen:* Powell.

Statistics of seal fisheries, Greenland. See Pini-artut.

**Stearns** (Winfrid Alden). Labrador | a sketch of | its peoples, its industries and its | natural history. | By | Winfrid Alden Stearns. |

Boston : | Lee and Shepard, 47 Franklin Street. | New York: Charles T. Dillingham. | 1884.

Title 1 l. pp. iii-viii, 1-295, 8°.—Numerals 1-10, 20, 30, of the Labrador Indians, and a vocabulary of 35 "other words" [not Eskimo), p. 291.—Labrador Indian terms passim.

*Copies seen:* Bureau of Ethnology, Congress.

**Steenholdt** (Wittus Frederik). Innûb nangminek isumaliornera Gudib'lo tekkotinera. Iunuktut nuktersimafok Wittus Frederik Steenholdtimit. Kjöbenhavnime, 1851.    *

*Literal translation:* Man's his own pondering and God's his revelation of himself. To men it is translated by Wittus Frederik Steenholdt. At Copenhagen.

75 pp. 8°. Religious tract in the Eskimo language of Greenland.

Title from Pinart sale catalogue, No. 352 (5).

—— Okalluktuæt Bibelimit pisimasut | Kristumiudlo Apostelit kingorneesigut | okalluktuarisauneræt tapusimavlune. | Aglæksimasut | Kavlunait Pelleseesa illænnit, Balslevimit; | nuktersimasut Wittus Frederik Steenholdtimit. | Kjöbenhavnime. | nakkittarsimasut Bianco Lunomit: | 1854.

*Literal translation:* Stories from the Bible made | and the Christian Apostles after them | their narratives having been included. | Written | Europeans their priests by some of them, by Balslev; | translated by Wittus Frederik Steenholdt. | At Copenhagen. | printed by Bianco Luno.

1 p. l. pp. 1-136, 16°. Bible stories in the Eskimo language of Greenland.

*Copies seen:* Harvard.

—— Tlerkuksamut imalôneet illuarnermik ajokensout . . . nuktersimarsok Wittus F. Steenholdtimit.

Noungme, 1860.

20 pp. 8°. Ethics in the Eskimo language of Greenland.—*Rink.*

Steenholdt was a native teacher. He died at Jakobshavn, Greenland, in 1862.

**Steiger** (E.). Steiger's | bibliotheca glottica, | part first. | A catalogue of | Dictionaries, Grammars, Readers, Expositors, etc. | of mostly | modern languages | spoken in all parts of the earth, | except of | English, French, German, and Spanish. | First division : | Abenaki to Hebrew. |

**Steiger (E.)**—Continued.

E. Steiger, | 22 & 24 Frankfort Street, | New York. [1874.]

Half-title on cover, title as above l l. notice 1 l. text pp. 1-40, 12°. Contains an Eskimo section, pp. 32-33. The second division of the first part was not published. Part second is on the English language, and Part third on the German language.

In his notice the compiler states: "This compilation must not be regarded as an attempt at a complete linguistic bibliography, but solely as a book-seller's catalogue for business purposes, with special regard to the study of philology in America."

*Copies seen:* Eames, Pilling.

**Steinthal** (*Dr.* H.). Charakteristik | der hauptsächlichsten | Typen des Sprachbaues. | Von | Dr. H. Steinthal, | Privatdocenten für allgemeine Sprachwissenschaft | an der Universität zu Berlin. | Zweite Bearbeitung | seiner | Classification der Sprachen. |

Berlin, | Ferd. Dümmler's Verlagsbuchhandlung | 1860.

Pp. i-ix, 1 l. pp. 1-336, 8°.—V. Die amerikanischen Sprachen, Einverleibung, pp. 202-231, includes: Die amerikanischen Sprachen überhaupt, mit besonderer Rücksicht auf das Grönländische, pp. 220-231.

*Copies seen:* Astor, Boston Athenæum, British Museum, Harvard, Trumbull.

**Stênberg** (Karl Junius Optatus). Bibelimit ujarsimmassut | okralluktuæt, | mêrkraeu illinniægæksait, | Kalâdlit nunnânne pællessiogalloab K. J. O. Stênberg-ib nuktigai. | Kjöbenhavnime. | Bianko-Lunomit nakkrittinnekratut. | 1854.

*Literal translation:* From the Bible selected | stories, | children's their instruction things, |

**Stênberg** (K. J. O.) — Continued.

Greenlanders' in their country the late priest K. J. O. Stênberg translated them. | At Copenhagen. | By Bianco Luno printed.

1 p. l. pp. 1-125, 16°. Bible stories in the Eskimo language of Greenland.

*Copies seen:* Harvard.

K. J. O. Stênberg was born in 1812, lived in Greenland from 1810 to 1853, and died while parish priest on the Island of Funen, Denmark, 1872.

—— See **Kattitsiomarsut**.

**Stimpson** (*Dr.* William) and **Hall** (*Prof.* Asaph). Chukchee vocabulary.

In Dall (W. H.), Alaska and Its Resources, pp. 552-554, Boston, 1870, 8°.

**Strale** (Frederick A.). The Lord's Prayer. Matt. Ch. VI. vv 9-13 | In upwards of Fifty different Languages, arranged mostly geographically according | to Fr.ᵏ Adelung's View.

New York Sept.ʳ 1841. Compiled by F. A. Strale. Lith. of Endicott—22 John Street.

Broadside, 25¼×19¾ inches. Contains among others the Lord's Prayer in the Greenland and Esquimaux of the Coast of Labrador, Nos. 50 and 51.

*Copies seen:* Powell.

**Stuart Island Vocabulary.** See Buschmann (J. C. E.).

**Stupart** (R. F.). The Eskimo of Stupart Bay.

In Canadian Institute Proc. new series, vol. 4, pp. 95-114, Toronto, 1886, 8°.

Eskimo vocabulary, pp. 113-115.

**Sutherland** (P. C.). On the Esquimaux. By P. C. Sutherland, M. D.

In Ethnological Soc. of London Jour. vol. 4, 1856, pp. 193-214, London, n. d. 8°. Numerals, 1-10, 16-30, of the Esquimaux, pp. 208-209.

# T.

Tales:

| | |
|---|---|
| Akudnirmiut. | See Boas (F.). |
| Greenland. | Böggild (O.), |
| | Kaladlit, |
| | Kjer (K.), |
| | Pok. |
| Okomiut. | Boas (F.). |
| Tchiglit. | Petitot (E. F. S. J.). |

**Tamedsa** Gudib kakkojanga.

*Literal translation:* Here is God's his bread.

No title-page; 1 l. pp. 1-8, sq. 24°. Bible lessons in the Eskimo language of Labrador.—Math. 9, 2-8, pp. 1-2.—Luc. 17, 11-19, pp. 3-4.—Luc. 19, 1-10, pp. 5-6.—Joh. 11, 41-44, pp. 7-8.

*Copies seen:* American Tract Society, Powell.

**Tamedsa** | Matthæousib, Markusib, | Lukasib, | Johannesiblo | okautsinnik tussarnertunnik | nalegapta pinlijipta Jesusib Kristusib pinuiarningit okausingillo. | Printed for | the British and Foreign Bible Society, | for the use of the Christian Esquimaux in the mission-settlements | of the United Brethren on the Coast of Labrador. |

London: | W. M'Dowall, Printer, Pemberton Row, Gough Square. 1839.

*Literal translation:* Here are | Matthew's, Mark's, | Luke's, | and John's | in their words pleasing to hear | our Lord our Savior | Jesus Christ's | his doings and his words.

**Tamedsa—Continued.**

Title 1 l. text pp. 1-277, 16°. Tho four gospels in tho Eskimo of Labrador.

Copies seen: British and Foreign Biblo Society.

Subsequently issued as a part of tho New Testament; see Testamentetak tamedsa.

**Tamedsa** Johanncsib. See **Kohlmeister (B. G.).**

**Tamersa** | Makperksaeket immakartut | Okautsinnik, Kristomi- | unnut | Ajokaersûtikscnnik Appersûtikscnnik | akkirsûtiksenniglo attortuksanrsunnik | Innûsiut ajokaersorniarlugit. | Budissime, | Nakkitarsimapnt Ernst Moritz Monscmit. | 1861.

Literal translation: Here are | tho books filled | with the words for christians | things to be used and instruction things | and things for answers to be used | children in teaching them. | At Bautzen, | they were printed by Ernst Moritz Mons.

Title verso blank 1 l. text pp. 3-72, 16°. Catechism entirely in the language of Greenland.

Copies seen: Pilling. Powell.

My copy, purchased at the Unitäts-Buchhandlung, Gnadau, Saxony, cost 80 pf.

**Tamerssa** Okautsit Testamentitokamo | agleksimarsut | illeit pirsariaglit, Ajokaersutinniglo ncvsniantik- | sennik, Tuksiantinniglo | illakartut | Nukter-simarsut Karadlit okausconnut. | [Design.] |

Budissime | nakkitarsimarsut Ernst Moritz Monsibme. [n. d.]

Literal translation: Here are | tho words in the Old Testament | written some of them | tho needful ones, | and with lessons things to serve for explanation | and psalms | united | translated Greenlanders into their speech. At Bantzen | printed at Ernst Moritz Mons's.

Title verso blank 1 l. pp. 3-225, 16°. Biblo stories from the Old Testament, entirely in the language of Greenland.

Copies seen: Pilling, Powell.

My copy, purchased of the Unitäts-Buchhandlung, Gnadau, Saxony, cost 2 M.

**Tamerssa** timminisant | killangmit pirsok. [Picture.]

Literal translation: Behold a supply-of-bread | from heaven come.

No title-page; heading only; 1 p. l. pp. 1-8, 24°. Biblo lessons in the language of Greenland.

Copies seen: American Tract Society.

**Tastamantitorkamik** | agdlagsimassut ilait oкalngtu- | arissat, ajoкersûtinik ilasi- | -massut. |

[Druck von Gustav Winter in Stolpen.] 1871.

**Tastamantitorkamik** —Continued.

Literal translation: By tho Old Testament | written some of tho tales, | with lessons | supplemented.

Title 1 l. text pp. 1-179, 12°. Biblo stories from tho Old Testament, entirely in the language of Greenland. For replies and queries to this see aperssûtit.

Copies seen: Pilling, Powell.

My copy, procured from the Unitäts-Buchhandlung, Gnadau, Saxony, cost 1 M.

Tchiglit:

Dictionary. See Petitot (E. F. S. J.).
Grammar. Henry (V.).
Grammatic treatise. Petitot (E. F. S. J.).
Legends. Petitot (E. F. S. J.).
Tales. Petitot (E. F. S. J.).

Tchongatche-Konega Vocabulary. See Balbi (A.).

Tchuktchi:

Grammatic treatise. See Radloff (L.).
Numerals. Pott (A. F.).
Songs. Hooper (W. II.).
Vocabulary. Balbi (A.),
    Gallatin (A.),
    Gilder (W. II.),
    Hooper (W. II.),
    Krauso (A.),
    Lesseps (J. B. B.),
    Pfizmaier (A.),
    Radloff (L.),
    Robeck (—),
    Romberg (II.),
    Stimpson (W.) and
    Hall (A.),
    Zagoskin (L. A.).

Ten Commandments:
Greenland. See Anderson (J.).
Hudson Bay. Peck (E. J.).

**Testamente** Nutak, eller. See **Egede (Paul).**

**Testamente** Nutak Kaladlin. See **Fabricius (O.).**

**Testamentetak** | tamedsa: | Nalegapta Piulijipta | Jesusib Kristusib | Apostelingitalo | pinniarningit okansingillo. | Printed for | The British and Foreign Bible Society, | for the use of the Christian Esquimaux in the mission-settlements | of the United Brethren on the coast of Labrador. |

London: | W. M'Dowall, printer, Pemberton-row, | Gough-square. | 1840.

Literal translation: The New Testament | behold it: | Our Lord our Savior | Jesus Christ's | and his Apostles' | their acts and their words.

2 p. ll. pp. 1-637, 12°, in tho language of Labrador.

Copies seen: Astor, British Museum, British and Foreign Biblo Society, Church Missionary Society, Congress.

**Testamentetak**—Continued.

At the Field sale, catalogue No. 644, a copy brought $1.62; at the Murphy sale, catalogue No. 907, 25 cents. Priced by Quaritch, No. 30047, at 5s.

A portion of this work, pp. 1–277, containing the four gospels only, was issued in 1839, with the title Tamedsa Matthaeusib; the remainder, pp. 277–637, was also issued separately with the heading Apostelit Piniaringut.

"In 1826 a complete edition of the [Labrador] Esquimaux New Testament left the [British and Foreign Bible] Society's press in London."—*Bagster.*

Reichelt speaks of "the first edition of the [Labrador Eskimo] New Testament having appeared in 1827 under the auspices of the British and Foreign Bible Society."

**Testamentetâk** terssa nalegauta annaursirsiuta Jesusib Kristusib ajokœrsugeisalo sullirseit okauseello. Translated into the greenlandish language by the missionaries of the Unitas fratrum. London, 1862.

*Literal translation:* The New Testament behold it, our Lord our Savior Jesus Christ's and his disciples' their acts and their words.

8°. New Testament in the Greenland. Title from the Pinart sale catalogue, No. 352. For earlier editions see Testamentitak terssa.

**Testamentetokak** Testamentitarlo.

*Literal translation:* The Old Testament and the New Testament.

In the language of Greenland. Title from Dr. Rink.

**Testamentetokak** Hiobib * * * Salomoblo. See **Erdmann** (F.).

**Testamentetotak** Josuab * * * Esterib. See **Erdmann** (F.).

**Testamentitak** | tamœdsa | nalegapta piulijipta | Jêsusib Kristusib | apostelingitalo | piniarningit ajokertusingillo. | Printed for | the British and Foreign Bible Society in London, | for the use of the Moravian Mission in Labrador. |

Stolpen: | Gustav Winterib Nênerlanktangit. | 1876.

*Literal translation:* The New Testament behold | our Lord our Savior | Jesus Christ's | and his apostles' | their acts and their teachings. | Stolpen: | Gustav Winter's his printings.

Pp. 1–282, 8°. The Four Gospels and the Acts of the Apostles in the language of Labrador.

*Copies seen:* British Museum.

A later edition, with additions, as follows:

**Testamentitak** | tamœdsa | nalegapta piulijipta | Jêsusib Kristusib | apostelingitalo | piniarningit ajokertusiu-

**Testamentitak**—Continued.

gillo. | Printed for | the British and Foreign Bible Society in London, | for the use of the Moravian Mission in Labrador. |

Stolpon, | Gustav Winterib Nênilauktangit. | 1876. 1878.

*Literal translation:* The New Testament | behold | our Lord our Savior | Jesus Christ's | and his apostles' | their acts and their teachings. | Stolpen, | Gustav Winter's his printings.

2 p. ll. pp. 1–282, 1–225, 8°, in the Eskimo of Labrador.—Matthew to Acts, pp. 1–282.—Romans to Revelation, pp. 1–222.

*Copies seen:* British and Foreign Bible Society, Pilling, Powell.

**Testamentitâk,** | terssa: | Nâlegauta annaursirsivta | Iesusib Kristusib, | ajokœrsugeisalo, sullurseit okauseello. | Translated | into the Greenland language | by the | Missionaries | of the | Unitas Fratenm; or United Brethren. | Printed for the use of the Mission | by | the British and Foreign Bible Society. |

London: | W. M'Dowall, Printer, 4, Pemberton Row, Gough Square. | 1822.

*Literal translation:* The New Testament | behold it: | our Lord our Savior | Jesus Christ's, | and his disciples', | their acts and their words.

2 p. ll. pp. 1–584, 2 ll. 12°, in the language of Greenland. The first edition of the revised version; 1,000 copies were printed for the above society.

*Copies seen:* British and Foreign Bible Society, British Museum, Shea, Trumbull, Watkinson.

Priced in Leclerc's Supplement, No. 2961, at 20 fr. The Murphy copy, catalogue No. 2929, brought $2.50.

**Testamentitâk** | terssa | Nâlegauta Annaursirsivta | Iesusib Kristusib, | ajokœrsugeisalo, | sullirseit okauseello. | The New Testament. | Translated | into the Greenland language | by the missionaries | of the | Unitas Fratrum or United Brethren | Second edition. | Printed for the use of the mission by | the British and Foreign Bible Society. | Budisimo | printed by Ernst Moritz Monse. | 1851.

*Literal translation:* The New Testament | behold | our Lord our Savior Jesus Christ's, | and his disciples', | their acts and their words. | At Bautzen.

2 p. ll. pp. 1–583, 8°, in the language of Greenland. According to Bagster's Bible of Every Land the edition consisted of 1,000 copies.

ХРИШТИАНАТѢ

ЛЮКѴДАХЧИЧАДА ЛѴААГИГА,

А͂ХАͅКѢ

МИКИ͂АГѴКѢ ТА͂НЦИШКАͅКѢ
ИШТѴͅЛӤКѢ

ЧАЛӤ

МИКИ͂АГѴКѢ КА͂ТИХИͅШИЦАͅКѢ.

Ильямъ Тыжповамъ пильл.

С. ПЕТЕРБУͅРГЪ.
Шинѵͅдамъ Типѵͅглаѵͅижͅни.
1847.

FAC-SIMILE OF TITLE-PAGE OF TISHNOFF'S CHRISTIAN GUIDE BOOK.

**Testamentiták**—Continuod.

*Copies seen:* Astor, Congress, Pilling, Powell.

My copy, procured from the Unitäts-Buchhandlung, Gnadau, Saxony, cost 5 M.

Dr. Rink has furnished mo with a similar title, no date, 553 pages, 8°. For a later edition see **Testamentiták terssa.**

**Testamentitokab** Makpérsægèjsa * * * Josvab. Seo **Kragh** (P.).

**Testamentitokab** makpérsægèjsa * * * profetit mingnerit. Seo **Kragh** (P.).

**Testamentitokab** makpérsegejsa * * * Mosesim. Seo **Kragh** (P.).

**Testamentitokamit** Davidim Ivngerutéj. Seo **Wolf** (N. G.).

**Testamentitokamit** Mosesim aglogèj. Seo **Fabricius** (O.).

**Testamentitokamit** Profetib Esaiasim. Seo **Wolf** (N. G.).

**Testamentitokamit** Salomonib. Seo **Wolf** (N. G.).

Texts:

| | |
|---|---|
| Aglogmiont. | Seo Pinart (A. L.). |
| Aleut. | Pinart (A. L.). |
| Kadiak. | Veniaminoff (J.). |

**Thomas** a Kempis. Seo **Egede** (Paul).

[**Thorhallesen** (Egil).] Tuksiutit | Sabbatit Ulloinnut | Napertorsaket, allello | Kallalingnut | Attuartukset; | Tuksiautillo Illacjartortut. | Apersoutingoello | Koekhorsunnut. |

Iglorpoksoinno Kiobenhavnimo | nakkitet Gerhard Gieso Salikath. | 1776.

*Literal translation:* Prayers | Sabbaths for their days | adapted, and other | for Greenlanders | things-to-bo-used; | and psalms selected. | And little questions | for candidates-for-baptism. | At the city at Copenhagen | printed by Gerhard Giese Salikath.

Title verso blank 1 l. preface signed by Paul Egede 1 l. text, entirely in the language of Greenland, pp. 1-110, index 2 ll. 16°. Pp. 54-110 are occupied with hymns.

*Copies seen:* British Museum.

—— Schema conjugationis Grönlandicæ Verborum in ok, vok et rpok definentium.

Hafn. 1776.				*

—— Expositio catechismi grönlandici. Kjøbh. 1776.				*

—— Precationes et hymni grönlandici in singulos septimanæ dics. Kjøbh. 1776.				*

Titles from Nyerup's Dansk-Norsk Litteraturlexicon, vol. 2, p. 609, Kjöbenhavn, 1818. This latter work is probably tho samo as that

**Thorhallesen** (E.)—Continuod.

of which full title, commencing Tuksiutit, is given above.

Thorhallesen was born in Iceland November 10, 1734. He graduated in 1758 and in 1765 became a missionary to Greenland. In 1776 he was made parson at Bogenso, in Fyen, and dean in Skovbo district. He died in 1789.

**Tishnoff** (Elias). [Seven lines Cyrillic characters.] | Ильямъ Тыжновамъ пильяп. | *[Two lines Cyrillic type.] | 1847.

*Translation:* Christian | Guido Book, | containing | Saint Michael | history | and | Michael Catechism. | Elias Tishnoff made. | St. Petersburg. | Synod Press.

Title 1 l. pp. 1-96, 8°, in the Aleutian language. In Cyrillic type, with the addition of several specially cast for the purpose. Seo p. 90 for fac-simile of title-page. The work is based on Veniaminoff (J.) and Netzvietoff (J.), Origin of Christian Creeds.

*Copies seen:* Pilling, Powell.

—— [Six lines Cyrillic characters. ] | На Алеутско-Кадьякскій языкъ перевелъ И. Тыжновъ. |

С. Петербургъ. | Въ суподальной типографіи. | 1848.

*Translation:* Of | Matthew | Saint | the Gospel. | Of | Matthew | Saint | the Gospel. | Into the Aleutian-Kadiak language translated by E. Tishnoff. | St. Petersburg. | Synod press. 1 p.l. pp.1-270, double columns, 11.8°. The first three lines of the title-page are in Aleut-Kadiak; the next three a Slavonic translation of the same.

*Copies seen:* Bancroft, Pilling, Powell.

—— [Two lines Cyrillic characters. ] | Алеутско-кадьякскій букварь. | Состав. Илья Тыжновъ.

С. Петербургъ. | Въ суподальной типографіи. | 1848.

*Translation:* Aleutian-Kadiak | Primer. | Aleutian-Kadiak | Primer. | Compiled by Elias Tishnoff. | St. Petersburg. | Synod press. Title 1 l. pp. 1-52, 16°. See p. 92 for fac-similo of title-page.

*Copies seen:* Pilling, Powell.

The three foregoing works sold at the Pinart sale, catalogue No. 14, to Leclerc for 15 fr.

—— [Two lines Cyrillic characters. ] | Алеутско-кадьякскій букварь. | Состав. Илья Тыжновъ. |

С. Петербургъ. | Въ суподальной типографіи. | 1848.

*Translation:* Aleutian-Kadiak | Primer. | Aleutian-Kadiak | Primer. | Compiled by Elias Tishnoff. | St. Petersburg. | Synod press. Pp. 1-33, 16°. Though identical in title with the one given above, it is not the same work; the two agree to the middle of page 8, but thereafter they differ materially.

*Copies seen:* Congress, Powell.

Вектамъ шуйда

лшмукатъ.

— ✦ —

АЛЕУТСКО-КАДЬЯКСКІЙ

БУКВАРЬ.

Состав. Ильл Тыжковъ.

С. ПЕТЕРБУРГЪ

Въ Стнодальной Типографіи.

1848.

FAC-SIMILE OF TITLE-PAGE OF TISHNOFF'S ALEUTIAN-KADIAK PRIMER.

**Tlerkuksamut** imalôucet illuarnermik. See **Steenholdt** (W. F.).

**Tomlin** (*Rev. J.*). A comparative vocabulary | of | forty-eight languages, | comprising | one hundred and forty-six | common English words, with their cognates in the other languages, | showing | their Affinities with the English and Hebrew. | By the | Rev. J. Tomlin, B. A., Author of "Missionary Journals and Letters during Eleven Years Residence in the East;" | [&c. three lines]. | Liverpool: | Arthur Newling, 27, Bold Street. | 1865.

Pp. i-xii, 1-32 (numbered odd on versos, even on rectos; recto of p. 1 and verso of p. 32 blank), pp. xiii-xxii, 1 l. 4°.—Includes an Esquimaux vocabulary (from a Moravian missionary).

*Copies seen:* British Museum, Watkinson.

**Toonooneenooshuk** Vocabulary. See Hall (C. F.).

Tract:

Greenland.  See Kragh (P.),
 Steenholdt (W. F.).
Labrador.  Bibelib.

**Trübner** (Nicolas): See **Ludewig** (H. E.).

**Trübner & Co.** A | catalogue | of | dictionaries and grammars | of the | Principal Languages and Dialects | of the World. | For sale by | Trübner & Co. | London: | Trübner & Co., 8 & 60 Paternoster Row. | 1872.

Title on cover as above, title as above 1 l. notice 1 l. text pp. 1-64, 1 l. alphabetically arranged.—List of Eskimo (Greenland) works, p. 18.

*Copies seen:* Pilling.

A later edition as follows:

**Trübner's** | catalogue | of | dictionaries and grammars | of the | Principal Languages and Dialects of the World. | Second edition, | considerably enlarged and revised, with an alphabetical index. | A guide for students and booksellers. | [Monogram.] | London: | Trübner & Co., 57 and 59, Ludgate Hill. | 1882.

Printed cover as above, title as above 1 l. pp. iii-viii, 1-170, 8°.—List of works in Eleuth [Aleut], p. 48; in Eskimo, p. 53.

*Copies seen:* Pilling.

**Trumbull:** This word following a title indicates that a copy of the work referred to was seen by the compiler in the library of Dr. J. Hammond Trumbull, Hartford, Conn.

**Tschuagmjute** Vocabulary. See Schott (W.).

Tschugazzi:
 Grammatic comments.  See Adelung (J. C.)
  and Vater (J. S.).
 Numerals.  Pott (A. F.).
 Vocabulary.  Adelung (J. C.)
  and Vater (J. S.),
  Baer (K. E. von),
  Buschmann (J. C. E.),
  Wowodsky (—).

**Tschuakak** Island Vocabulary. See Buschmann (J. C. E.).

**Tugsiautit** | augnerit | Katángutigingniannut | kalâtdlit nunânïtunut atortugssat. | Stolpen, | Druck von Gustav Winter. | 1878.

*Literal translation:* Psalms | the greatest | for the brethren | Greenlanders in-their-land being things-to-be-used.

*Free translation:* The most important psalms for the use of the brethren who are in the country of the Greenlanders.

Title verso blank 1 l. contents pp. iii-vi, text pp. 7-442, alphabetic list of hymns pp. 443-494, 12°. Hymn-book entirely in the language of Greenland.

*Copies seen:* Pilling, Powell.

My copy, bought of the Unitäts-Buchhandlung, Gnadau, Saxony, cost 4 M.

**Tuksiarutsit,** | attorekset | Illagěktunnut | Labradoremetunnut. | Londonneme: | W. McDowallib; Nenilanktangit. | 1809. | Printed for the Brethren's Society for the Furtherance of the Gospel; for the Use of the Christian Esquimaux in the | Brethren's settlements, Nain, Okkak, and Hopedale, on | the Coast of Labrador.

*Literal translation:* Psalms, | things-to-be-used | for the communities | that-are-in-Labrador. | At London: | W. McDowall's; his printings.

Pp. i-iv, text pp. 1-277, index pp. 1-34, 16°. Hymn-book entirely in the Eskimo language of Labrador.

*Copies seen:* British Museum.

Priced by Trübner, 1856, No. 670, at 6s. A copy (dated 1819) at the Pinart sale, catalogue No. 902, brought 1 fr. 50 c.

**Tuksiarutsit** | uvlâkut unnukullo, | uvlunut tamainut illingajut | Wocheme. | *Colophon:* E. Bastaniermullo & Dunskymullo nêuertanlankput Læbaume. | [1871.]

*Literal translation:* Psalms | for morning and for evening, | for the days all made | in the week. | By E. Bastanier & Dunsky they are printed at Löbau.

**Tuksiarutsit**—Continued.

Half-title as above verso blank 1 l. text (prayers) entirely in the language of Labrador, pp. 3-19, colophon verso of p. 19, 16°.

*Copies seen:* Pilling, Powell.

My copy, bought of the Unitäts-Buchhandlung, Gnadau, Saxony, cost 35 pf.

**Tuksiautit** attuagækset | illageennut | innuit nunaennetunnut. | [Design.] | Barbimo, 1785.

*Literal translation:* Psalms things-to-be-used | for the congregations | the Eskimo in-their-country-being. | At Barby.

*Free translation:* Psalms for the use of the congregations that are in the country of the Eskimo.

Title verso blank 1 l. contents 2 ll. text (canticles) in Greenland Eskimo, Danish headings (German letter), pp. 7-304, index 16 ll. 16°. Leclerc says probably by Paul Egede. The work itself bears no such indication.

*Copies seen:* Maisonneuve.

Priced by Leclerc, 1878, No. 2235, at 60 fr. The Pinart copy, catalogue No. 903, sold to Leclerc for 13 fr.

**Tuksiautit** | attuagækset | Ingmikortartunnut | Illageeksunnetunnut. | [Design.]

[Zerbst, gedruckt bey Andreas Füchsel.] | 1822.

*Literal translation:* Psalms | things-to-be-used | for separate | congregations.

Pp. 1-47, 16°. Litany catechism entirely in the Greenland Eskimo.

*Copies seen:* Pilling, Powell.

My copy cost 80 pf.

**Tuksiautit** erinaglit. See **Muller** (V.).

**Tuksiautit** Julesiutit makko. See **Kjer** (K.).

**Tuksiautit** Kikiektugarursomik. See **Kjer** (K.).

**Tuksiautit** | ussornautiksaglit, | attuagækset | Illageenut Innuit nunaennetunnut. | [Design.]

[No place.] 1822.

Title verso blank 1 l. text pp. 3-160, 16°. Liturgic manual with prayers for public worship entirely in the language of Greenland. For translation see next title.

*Copies seen:* Pilling, Powell.

My copy, purchased from the Unitäts-Buchhandlung, Gnadau, Saxony, cost 80 pf.

**Tuksiautit** | ussornautiksaglit, | attuagækset | Illageenut Innuit nunaennetunnut. |

Loebaume, | J. A. Duroldtib nakittagei. | 1852.

**Tuksiautit**—Continued.

*Literal translation:* Psalms | with-means-for-worshiping | a manual | for the congregations the Eskimo in-their-land-being. | At Löban, | J. A. Duroldt printed them.

Title verso blank 1 l. pp. 3-72, 16°. Small liturgy entirely in the language of Greenland.

*Copies seen:* Pilling, Powell.

My copy, bought of the Unitäts-Buchhandlung, Gnadau, Saxony, cost 80 pf.

**Tuksiutit** Sabbatit Ulloinnut. See **Thorhallesen** (E.).

**Turner** (Lucien McShan). Contributions | to the | natural history of Alaska. | Results of investigations made chiefly in the Yukon | District and the Aleutian Islands; conducted | under the auspices of the Signal Service, | United States Army, extending from | May, 1874, to August, 1881. | Prepared under the direction of | Brig. and Bvt. Maj. Gen. W. B. Hazen, | Chief Signal Officer of the Army, | by | L. M. Turner. | No. II. | Arctic series of publications issued in connection with the Signal Service, U. S. Army. | With 26 plates. | Washington: | Government Printing Office. | 1886.

Title reverse blank 1 l. pp. 3-216, plates, 4°.—Scattered through the volume are many Unalit and Aleut names of fishes, birds, and mammals.

—— [Contribution to the natural history of North America. Report on observations made in Ungava and Labrador in 1882-1884 by L. M. Turner.] *

Manuscript, 3900 pp. folio, in course of preparation.—Ethnology of the Innuit, pp. 1842-2127.—Vocabulary of the Koksoagmyut, over 7,000 words, pp. 2128-2867.—Notes on the linguistics of the Koksoagmyut, pp. 2868-3011.—Over 1,000 sentences, Koksoagmyut-English, pp. 3012-3185.—Unalit (Norton Sound, Alaska) vocabulary, including over 3,000 words, besides sentences and notes, together with conjugation of verb *to go*, pp. 3186-3475.—Vocabulary of the Malimyut (Norton Sound, Alaska), 250 words, pp. 3475a-3495.—Unalashkan Alyut-English vocabulary, together with sentences and conjugations, over 1,900 words, pp. 3496-3673.

—— [Descriptive catalogue of Innuit collections made in 1882-1884 in Ungava and Labrador by L. M. Turner for the use of the U. S. National Museum.] *

Manuscript, about 600 pp. folio, in course of preparation. Includes traditions, legends, and narratives, and contains many names of objects in the Koksoagmyut dialect.

**Turner** (L. M.)—Continued.

—— [Descriptive catalogue of ethnologic collections made in 1880–1881 by L. M. Turner on Attu Island, Aleutian Chain, Alaska. Prepared for the use of the U. S. National Museum.]  *

Manuscript, about 300 pp. folio, in course of preparation, describing implements, characteristics, customs and traditions; notes on names of village sites, &c., giving the native names of the articles described, of villages, &c.

—— [Descriptive catalogue of ethnologic collections made in 1874–1877 by L. M. Turner in Norton Sound, Alaska. Prepared for the use of the U. S. National Museum.]  *

Manuscript, about 800 pp. folio, in course of preparation, describing implements, uses, &c., together with chapters on the characteristics and customs of the Unalit of Norton Sound. Contains many native terms.

—— [Innuit names of birds, compiled from various sources by L. M. Turner.]  *

Manuscript, 62 pp. folio, in possession of the author. Remarks on distribution of birds in the Innuit land; descriptive names of parts of birds; authorities quoted; remarks on spelling and pronunciation of names given, pp. 1–11.—Names of 155 species of birds (arranged

**Turner** (L. M., —Continued.

according to the American Ornithological Union Check-list), pp. 12–62.

Titles from the author, who has also furnished me the following brief of his work among the Eskimo:

"From May, 1874, to July, 1877, at St. Michael's, Norton Sound, Alaska, among the Unalit, Malimyut, Kavyaagmyut, and Kvichpagmyut tribes of the Innuit of that region. From May, 1878, to July, 1881, among the Alyut of Unalashka, Atkha, and Attu; also visited Bristol Bay region, mouth of Kuskokvim River, Ugasik, and Kadiak during that time. From June, 1882, to September, 1884, along coast of Labrador and south of Hudson Strait, among the Innuit of those regions and the Naskopie (Naynaynots) Indians of the Ungava District, Hudson Bay Territory."

Since his return, in 1884, Mr. Turner, under the direction of the Secretary of the Smithsonian Institution, has been preparing his material for publication.

**Turner** (William Wadden). See **Ludewig** (H. E.).

**Tussajungnik** siutelik tussarle. | [Design.]

*Literal translation:* About · what · is · to · be· heard (?) he who has ears let him hear.

No title-page; 1 p. l. pp. 1–8, sq. 24°. Bible lessons in the language of Labrador.

*Copies seen:* American Tract Society.

# U.

**Ugalenzi:**
| | |
|---|---|
| Vocabulary. | See Baer (K. E. von), |
| | Buschmann (J. C. E.), |
| | Wrangell (F. von). |
| Words. | Buschmann (J. C. E.). |

**Ugaljachmutzi:**
| | |
|---|---|
| Grammatic comments. | See Adelung (J. C.) and Vater (J. S.). |
| Remarks. | Radloff (L.). |
| Vocabulary. | Adelung (J. C.) and Vater (J. S.), |
| | Balbi (A.), |
| | Dall (W. H.), |
| | Fisher (J.), |
| | Prichard (J. C.). |
| Words. | Buschmann (J. C. E.), |
| | Uméry (J.). |

**Uméry** (J.). Sur l'identité du mot *Mère* dans les idiomes de tous les peuples.

In Revue Orientale et Américaine, vol. 8, pp. 335–338, Paris, 1863, 8°. (*)

Contains the word for *mother* in Ugaljachmoutzi, Greenland, Aleut of Unalaska.

**Unalaska:**
| | |
|---|---|
| Conjugations. | See Turner (L. M.). |

**Unalaska** — Continued.
| | |
|---|---|
| Numerals. | See Baer (K. E. von). |
| Sentences. | Turner (L. M.). |
| Vocabulary. | Adelung (J. C.) and Vater (J. S.), |
| | Bryant (—), |
| | Dall (W. H.), |
| | Davidson (G.), |
| | Fry (E.), |
| | Gallatin (A.), |
| | Latham (R. G.), |
| | Lisiansky (U.), |
| | Lutké (F.), |
| | Turner (L. M.), |
| | Veniaminoff (J.), |
| | Wowodsky (—). |
| Words. | Campbell (J.). |

**Unaligmut** Vocabulary. See Dall (W. H.).

**Unalit:**
| | |
|---|---|
| Conjugations. | See Turner (L. M.). |
| Vocabulary. | Nelson (E. W.), |
| | Turner (L. M.). |

**Underretning** * * * Grøuland. See **Kragh** (P.).

**Unipkautsit** 52git maggoertorlugit Bibelemit. Illinniarringnut kittorngarenullo illingajut.

**Unipkautsit**—Continued.

Calev, Barthib sonnalauktaugit;
Stuttgart, J. F. Steinkopfib nelilauk-
tangit, 1852.                                        *

 *Literal translation:* Stories 52-in-number
 repeated from the Bible. For schools and families adapted. Caleb Barth's his works; Stuttgart, J. F. Steinkopf's his printings.

 Pp. vi, 205, 12°, in the Eskimo language of
 Labrador.

 Title from Sabin's Dictionary, No. 3703.

**Unipkautsit** | 52git maggoertordlugit
Bibelemit. | Illiniarvingnut kittorn-
garénullo | illingajut. | Biblische Ge-
schichten. |
  Stolpen, | Gustav Winterib nênilauk-
tangit. | 1878.

**Unipkautsit**—Continued.

 Title verso blank 1 l. contents pp. i-viii, text,
 Old Testament stories (52), pp. 1-342, New
 Testament stories (52), pp. 343-520, 16°. In
 the Eskimo language of Labrador.

 *Copies seen:* Pilling, Powell.
 My copy cost 6 M.

**Unnersòutiksak** ernisûksiortunnut. See
Kragh (P.).

**Ursini** (G. F.).    See **Kragh** (P.).

**Ussornakaut** nákinniktut. | [Picture.]

 *Literal translation:* Blessed are the merciful.
 No title-page; 1 p. 1. pp. 1-8, 16°. Bible
 lessons in the language of Labrador. I have
 seen the same tract with outside title; Pil-
 loridlarput nápkiniktut.

 *Copies seen:* American Tract Society.

# V.

**Vater** (Johann Severin).  Untersuchun-
gen | über | Amerika's Bevölkerung |
aus dem | alten Kontinente | dem |
Herrn Kammerherrn | Alexander von
Humboldt | gewidmet | von | Johann
Severin Vater | Professor und Biblio-
thekar. |                             *
  Leipzig, | bei Friedrich Christian
Wilhelm Vogel. | 1810.

 Pp. i-xii, 1-212, 12°.—A few words in the
 language of Greenland, pp. 47, 156, 195; Eskimo, p. 203.

 *Copies seen:* Astor, British Museum, Congress, Harvard, Watkinson.

 At the Fischer sale, No. 2879, a copy was
 bought by Quaritch for 1s. 6d.

—— Linguarum totius orbis | Index |
alphabeticus, | quarum | Grammaticae,
Lexica, | collectiones vocabulorum |
recensentur, | patria significatur, his-
toria adumbratur | a | Joanne Severino
Vatero, | Theol. Doct. [&c. 2 lines]. |
  Berolini | In officina libraria Fr.
Nicolai. | MDCCCXV [1815].

 Latin title verso l. 1, German title recto l. 2,
 verso blank, dedications 2 ll. preface pp. i-iv,
 half-title 1 l. text pp. 3-259, 8°. Alphabetically
 arranged by families, double columns, German
 and Latin.

 Notices of works in Aleut, p. 11; Andre-
 owsk, pp. 13-14; Greenland, pp. 85-86; Kadjak,
 p. 110; Kamtschadka, pp. 112-113; Norton
 Sound, p. 170; Prinz-Williams-Sund, p. 193;
 Tschugazzi, pp. 240-241; Tschuktschi, p. 241;
 Ugaljachmutz, p. 247.

 *Copies seen:* Bureau of Ethnology.

 A later edition in German as follows:

—— Litteratur | der | Grammatiken, |
Lexika | und | Wörtersammlungen |

**Vater** (J. S.)—Continued.
aller Sprachen der Erde | von | Johann
Severin Vater. | Zweite, völlig umgear-
beitete Ausgabe | von | B. Jülg. |
  Berlin, 1847. | In der Nicolaischen
Buchhandlung.

 Pp. i-xii, 1-592, 2 ll. 8°, arranged alphabetically by languages, with family and author
 indexes.

 List of works in Aglegmute, p. 453; Aleut, pp.
 12-13, 454; Andreauowski, p. 19; Atuah, p. 38;
 Eskimo, pp. 113-114, 481; Hudson Bay, p. 173;
 Kadjak, pp. 194, 499; Kamtschadale, pp. 196,
 501; Kinai, Ugaljaschmutzi, pp. 204, 504; Kor-
 jaken, pp. 210-211, 508; Kuskokwim, p. 509;
 Norton Sound, pp. 266-267; Prince Williams
 Sound, p. 296; Tschugatschen, pp. 408-409;
 Tschuktschen, p. 409; Ugalenzen, p. 425; Una-
 laschka, pp. 427-428.

 *Copies seen:* Congress, Eames, Harvard.

 In the Fischer catalogue, No. 1710, a copy
 sold for 1s.

—— See **Adelung** (J. C.) and **Vater** (J.
S.).

**Veniaminoff** (*Rev.* John). Указаніе ,нути
въ | царьтвіе небесное, | поученіе. | На |
Алеутско-Лисьевскомъ | языкѣ, сочиненное |
Священникомъ Іоанномъ | Веніаминовымъ. |
1833 года. |
  Москва. | Въ Синодальной типографіи, |
1840.

 *Translation:* Guide | road | into | kingdom
 heavenly | taught. | In Aleutian-Fox | dialect;
 | written | by Reverend John | Veniaminoff. |
 1833 year. | Moscow. | At Synod press.

 Russian title, reverse blank, 1 l. title-page in
 Cyrillic characters, reverse blank, 2 ll. 67 other
 ll. in Cyrillic characters, 16°. See fac-simile
 of title-page, page 97.

 *Copies seen:* Congress, Powell.

# УКАЗАНIЕ

## ПУТИ

### ВЪ

# ЦАРСТВIЕ НЕБЕСНОЕ,

# НОУЧЕНIЕ.

### НА

# Алеутско-Лисьевскомъ

# ЯЗЫКѢ,

соЧиненное

Священникомъ *Iоанномъ*
*Венiаминовымъ.*

1833 года.

———— ✳ ————

# МОСКВА.

Въ Сvнодальной Типографiи,

# 1840.

FAC-SIMILE OF TITLE-PAGE OF VENIAMINOFF'S GUIDE ROAD.

# ЗАМѢЧАНІЯ

## О КОЛОШЕНСКОМЪ И КАДЬЯКСКОМЪ

### ЯЗЫКАХЪ

и

ОТЧАСТИ О ПРОЧИХЪ РОССІЙСКО-АМЕРИКАНСКИХЪ,

съ присовокупленіемъ

### РОССІЙСКО-КОЛОШЕНСКАГО

## СЛОВАРЯ,

СОДЕРЖАЩАГО БОЛѢЕ 1000 СЛОВЪ, ИЗЪ КОИХЪ НА НѢКОТОРЫЯ СДѢЛАНЫ
ПОЯСНЕНІЯ.

*Составилъ Иванъ Веніаминовъ,*

### ВЪ СИТХѢ.

САНКТПЕТЕРБУРГЪ

Въ типографіи Императорской Академіи Наукъ

## 1846.

FAC-SIMILE OF VENIAMINOFF'S REMARKS, &C.

**Veniaminoff (J.)—Continued.**

——Записки | объ островахъ | уналашкинскаго | отдѣла, | составленныя | И. Веніаминовымъ | Часть первая [-вторая]. | Издано иждивеніемъ Россійско-Американской | компаніи. | Санктпетербургъ. | 1840.

*Translation:* Notes | on the islands | of the Unalashkan | district, | Compiled | by J. Veniaminoff. | Part first [-second]. | Published at the expense of the Russian-American | Company. | St. Petersburg.

2 vols.: 4 p. ll. pp. i-ix, 1-364 ; 4 p. ll. pp. 1-409, 8 ll. and table, 8°. Vol. 3 has a different title, as follows:

——Записки | объ | атхинскихъ алеутахъ | и | Колошахъ. | И. Веніаминова, | составляющіе | третію часть | записокъ | объ островахъ | упалашкинскаго отдѣла. | издано иждивеніемъ Россійско-Американской | Компаніи. | Санктпетербургъ, | 1840.

*Translation:* Notes | on | the Atkhan Aleuts | and | Koloshians. | By J. Veniaminoff, | being | the third part | of notes | on the islands | of the Unalashkan district. | Published at the expense of the Russian-American | Company. | St. Petersburg.

2 p. ll. pp. 1-155, 8°.—Aleutian words, with Russian synonyms, scattered throughout.— Vol. 2, part 2, pp. 204-271, gives some account of the Aleutian grammar. Chap. 16, pp. 298-305, on the songs, gives five songs in parallel columns of Aleut and Russian.—Vol. 3, chap. 1, relates to the Atkhaus, and treats chiefly of the distinctions in language between the Atkhans and Unalashkans; pp. 20-26 give songs and stories in Atkhan and some in Russian. Chap. 2 relates to the Koloshians; pp. 135-154 treat of their language and grammar and include numerals 1-200, pp. 148-149; pp. 152-154 contain sentences, &c. in Tlinkit and Russian.

*Copies seen:* Bancroft, British Museum, Congress.

——Замѣчанія | о Колошенскомъ и Кадьякскомъ | языкахъ | и | отчасти о прочихъ Россійско-Американскихъ, | съ присовокупленіемъ | Россійско-Колошенскаго | словаря, | содержащаго болѣе 1000 словъ, изъ конхъ на нѣкоторыя сдѣланы | поясненія. | Составилъ Иванъ Веніаминовъ, | въ ситхѣ. |

Санктпетербургъ | въ типографіи Императорской Академіи наукъ. | 1846.

*Translation:* Remarks | on the Koloshian and Kadiak | languages | and | in part concerning other Russian-American [languages] | with the addition | of a Russian-Koloshian | vocabulary, | containing over 1,000 words, some of which are fully defined. | Compiled by Ivan Veniaminoff, | at Sitka. | St. Petersburg, | in the Printing Office of the Imperial Academy of Sciences. |

**Veniaminoff (J.)—Continued.**

Printed cover, with title briefer than above, 1 l. title as above 1 l. text pp. 3-81, errata 1 l. 8°.—General remarks on the language and grammar of the Koloshian, pp. 1-24.— Translations, pp. 25-26.—Kadiak grammar, pp. 27-35.— Kadiak translations, pp. 36-37.—Russian-Koloshian vocabulary, pp. 40-81.

See fac-simile of title-page, page 98.

*Copies seen:* British Museum, Powell.

Leclerc, 1878, No. 2987, prices a copy at 15 fr.

——Опытъ | грамматики | Алеутско-Лисьевскаго языка. | Священника И. Веніаминова, | въ Уналашкѣ. |

Санктпетербургъ | въ типографіи императорской академіи наукъ. | 1846.

*Translation:* An essay | upon the grammar | of the Fox dialect of the Aleutian language. | By Reverend J. Veniaminoff, | of Unalashka. | St. Petersburg | in the press of the Imperial Academy of Sciences.

2 p. ll. pp. i-xv, 1-87, i-iii, 1-120, i-vi, and 2 folding tables, 8°.—The grammar occupies pp. 1-87.—Introduction to dictionary, pp. i-iii.—Aleut-Russian dictionary, pp. 1-76.—Russian-Aleut dictionary, pp. 77-111.—Aleut phrases, with Russian translation, pp. 113-120.—Errata, pp. i-vi, and two folding leaves, conjugation of verbs.

*Copies seen:* Bancroft, British Museum.

Priced by Leclerc, 1878, No. 2090, at 35 fr. and by Trübner, 1882 (p. 48), at 5s. 6d.

——— Langues de l'Amérique Russe. Par Ivan Veniaminoff.

In Nouvelles Annales des Voyages, vol. 1, 1850 (vol. 125 of the collection), pp. 359-364. Paris, n. d. 8°.

For extracts from Veniaminoff see **Henry** (V.); also Schott (W.).

—— and **Netzvietoff** (*Rev.* Jacob). Начатки | христіанскаго ученія | или | краткая священная | исторія | и | краткій христіанскій | катихизисъ. | съ Русскаго языка на Алеутско-Лисьевскій переведъ | Священникъ Іоаннъ Веніаминовъ 1827 года, и въ 1837 | году исправилъ; а Священникъ Іаковъ Нецвѣтовъ | разсматривая оныя, своими поясненіями сдѣлалъ ихъ | понятными и для Атхинцовъ, имѣющихъ свое нарѣчіе. |

Санктпетербургъ, | Въ Синодальной типографіи. | 1840.

*Translation:* The rudiments | of Christian instruction | or | Short Sacred | History | and | Short Christian | Catechism. | From the Russian tongue into Aleutian-Fox translated | by Reverend John Veniaminoff in the year 1827, and in 1837 | year revised; and Reverend Jacob Netzvietoff | has examined it and with notes made it | intelligible for the Atkhans, who have a dialect of their own. | St. Petersburg, | At Synod Press.

# НАЧАТКИ

## ХРИСТІАНСКАГО УЧЕНІЯ

## ИЛИ

# КРАТКАЯ СВЯЩЕННАЯ

# ИСТОРІЯ

## и

# КРАТКІЙ ХРИСТІАНСКІЙ

# КАТИХИЗИСЪ.

съ Русскаго языка на Алеутско-Лисьевскій перевелъ Священникъ Іоаннъ Веніаминовъ 1827 года, и въ 1837 году исправилъ; а Священникъ Іаковъ Нецвѣтовъ разсматривалъ оный, своими пополнеиіями сдѣлалъ ихъ понятными и для Атхинцовъ, имѣющихъ свое нарѣчіе.

———————————

# САНКТПЕТЕРБУРГЪ,

Въ Сунодальной Типографіи

# 1840.

**Veniaminoff (J.)—**Continued.

Half-title in Cyrillic type and Russian, reverse title in Russian, as above, 1 l. title in Cyrillic type (same as Russian title minus the imprint) 1 l. preface by Veniaminoff in parallel columns of Aleutian (Cyrillic type) and Russian, pp. i-vii; preface by Netzvietoff in parallel columns, Aleutian (Cyrillic type) and Russian, pp. ix-xix; primer in Aleut and Russian, pp. 1-24; Short Sacred History in Aleutian, pp. 1-104; Short Christian Catechism in Aleutian, pp. 1-51, 8°. See fac-simile of title-page, page 100.

*Copies seen:* Pilling, Powell. ✎

For a later edition of the Sacred History see **Tishnoff** (E.).

———— Господа нашего | Iисуса Христа | Евангеліе, | написанное | апостоломъ Матеемъ. | Съ Русскаго языка на Алеутско-Лисьевскоꙗ переведъ | Священникъ Iоаннъ Веніаминовъ 1828 года, и въ | 1836 году исправилъ; а Священникъ Iаковъ Нецвѣтовъ разсматривая его | окончательно, своими пополненіами сдѣлалъ понятнымъ | и для Атхинцовъ, имѣющихъ свое нарѣчіе. |

[Moscow: Synod Press, about 1848.]

*Translation:* Of our Lord | Jesus Christ | the Gospel, | written | by the apostle Matthew. | From the Russian tongue into the Aleutian-Fox translated | by Reverend John Veniaminoff, in the year 1828, and in | 1836 year revised; | and Reverend Jacob Netzvietoff revising it | finally, with notes has made it intelligible | also for the Atkhans, who have a dialect of their own.

Half-title 1 l. title in Cyrillic type (12 lines), verso of l. 2; Russian title, recto l. 3; Preface, by Veniaminoff, in parallel columns of Aleut (in Cyrillic type) and Russian, pp. i-v; Preface, by Netzvietoff, in parallel columns Aleutian (Cyrillic type) and Russian, pp. vi-xiv; Gospel of Matthew, parallel columns Aleutian (Cyrillic type) and Russian, pp. 15-237 (erroneously numbered 247); Form of worship for the paschal feast, and first and second chapters of Luke, in Cyrillic type only, pp. 1-21, 8°. See fac-similes of title-pages, pages 102, 103.

*Copies seen:* Pilling, Powell.

[**Vocabularies** (60 words each) of the Asiagmut, of Norton Bay; Kuskokwims, of Norton Bay; of the Indians near Mount St. Elias; of Kadiak Island; and of the Indians of Bristol Bay.]

Manuscript, 5 ll. folio, in the library of the Bureau of Ethnology.

Vocabulary:

| | |
|---|---|
| Aglemiut. | See Balbi (A.), |
| Aglemiut. | Pinart (A. L.), |
| Aglemiut | Wowodsky (—). |
| Aleut | Baer (K. E. von), |
| Aleut. | Dalitz (A.), |
| Aleut. | Balbi (A.), |
| Aleut. | Bancroft (H. H.), |

**Vocabulary—**Continued.

| | |
|---|---|
| Aleut. | See Buynitzky (S. N.), |
| Aleut. | Drake (S. G.), |
| Aleut. | Everette (W. E.), |
| Aleut. | Gallatin (A.), |
| Aleut. | Herzog (W.), |
| Aleut. | Lowe (F.), |
| Aleut. | Müller (F.), |
| Aleut. | Robeck (—), |
| Aleut. | Russkie, |
| Aleut. | Sauer (M.). |
| Androanowski [Atkan]. | Adelung (J. C.) and Vater (J. S.), |
| Androanowski [Atkan]. | Robeck (—). |
| Aretle. | Everette (W. E.), |
| Arctic. | Petitot (E. F. S. J.). |
| Argalaxamut. | Hoffman (W. J.). |
| Aslagmut. | Furuhelm (H.), |
| Aslagmut. | Vocabularies. |
| Atka. | Dall (W. H.), |
| Atka. | Gibbs (G.), |
| Atka. | Veniaminoff (J.). |
| Baffin Bay. | Notice. |
| Bathurst. | Petitot (E. F. S. J.) |
| Bristol Bay. | Johnson (J. W.), |
| Bristol Bay. | Vocabularies. |
| Chiagmiut. | Zagoskin (L. A.). |
| Chugátchigmút. | Dall (W. H.). |
| Chuklukmut. | Dall (W. H.). |
| Coyukon. | Whymper (F.). |
| Cumberland Strait. | Gilder (W. H.), |
| Cumberland Strait. | Kumlien (L.). |
| Davis Strait. | Gibbs (G.) |
| Ekogmut. | Dall (W. H.). |
| Eskimo. | Adelung (J. C.) and Vater (J. S.), |
| Eskimo. | Beechey (F. W.), |
| Eskimo. | Bryant (—), |
| Eskimo. | Buschmann (J. C. E.), |
| Eskimo. | Chappell (E.), |
| Eskimo. | Dobbs (A.), |
| Eskimo. | Herzog (W.), |
| Eskimo. | Jéhan (L. F.), |
| Eskimo. | Kalm (P.), |
| Eskimo. | Latham (R. G.), |
| Eskimo. | Long (J.), |
| Eskimo. | M'Keevor (T.), |
| Eskimo. | Murdoch (J.), |
| Eskimo. | Nelson (E. W.), |
| Eskimo. | Newton (A.), |
| Eskimo. | Parry (W. E.), |
| Eskimo. | Petroff (I.), |
| Eskimo. | Rand (S. T.), |
| Eskimo. | Ross (J.), |
| Eskimo. | Schorer (J. B.), |
| Eskimo. | Schubert (— von), |
| Eskimo. | Tomlin (J.), |
| Eskimo. | Washington (J.). |
| Fox Channel. | Hall (C. F.). |
| Greenland. | Balbi (A.), |
| Greenland. | Bartholinus (C.), |
| Greenland. | Barton (B. S.), |
| Greenland. | Bryant (—), |
| Greenland. | Court de Gebelin (A. de), |
| Greenland. | Dall (W. H.), |

ТУ́МА́ЙНЪ ЛГУ́ГУМЪ

ЙПСУ́СЪ ХРИСТУ́САМЪ

ТУ́НУС́ОЛЧХИСЛИГИНЪ

ЛПУ́СТУЛЛМЪ МАТѲИ́ЖЪ

ЙЛАХ́ТА́ГЛНЪ А́ЛУХ́ТАСАКА́НИНЪ.

КА́МГА — ТУ́ККУМЪ ІОА́ННЪ ВЕНІАМИ́НОВЪ ЙЛАХ́ТА́ГА
КАСА́КАМЪ ТУ́НУ́ГАНЪ КУ́ЙГИНЪ УНА́ЙГАМЪ ТУ́НУ́ГАНЪ ЙЛИ
1828 ТУ́ЛМАЧИ́САЛНКЪ, КА́ЮХЪ 1836 СЛЮ́ЛАГАНЪ ЙЛА
АТХАГУ́САКА́НИНЪ;

ТА́ГА КА́МГА — ТУ́ККУМЪ ІА́КОВЪ НИЦВѢ́ТОВЪ ЙЛАХ́ТА́ГА
АТХАГУ́САГУ́САЛНКЪ КА́ЮХЪ НИГУ́ГИМЪ, ТУ́НУ́МЪ ИПАКАХ́Т
МАТАНА́ГАНЪ, А́ДА́ИГИНЪ КАНЧИ́МЛДУ́СИГИНЪ И́ТХА́ИГИНЪ.

FAC-SIMILE OF CYRILLIC TITLE-PAGE OF VENIAMINOFF AND NETZVIETOFF'S ALÉUT-FOX GOSPEL OF MATTHEW.

# ГОСПОДА НАШЕГО

# IИСУСА ХРИСТА

# ЕВАНГЕЛIЕ,

## НАПИСАННОЕ

## АПОСТОЛОМЪ МАТѲЕѢМЪ.

ъ Русскаго языка на Алеутско-Лисьевской перевелъ
вященникъ Iоаннъ Вениаминовъ 1828 года, и въ
1836 году исправилъ;

а Священникъ Iаковъ Нецвѣтовъ разсматривал его
окончательно, своими поясненiями сдѣлалъ понятнымъ
и для Атхинцовъ, имѣющихъ свое нарѣчiе.

FAC-SIMILE OF RUSSIAN TITLE-PAGE OF VENIAMINOFF AND NETZVIETOFF'S ALEUT-FOX
GOSPEL OF MATTHEW.

**Vocabulary—Continued.**

| | |
|---|---|
| Greenland. | See Egede (II.), |
| Greenland. | Egede (Paul), |
| Greenland. | Franklin (J.), |
| Greenland. | Fry (E.), |
| Greenland. | Gallatin (A.), |
| Greenland. | Gilder (W. II.), |
| Greenland. | Graah (W. A.), |
| Greenland. | Klaproth (A.), |
| Greenland. | Konigseor (C.M.), |
| Greenland. | Markham (C. R.), |
| Greenland. | Morgan (L. II.), |
| Greenland. | O'Reilly (B.), |
| Greenland. | Olearius (A.), |
| Greenland. | Pfizmaier (A.), |
| Greenland. | Prichard (J. C.), |
| Greenland. | Rink (II. J.), |
| Greenland. | Scherer (J. B.). |
| Hudson Bay. | Gallatin (A.), |
| Hudson Bay. | Gilder (W. II.), |
| Hudson Bay. | Morgan (L. II.). |
| Inkalik. | Buschmann (J. C. E.), |
| Inkalik. | Schwatka (F.), |
| Inkalik. | Schott (W.), |
| Inkalik. | Zagoskin (L. A.). |
| Inkalit-Jug-eljnut. | Buschmann (J. C. E.), |
| Inkalit-Jug-eljnut. | Schott (W.), |
| Inkalit-Jug-eljnut. | Zagoskin (L. A.). |
| Inkulnklates. | Wrangell (F.von). |
| Innuit. | Buschmann (J. C. E.), |
| Innuit. | Müller (F.), |
| Inuuit. | Woolfe (H. D.). |
| Kadiak. | Baer (K. E. von), |
| Kadiak. | Buschmann (J. C. E.), |
| Kadiak. | Davidoff (G. I.), |
| Kadiak. | Davidson (G.), |
| Kadiak. | Gallatin (A.), |
| Kadiak. | Gibbs (G.), |
| Kadiak. | Klaproth (J.), |
| Kadiak. | Khromchenko (V. S.), |
| Kadiak. | Latham (R. G.), |
| Kadiak. | Lisiansky (U.), |
| Kadiak. | Petroff (I.), |
| Kadiak. | Robeck (—), |
| Kadiak. | Sauer (M.), |
| Kadiak. | Schott (W.), |
| Kadiak. | Vocabularies, |
| Kadiak. | Zagoskin (L. A.), |
| Kadiak. | Zelenic (S. J.). |
| Kagcagemut. | Fisher (W. J.). |
| Kamchatka. | Gallatin (A.), |
| Kamchatka. | Klaproth (J.), |
| Kamchatka. | Sauer (M.). |
| Kamskadalo. | Drake (S. G.), |
| Kamskadalo. | Golovnin (M.), |
| Kamskadalo. | Lessops (J. B. B.). |
| Kangjulit. | Zelenic (S. J.). |
| Kaviagmût. | Dall (W. H.). |
| Kenai. | Davidson (G.), |
| Kenai. | Lisiansky (U.). |

**Vocabulary—Continued.**

| | |
|---|---|
| Kiatexemut. | See Hoffman (W. J.). |
| King William's Land. | Hall (C. F.). |
| Koikhpagmint. | Zagoskin (L. A.). |
| Konega. | Bancroft (II. II.). |
| Koniagmut. | Dall (W. H.), |
| Koniagmut. | Gibbs (G.). |
| Koriak. | Lesseps (J. B. B. de). |
| Kotzebuo Sound. | Gallatin (A.). |
| Kuskivigmut. | Schott (W.), |
| Kuskivigmut. | Zagoskin (L. A.). |
| Kuskokwim. | Baer (K. E. von), |
| Kuskokwim. | Furuhelm (II.), |
| Kuskokwim. | Kuskokwim, |
| Kuskokwim. | Vocabularies, |
| Kuskokwim. | Wrangell (F. von). |
| Kuskutchewac. | Latham (R. G.), |
| Kuskutchewac. | Morgan (L. II.), |
| Kuskutchewac. | Richardson (J.). |
| Kuskutchewak. | Baer (K. E. von). |
| Kuskwôgmût. | Dall (W. II.). |
| Kwigpak. | Schott (W.). |
| Labrador. | Fry (E.), |
| Labrador. | Latrobe (P.) and Washington (J.), |
| Labrador. | Morgan (L. II.), |
| Labrador. | Richardson (J.), |
| Labrador. | Stearns (W. A.). |
| Lamouto. | Lesseps (J. B. B. de). |
| Mahlemut. | Bannister (II.M.), |
| Mahlemut. | Dall (W. H.), |
| Mahlemut. | Pinart (A. L.), |
| Mahlemut. | Smith (E. E.), |
| Mahlemut. | Whymper (F.). |
| Meduovskie. | Wrangell (F. von). |
| Namoller. | Schott (W.). |
| Noonatarghmentes. | Oldmixon (G. S.). |
| Noowookmentes. | Oldmixon (G. S.). |
| Northumberland Inlet. | Morgan (L. II.). |
| Norton Sound. | Adelung (J. C.) and Vater (J. S.), |
| Norton Sound. | Bryant (—), |
| Norton Sound. | Fry (E.). |
| Nuniwok Island. | Buschmann (J. C. E.). |
| Nushergágmût. | Dall (W. II.). |
| Point Barrow. | Ray (P. H.), |
| Point Barrow. | Simpson (J.). |
| Pond Bay. | Hall (C. F.). |
| Prince William Sound. | Anderson (W.), |
| Prince William Sound. | Buschmann (J. C. E.), |
| Prince William Sound. | Forster (J. G. A.), |
| Prince William Sound. | Fry (E.), |
| Prince William Sound. | Portlock (N.). |
| St. Michael. | Everette (W. E.). |
| Skitaget. | Gibbs (G.), |
| Stupart Bay. | Stupart (R. F.). |
| Stewart Island. | Buschmann (J. C. E.). |

**Vocabulary—Continued.**

| | |
|---|---|
| Tchougatche-Kouoga. | See Balbi (A.). |
| Tchuktchi. | Balbi (A.), |
| Tchuktchi. | Gallatin (A.), |
| Tchuktchi. | Gilder (W. H.), |
| Tchuktchi. | Hooper (W. II.), |
| Tchuktchi. | Krause (A.), |
| Tchuktchi. | Lesseps (J. B. B. de), |
| Tchuktchi. | Pützmaier (A.), |
| Tchuktchi. | Stimpson (W.) and Hall (A.), |
| Tchuktchi. | Robeck (—), |
| Tchuktchi. | Romberg (II.), |
| Tchuktchi. | Radloff (L.), |
| Tchuktchi. | Zagoskin (L. A.). |
| Toonoonoenooshuk. | Hall (C. F.). |
| Tschuagmjuten. | Schott (W.). |
| Tschugazzen. | Adelung (J. C.) and Vater (J. S.), |
| Tschugazzen. | Baer (K. E. von), |
| Tschugazzen. | Buschmann (J. C. E.), |
| Tschugazzon. | Wowodsky (—). |
| Tschnkak Island. | Buschmann (J. C. E.). |
| Ugalakmut. | Dall (W. H.). |

**Vocabulary—Continued.**

| | |
|---|---|
| Ugalenzi. | See Baer (K. E. von), |
| Ugalenzi. | Buschmann (J. C. E.), |
| Ugalenzi. | Dall (W. II.), |
| Ugalenzi. | Wrangell (F. von). |
| Ugaljachmutzi. | Adelung (J. C.) and Vater (J S.), |
| Ugaljachmutzi. | Balbi (A.), |
| Ugaljachmutzi. | Prichard (J. C.). |
| Ugashachmut. | Fisher (J.). |
| Unalaska. | Adelung (J. C.) and Vater (J. S.), |
| Unalaska. | Bryaut (—), |
| Unalaska. | Dall (W. II.), |
| Unalaska. | Davidson (G.), |
| Unalaska. | Fry (E.), |
| Unalaska. | Gallatin (A.), |
| Unalaska. | Latham (R. G.), |
| Unalaska. | Lisiansky (U.), |
| Unalaska. | Lutké (F. P.), |
| Unalaska. | Wowodsky (—). |
| Unaligmut. | Dall (W. II.). |
| Yukon River. | Everette (W. E.). |

# W.

**Wandall (Erik Adolf).** Kissitsisillior-nermik | iliniarkautiksæt | Kaladlinnut attnægoksaursut. | Kaladlisut nukter-simagalloæt | nark'iksarej sennak' iglu-gidlo | Erik Adolf Wandall-ib, | Tol-strupimiut pellesiæta. |
Aalborgime. | 1845.

*Literal translation:* About-figure-making | fundamental-instructions | for Greenlanders being-intended-for-a-thing-to-be-used. | After the fashion of the Greenlanders already trans-lated | Corrected them and partly remodeled them | Erik Adolf Wandall, | the people of Tolstrup their priest. | At Aalborg.

*Second title:* Bogyndelsesgrundone | i | Reg-ning | til Brug for Grønlænderne. | Oversat-telsen paa Grønlandsk | rettet og tildeels omarbeidet | af | Erik Adolph Wandall, | Praest i Tolstrup. |
Aalborg. | 1845.

Eskimo title verso l. 1, Danish title recto l. 2, text, alternate pp. Danish and Greenland, pp. 4-91, 16°. Elements of arithmetic in the lan-guage of Greenland.

*Copies seen:* Harvard.

—— Naitsungordlugo nunab aglautigen-era Stoud-Platoumit.

Aalborgime, 1846.

8°. Title from the Pinart sale catalogue, No. 948, which copy brought 1 fr.

A later edition as follows:

**Wandall (E. A.)—Continued.**

—— Naitsungordlugo | nunab aglautige-nera Stond-Platoumit. | Kaladlit okau-zeennut nuktersimaga | E. A. Wandall-ib, | Tolstrupimiut | pellesiæta. | Aalborgime. | Stiftib nakk'iteriviane-nakk'ittarsimarsut. | 1848.

*Literal translation:* So that it became short | the earth's its description by Stoud-Platon. | Greenlanders into their speech translated it | E. A. Wandall | the people of Tolstrap | their priest. | At Aalborg. | The diocese's on its printing-press printed.

Pp. 1-109, 12°. Geography in Greenland Eskimo.

At the Pinart sale, catalogue No. 949, a copy brought 1 fr.

*Copies seen:* Harvard.

"Wandall was born in 1807, lived in Green-land from 1834 to 1840, and died, in 1869, at Seo-land, Denmark, where he had served as parish priest and teacher of the Greenland language to missionary students since 1849."—*Rink.*

**Wanderings of the Apostles,** Greenland. See Egede (Paul).

**Warden (David Baillie).** Recherches | sur | les Antiquités | de l'Amérique du Nord | et de | l'Amérique du Sud, | et sur | la Population primitive | de ces deux continents, | par | M. Warden, |

**Warden** (D. B.)—Continued.

Ancien Consul-Général [&c., three lines]. | [Design.] |

Paris, | Imprimerie et Fonderie normales de Jules Didot l'aîné, | Boulevart d'Enfer, No. 4. | 1834.

Pp. 1-224, folio. Forms deuxième partie, deuxième division, tome second, Antiquités Américaines, Paris, 1834, 2 vols. folio.—A few words of scripture, St. Matthew and St. John, in the Esquimaux of Labrador and of Greenland compared.

*Copies seen:* Astor, Bancroft, British Museum.

The earlier edition of this work (1827) does not contain the Eskimo material. (Congress.)

**[Washington** (*Capt.* John).] Eskimaux and English vocabulary, | for the use of the Arctic expedition. | Published by order of the lords commissioners of the admiralty. |

London: | John Murray, Albemarle Street. | 1850.

Pp. i-xvi, 1-160, oblong 12°. "Compiled for the use of the Arctic expeditions fitted out at the expense of the British Government to carry reliefto Sir John Franklin and his companions." Extract from preface, signed John Washington, Captain, R. N.—Brief sketch of the Eskimaux Grammar, pp. xi-xvi.—English and Eskimaux vocabulary [Labrador, or Eastern; Winter Island and Iglûlik, or Central; Kotzebue Sound, or Western], pp. 1-100.—Specimen of Dialogues [Labrador-Eskimaux], pp. 101-107.—Eskimaux or Innuit Names of Places in or near Melville Peninsula [Labrador-Eskimaux], pp. 108-109.—Comparative Table of a few words of the Eskimaux (or Innuit), Chukchi, Aleutian, and Karyak languages, chiefly from Balbi's Atlas Ethnographique and Klaproth's Sprach-Atlas, pp. 110-113.—Eskimaux and English vocabulary, pp. 115-160.

*Copies seen:* Astor, Brinley, British Museum, Congress, Shea, Wisconsin Historical Society.

At the Brinley sale, catalogue No. 5643, a copy was disposed of for $5.75. The Murphy copy, No. 905, brought $5. Priced by Quaritch, No. 30049, at 3s. 6d.

—— [Greenland-Eskimo and English Vocabulary. Compiled by Capt. Washington, R. N.

London, 1853.]

Oblong 12°.

Priced by Quaritch, No. 12580, at 2s. 6d.; by Trübner, 1882 (p. 53), at 7s. 6d.

**Watkinson**: This word following a title indicates that a copy of the work referred to was seen by the compiler in the Watkinson library, Hartford, Conn.

**Watts's** First Catechism. See **Peck** (E. J.).

**Western** Esquimaux Primer. See **Bompas** (W. C.).

**Wexel** (W. A.). See **Kragh** (P.).

**Whymper** (Frederick). Travel and adventure | in the | territory of Alaska, | formerly Russian America—now ceded to the | United States—and in various other | parts of the North Pacific. | By Frederick Whymper. | [Design.] | With map and illustrations. |

London: | John Murray, Albemarle street. | 1868. | The right of Translation is reserved.

Pp. i-xx, 1-331, map, plates, 8°.—Appendix V. Indian dialects of Northern Alaska (late Russian America), pp. 318-328, contains: Malemute vocabulary, words from the dialect of the Malemutes, Norton Sound, Northern Alaska, pp. 318-319.—Co-yukon vocabulary, words from the Co-yukon dialect, spoken (with slight variations) on the Yukon River for at least 500 miles of its lower and middle course (Ingelete, a variety of same dialect), pp. 320-321.

*Copies seen:* Boston Public, British Museum, Congress.

At the Field sale, catalogue No. 2539, a copy brought $2.75.

—— Travel and adventure | in the | territory of Alaska, | formerly Russian America—now ceded to the | United States—and in various other | parts of the North Pacific. | By Frederick Whymper. | [Design.] | With map and illustrations. |

New York: | Harper & Brothers, Publishers, | Franklin square. | 1869.

Pp. i-xix, 21-353, maps and plates, 8°.—Linguistics as in London edition, pp. 341-350.

*Copies seen:* Bancroft, Boston Athenæum, Powell.

Reprinted 1871, pp. xix, 21-353, 8°.

I have seen mention of an edition in French. Paris, 1871, 8°. (*)

—— Russian America, or "Alaska": the Natives of the Youkon River and adjacent country. By Frederick Whymper, Esq.

In Ethnological Soc. of London Trans. vol. 7. pp. 167-185, London, 1869, 8°.

A few words of the Malemute of Norton Sound and the Greenland Esquimaux compared, p. 180.—Malemute vocabulary, Norton Sound, Russian America, pp. 180-182.—Coyonkon vocabulary, Yukon River, pp. 182-183.

**Winkler** (*Dr.* Heinrich). Uralaltaische Völker und Sprachen | von | Dr. Heinrich Winkler. |

**Winkler (H.)**—Continued.

Berlin | Ferd. Dümmlers Verlags-
buchhandlung | Harrwitz und Goss-
man | 1884.

Title verso blank 1 l. contents 1 l. text pp.
1-480, 8°.—General remarks on the Eskimo,
Aleut, and Tschuktschi languages and on
their principal parts of speech, pp. 115-118,
119-121.

*Copies seen:* Brinton.

"Dr. Heinrich Winkler, in his recently published 'Uralaltaische Völker und Sprachen,'
has made a careful comparison of the Eskimo
with the languages of northern and northeastern Asia. He reaches the result that it is in
unmistakably close relation to the Kadyak,
Tschiglit, and Namollo of the Asiatic coast,
but is in no way connected with the Ural-altaic
tongues. It may have originally proceeded
from the same elementary conception of
speech; but it has developed a type of its own,
differing widely from Asiatic standards, and
much more closely approaching the structure
typical of the great mass of American tongues,
though in many respects presenting features
peculiar to itself."—*Brinton.*

**Wisconsin Historical Society:** These words following a title indicate that a copy of the work
referred to was seen by the compiler in the
library of that society, Madison, Wis.

**Wöldike (Marcus).** Betænkning om det
Grønlandske Sprogs Oprindelse og
Uliighed med andre Sprog. Forfattet
af M. W.

In Kjøbenhavnske Selskab, Skrifter, ɬol. 2,
pp. 129-156, Kjøbenhavn, 1746, 4°.

—— Meletema de Lingvæ Groenlandicæ
origine, ejusque a cæteris lingvis diffe-
rentia, autore M. W.

In Kjøbenhavnske Selskab, Scriptorum à
Soc. Hafn. vol. 2, pp. 137-162, Hafniæ, 1746, 4°.

**Wolf (Niels Gjessing).** Testamentitoka-
mit | Davidim Ivngerutéj | Kaladlin
okàuzeeunut | nuktersimarsut | Pelle-
simit | Nielsimit Wolfimit, | attuægek-
säukudlugin innungnut koïsimarsun-
nut. |

Kjöbenhavnime | Illiârsuïn gloænne
nakkitarsimarsut | 1824. | C. F. Schu-
bartimit.

*Literal translation:* From the Old Testament
| David's his psalms | Greenlanders' into their
speech | translated | by the priest Niels Wolf
| being intended for a manual for people
christened. | At Copenhagen | at the orphans'
their house [Waisenhaus] printed | 1824. |
From [issued by] C. F. Schubart.

Pp. 1-238, 16°.

*Copies seen:* Astor, British and Foreign
Bible Society, British Museum, Congress,
Harvard, Powell, Watkinson.

**Wolf (N. G.)**—Continued.
The Fischer copy, catalogue No. 2337,
bought by Trübner, brought 2s.

—— Testamentitokamit | Profetib Esaia-
sim | Aglegêj. | Kaladlin okàuzeeunnut |
nuktersimarsut | P[e]llesimit | N. G.
Wolfimit, | attuægeksäukudlugit in-
nungnut koïsimarsunnut. |

Kjöbenhavnime | Illiârsuïn igloænne
nakittarsimarsut | 1825. | C. F. Schu-
bartimit.

*Literal translation:* From the Old Testament
| the prophet Isaiah's | his written things
[book]. | Greenlanders' into their speech |
translated | by the priest | N. G. Wolf, | being
intended for a manual for people christened. |
At Copenhagen | at the orphans' their house
[Waisenhaus] printed | 1825. | From [issued
by] C. F. Schubart.

Pp. 1-200, 16°. See Pfizmaier (A.).

*Copies seen:* Astor, British and Foreign Bible
Society, British Museum, Congress, Harvard,
Powell, Watkinson.

Bought by Trübner at the Fischer sale, No.
2338, for 2s. 6d.

—— Testamentitokamit | Salomonib |
Ajokœrsutéj Erkäïrseksæt | Kaladlin
okàuzeeunnut | nuktersimarsut. | Pelli-
simit | N. G. Wolfimit attuægeksäuku-
dlugit innungnut koïsimarsunnut. |

Kjöbenhavnime. | Nakkittarsimarsut
Fabritius de Tongnagelmit. | 1828.

*Literal translation:* From the Old Testament
| Solomon's | his teachings things which shall
be remembered | Greenlanders' into their
speech | translated. | By the priest | N. G.
Wolf | being intended for a manual for people
christened. | At Copenhagen | Printed by
Fabricius de Tengnagel.

2 p. ll. pp. 1-73, 16°. Prover bs of Solomon.

*Copies seen:* Astor, Powell.

Priced by Quaritch, No. 12582, at 2s. 6d. The
Murphy copy, No. 2763, brought 25 cts. Priced
by Quaritch, No. 30057, at 2s.

—— See Fabricius (O.).

Wolf was born at Copenhagen August 6, 1779.
He received instruction from his father, and
in 1791 entered the Vordenborg Latin school,
and in 1796 entered the university, passing his
final examination in January, 1803. In December, 1803, he was sent as missionary to
Greenland, first to the colony of Holsteinborg
and Sukkertoppen, and in the fall of 1807 to
Godthaab. He remained in Greenland until
1811. He died in Copenhagen October 16, 1848.

**Woolfe (Henry D.).** [Vocabulary of the
Innuit language.]

Manuscript. In a letter of November, 1886,
to the secretary of the Smithsonian Institution, Mr. Woolfe, who is connected with the
Pacific Steam Whaling Company, says he has

**Woolfe (H. D.)—Continued.**
compiled a "Muhtes," or Innuit, vocabulary of 3,000 words.

Words:

| | |
|---|---|
| Aglemonte. | See Schomburgk (R. H.). |
| Aleut. | Campbell (J.), |
| | Coxe (W.), |
| | Pinart (A. L.), |
| | Uméry (J.). |
| Davis Strait. | Brown (R.). |
| Eskimo. | Balbi (A.), |
| | Buschmann (J. C. E.), |
| | Duncan (D.), |
| | Hooper (W. H.), |
| | Latham (R. G.), |
| | Pinart (A. L.), |
| | Yankiewitch (F.). |
| Greenland. | Buschmann (J. C. E.), |
| | Lesley (J. P.), |
| | Rink (H. J.), |
| | Uméry (J.), |
| | Vater (J. S.), |
| | Whymper (F.). |
| Hudson Bay. | Schomburgk (R. H.). |
| Kadiak. | Campbell (J.), |
| | Davidoff (G. I.), |
| | Lesley (J. P.). |
| Norton Sound. | Yankiewitch (F.). |
| Ugalenzen. | Buschmann (J. C. E.). |
| Ugaljachmutzi. | Buschmann (J. C. E.), |
| | Uméry (J.). |
| Unalaska. | Campbell (J.). |

**Wowodsky (Gor. —.).** Vocabulary of the Aglemint (Bristol Bay).

**Wowodsky (Gov.)—Continued.**
Manuscript, 2 ll. foolscap, 50 words and numerals 1-10; in the library of the Bureau of Ethnology.

—— Vocabulary of the Kadiak.
Manuscript, 2 ll. foolscap, 50 words and numerals 1-10; in the library of the Bureau of Ethnology.

—— Vocabulary of the Tchugatz (Prince William Sound).
Manuscript, 2 ll. foolscap, 50 words and numerals 1-10; in the library of the Bureau of Ethnology.

—— Vocabulary of the Oonalashka.
Manuscript, 2 ll. foolscap, 50 words and numerals 1-10; in the library of the Bureau of Ethnology.

**Wrangell** (*Admiral* Ferdinand von). Observations recueillies par l'Amiral Wrangell sur les habitants des Côtes Nord-ouest de l'Amérique; extraites du russe par M. le prince Emanuel Galitzin.

In Nouvelles Annales des Voyages, vol. 1, 1853 (vol. 137 of the collection), pp. 195-221, Paris, n. d. 8°.

Short vocabulary of the Mednovskie [Copper Islanders] and the Ougalantsi, p. 199.—Short vocabulary of the Inkuluklates, pp. 209-210.—Names of some of the constellations and of the months in Kouskovimtsi, p. 220.

*Copies seen:* British Museum, Congress.

—— See **Baer** (K. E. von).

# Y.

Yale: This word following a title indicates that a copy of the work referred to was seen by the compiler in the library of Yale College, New Haven, Conn.

**[Yankiewitch** (Feodor de Miriewo).]
Сравнительный | словарь | всѣхъ | языковъ и нарѣчій, | по азбучному порядку | расположенныи. | часть первая | [-четвертая] А-,[ [С-Ѳ].

Въ Санктпетербургѣ, 1790[-1791].

*Translation:* Comparative | dictionary | of all | languages and dialects | in alphabetical order | arranged. | Part first [-fourth]. A-D [S-Th]. | At St. Petersburg.

4 vols. 4°.

**Yankiewitch (F. de M.)—Continued.**
Scattered throughout the work are words in Eskimo and in the language of Norton Sound.

"Pallas having published, in 1786 and 1789, the first part of the Vocabularium Catharinæ um (a comparative vocabulary of 286 words in the languages of Europe and Asia), the material contained therein was published in the above edition in another form, and words of American languages added. The book did not come up to the expectations of the government, and was therefore not published, so that but few copies of it can be found."—*Ludewig.*

*Copies seen:* British Museum.

**Yukon River Vocabulary.** See **Everette** (W. E.).

# Z.

ЗАГОСКИНЪ (Лент. Лаврентій Алексѣй). [Za-goskin (*Lieut.* Laurenti Alexie).] Пе-шеходная опись | части русскихъ владѣній | въ Америкѣ. | Произведенная | лейтенантомъ Л. Загоскинымъ | въ 1842, 1843 и 1844 го-дахъ. Съ Меркаторскою картою гравированною на мѣди. | Часть первая [-вторая]. | Санктпетербургъ. | Печатано въ типографіи карла крайя. | 1847[-1848].

*Translation:* Pedestrian Exploration | of parts of the Russian Possessions | in America. | Accomplished | by Lieutenant L. Zagoskin | in the years 1842, 1843 and 1844. | With a Mer-cator's chart engraved on copper. | Part first [-second]. | St. Petersburg. | Printed in the Printing Office of Karl Krai. | 1847[-1848].

2 vols.: 1 p. l. pp. 1-183; 1 p. l. pp. 1-120, 1-15, 1-45, 8°.—Vocabulary of the Inkilik and Inka-lit Yugehunt, vol. 2, appendix, pp. 17-20.—Vo-cabulary of the Chiagmiut, Kuskivigmut, Ka-ciak (from Billings and Lisiansky), and Seden-tary Chukche, or Namollos (from Robeck), vol. 2, appendix, pp. 21-36.—List of villages, with population statistics, vol. 2, appendix, pp. 39-

ЗАГОСКИНЪ (Л. А.)—Continued.

41.—List of birds in Koikhpagmiut and Inki-lik, vol. 2, appendix, pp. 42-43.

*Copies seen:* Bancroft, British Museum.

For reprints, in whole or in part, see Busch-mann (J. C. E.); Schott (W.); and Zelenie (S. I.).

ЗЕЛЕНЫЙ (С. П.) [Zelenie, S. I.]. Извлече-ніе изъ дневника лейтенанта Загоскина, веденнаго въ экспедиціи, совершенной имъ по материку сѣверо-западной Америки. (Соста-влено Л. Чл. С. П. Зеленымъ.)

*Translation:* Extract from the daily journal of Lieut. Zagoskin, who led an expedition clear to the continent of Northwest America. Compiled by active member S. I. Zelenie [Green].

In Russian Geographical Society Journal, vols. 1 and 2 (second edition), pp. 211-266, St. Petersburg, 1849, 8°.

Comparative vocabulary in parallel columns, Russian, Chuagmut, Yukon and Kuskokwim-mut, Zuzentseff of Kadiak Island, and Na-mollo or Sedentary Chukchee, pp. 250-266.

# CHRONOLOGIC INDEX.

## LIST OF AUTHORS, IN CHRONOLOGIC ORDER, WHO HAVE WRITTEN IN OR UPON THE ESKIMO LANGUAGE.

| | | |
|---|---|---|
| 1656 | Olearius (A.). | Greenland. |
| 1656 | Olearius (A.). | Greenland. |
| 1659 | Olearius (A.). | Greenland. |
| 1662 | Olearius (A.). | Greenland. |
| 1663 | Olearius (A.), note. | Greenland. |
| 1669 | Olearius (A.). | Greenland. |
| 1669 | Olearius (A.), note. | Greenland. |
| 1671 | Olearius (A.), note. | Greenland. |
| 1675 | Bartholinus (C.). | Greenland. |
| 1676 | Crespieul (F. X.). | Eskimo. |
| 1679 | Olearius (A.). | Greenland. |
| 1690 | Olearius (A.), note. | Greenland. |
| 1691 | Olearius (A.), note. | Greenland. |
| 1719 | Olearius (A.). | Greenland. |
| 1727 | Olearius (A.). | Greenland. |
| 1728 | Olearius (A.), note. | Greenland. |
| 1729 | Egede (H.). | Greenland. |
| 1730 | Egede (H.). | Greenland. |
| 1741 | Egede (H.). | Greenland. |
| 1742 | Egede (H.). | Greenland. |
| 1742 | Egede (H.), note. | Greenland. |
| 1744 | Dobbs (A.). | Eskimo. |
| 1744 | Egede (Paul). | Greenland. |
| 1745 | Egede (H.). | Greenland. |
| 1746 | Anderson (J.). | Greenland. |
| 1746 | Egede (H.). | Greenland. |
| 1746 | Wöldike (M.). | Greenland. |
| 1746 | Wöldike (M.). | Greenland. |
| 1747 | Anderson (J.). | Greenland. |
| 1750 | Anderson (J.). | Greenland. |
| 1750 | Anderson (J.). | Greenland. |
| 1750 | Beyer (J. F.). | Greenland. |
| 1750 | Egede (Paul). | Greenland. |
| 1753-1764 | Kalm (P.). | Eskimo. |
| 1754-1764 | Kalm (P.). | Eskimo. |
| 1756 | Anderson (J.). | Greenland. |
| 1756 | Egede (Paul). | Greenland. |
| 1756 | Egede (Peter). | Greenland. |
| 1756 | Indrenius (A. A.). | Greenland. |
| 1758 | Egede (Paul), note. | Greenland. |
| 1760 | Egede (Paul). | Greenland. |
| 1760 | Groenlandsk. | Greenland. |
| 1760 | Jefferys (T.). | Eskimo. |
| 1761 | Brun (R.). | Greenland. |
| 1761 | Jefferys (T.). | Eskimo. |
| 1763 | Egede (H.). | Greenland. |
| 1763 | Egede (H.). | Greenland. |
| 1765 | Cranz (D.). | Greenland. |
| 1766 | Egede (Paul). | Greenland. |
| 1767 | Cranz (D.) | Greenland. |
| 1767 | Cranz (D.). | Greenland. |
| 1769 | Cranz (D.). | Greenland. |
| 1770-1771 | Kalm (P.). | Eskimo. |
| 1772 | Kalm (P.). | Eskimo. |
| 1772 | Kalm (P.). | Eskimo. |
| 1776 | Beck (J.). | Greenland. |
| 1776 | Thorhallesen (E.). | Greenland. |
| 1776 | Thorhallesen (E.). | Greenland. |
| 1776 | Thorhallesen (E.). | Greenland. |
| 1776 | Thorhallesen (E.). | Greenland. |
| 1777 | Scherer (J. B.). | Greenl'd & Lab. |
| 1779-1786 | Giessing (C.). | Eskimo. |
| 1779-1797 | Cranz (D.), note. | Greenland. |
| 1780 | Coxe (W.). | Aleut. |
| 1780 | Coxe (W.), note. | Aleut. |
| 1780 | Konigseer (C. M.). | Greenland. |
| 1780 | Konigseer (C. M.). | Greenland. |
| 1780-1801 | La Harpe (J. F.). | Greenland. |
| 1781 | Court de Gebelin(A.). | Esk. & Greenl'd. |
| 1783 | Abel (L.). | Greenland. |
| 1783 | Egede (Paul). | Greenland. |
| 1784 | Anderson (W.). | Pr. Wm. Sound. |
| 1784 | Anderson (W.), note. | Pr. Wm. Sound. |
| 1784 | Anderson (W.), note. | Pr. Wm. Sound. |
| 1784 | Anderson (W.), note. | Pr. Wm. Sound. |
| 1784 | Bryant (—). | Various. |
| 1784 | Bryant (—). note. | Various. |
| 1784 | Bryant (—), note. | Various. |
| 1784 | Hervas (L.). | Greenland. |
| 1785 | Anderson (W.), note. | Pr. Wm. Sound. |
| 1785 | Anderson (W.), note. | Pr. Wm. Sound. |
| 1785 | Anderson (W.), note. | Pr. Wm. Sound. |
| 1785 | Anderson (W.), note. | Pr. Wm. Sound. |
| 1785 | Bryant (—), note. | Various. |
| 1785 | Bryant (—), note. | Various. |
| 1785 | Bryant (—), note. | Various. |
| 1785 | Bryant (—), note. | Various. |
| 1785 | Jensim. | Greenland. |
| 1785 | Tuksiantit. | Greenland. |
| 1786-1792 | Broderson (J.). | Greenland. |
| 1787 | Anderson (W.). | Pr. Wm. Sound. |
| 1787 | Bryant (—), note. | Various. |
| 1787 | Coxe (W.). | Aleut. |
| 1787 | Egede (Paul). | Greenland. |
| 1787 | Hervas (L.). | Greenland. |
| 1787-1788 | Anderson (W.), note. | Pr. Wm. Sound. |
| 1788 | Egede (Paul). | Greenland. |
| 1788 | Fabricius (O.), note. | Greenland. |
| 1789 | Bergmann (G. von). | Greenland. |
| 1789 | Dixon (G.). | Various. |

111

ESK——8

| 1851 | Richardson (J.). | Various. |
|---|---|---|
| 1851 | Steenholdt (W. F.). | Greenland. |
| 1851 | Testamentitâk. | Greenland. |
| 1852 | Hooper (W. H.). | Esk. and Tchukt. |
| 1852 | Richardson (J.). | Various. |
| 1852 | Tuksiautit. | Greenland. |
| 1852 | Unipkautsit. | Labrador. |
| 1853 | Bock (C. W.). | Greenland. |
| 1853 | Buschmann (J. C. E.). | Various. |
| 1853 | Buschmann (J. C. E.). | Various. |
| 1853 | Hooper (W. H.). | Tchuktchi. |
| 1853 | Kragh (P.). | Greenland. |
| 1853 | Scemann (B.). | Eskimo. |
| 1853 | Seemann (B.). | Eskimo. |
| 1853 | Washington (J.). | Greenland. |
| 1853 | Wrangell (F. von). | Various. |
| 1854 | Buschmann (J. C. E.). | Various. |
| 1854 | Drake (S. G.). | Al. & Kam'd'le. |
| 1854 | Steenholdt (W. F.). | Greenland. |
| 1854 | Stenberg (K. J. O.). | Greenland. |
| 1855 | Buschmann (J. C. E.). | Various. |
| 1855 | Buschmann (J. C. E.). | Various. |
| 1855 | Simpson (J.). | Eskimo. |
| 1856 | Buschmann (J. C. E.). | Eskimo. |
| 1856 | Buschmann (J. C. E.). | Various. |
| 1856 | Cull (R.). | Cumb. Str. & Lab. |
| 1856 | Kjer (K.). | Greenland. |
| 1856 | Richardson (J.), note. | Various. |
| 1856 | Schott (W.). | Greenland. |
| 1856 | Sutherland (P. C.). | Eskimo. |
| 1857 | Buschmann (J. C. E.). | Eskimo. |
| 1857 | Buschmann (J. C. E.). | Eskimo. |
| 1857 | Drake (S. G.), note. | Al. & Kam'd'le. |
| 1857 | Gibbs (G.). | Various. |
| 1857 | Gibbs (G.). | Davis Strait. |
| 1857 | Gibbs (G.). | Kadiak. |
| 1857 | Pok. | Greenland. |
| 1857 | Rink (H. J.). | Greenland. |
| 1857 | Sutherland (P. C.). | Eskimo. |
| 1858 | Buschmann (J. C. E.). | Various. |
| 1858 | Buschmann (J. C. E.). | Various. |
| 1858 | Drake (S. G.), note. | Al. & Kam'd'le. |
| 1858 | Janssen (C. E.). | Greenland. |
| 1858 | Jéhan (L. F.). | Eskimo. |
| 1858 | Kalatdlit. | Greenland. |
| 1858 | Ludewig (H. E.). | Various. |
| 1858 | Nunalerutit. | Greenland. |
| 1858 | Radloff (L.). | Ugalachmut. |
| 1859 | Buschmann (J. C. E.). | Various. |
| 1859 | Buschmann (J. C. E.). | Various. |
| 1859 | Kalatdlit. | Greenland. |
| 1859 | Kleinschmidt (S. P.). | Greenland. |
| 1859 | Radloff (L.). | Ugalachmut. |
| 1859–1863 | Kaladlit. | Greenland. |
| 1860 | Bagster (J.). | Greenl'd & Lab. |
| 1860 | British and F. B. S. | Greenl'd & Lab. |
| 1860 | Buschmann (J. C. E.). | Various. |
| 1860 | Buschmann (J. C. E.). | Various. |
| 1860 | Drake (S. G.). | Al. & Kam'd'le. |
| 1860 | Haldeman (S. S.). | Eskimo. |
| 1860 | Kaladlit. | Greenland. |
| 1860 | Kaladlit. | Greenland. |
| 1860 | Kaladlit. | Greenland. |
| 1860 | Latham (R. G.). | Various. |
| 1860 | Romberg (H.). | Tchuktchi. |
| 1860 | Steenholdt (W. F.). | Greenland. |

| 1860 | Steinthal (H.). | Greenland. |
|---|---|---|
| 1861 | Abecedarium. | Greenland. |
| 1861 | Golovnin (V. M.). | Kamschatka. |
| 1861 | Janssen (C. E.). | Greenland. |
| 1861 | Radloff (L.). | Tchuktschi. |
| 1861 | Tamersa. | Greenland. |
| 1861–1865 | Atuagagdliutit. | Greenland. |
| 1862 | Furuhelm (H.). | Asiagmut. |
| 1862 | Furuhelm (H.). | Kuskokwim. |
| 1862 | Janssen (C. E.). | Greenland. |
| 1862 | Latham (R. G.). | Various. |
| 1862 | Lesley (J. P.). | Various. |
| 1862 | Preces. | Greenland. |
| 1862 | Testamentêtak. | Greenland. |
| 1862–1867 | Nalunaerutit. | Greenland. |
| 1863 | Uméry (J.). | Various. |
| 1864 | Erdmann (F.). | Labrador. |
| 1864 | Hall (C. F.). | Eskimo. |
| 1864 | Jéhan (L. F.), note. | Eskimo. |
| 1864 | Kleinschmidt (S. P.). | Greenland. |
| 1865 | British and F. B. S. | Greenl'd & Lab. |
| 1865 | Erdmann (F.), note. | Labrador. |
| 1865 | Hall (C. F.). | Eskimo. |
| 1865 | Tomlin (J.). | Eskimo. |
| 1866 | Hagen (C.). | Greenland. |
| 1866 | K'einschmidt (S. P.), note. | Greenland. |
| 1866 | Markham (C. R.). | Greenland. |
| 1866 | Rink (H. J.). | Greenland. |
| 1867 | Jesuajb. | Labrador. |
| 1867 | Kragh (P.). | Greenland. |
| 1867 | Leclerc (C.). | Eskimo. |
| 1867 | Liturgiit. | Labrador. |
| 1867 | Liturgiit. | Labrador. |
| 1867 | Okautsit. | Labrador. |
| 1868 | British and F. B. S. | Greenl'd & Lab. |
| 1868 | Whymper (F.). | Various. |
| 1868–1870 | Nalunaerutit. | Greenland. |
| 1868–1886 | Sabin (J.). | Eskimo. |
| 1869 | Balitz (A.). | Aleut. |
| 1869 | Davidson (G.). | Various. |
| 1869 | Davidson (G.). | Various. |
| 1869 | Erdmann (F.). | Labrador. |
| 1869 | Janssen (C. E.). | Greenland. |
| 1869 | Naphegyi (G.). | Greenland. |
| 1869 | Whymper (F.). | Various. |
| 1869 | Whymper (F.). | Various. |
| 1870 | Dall (W. H.). | Various. |
| 1870 | Dall (W. H.). | Various. |
| 1870 | Dall (W. H.), note. | Various. |
| 1870 | Gebet. | Various. |
| 1870 | Marietti (P.). | Greenland. |
| 1870 | Okálautsit. | Labrador. |
| 1870 | Rudolph (—). | Greenland. |
| 1870 | Stimpson (W.) and Hall (A.). | Chukchee. |
| 1870–1871 | Nalunaerutit. | Greenland. |
| 1871 | Buynitzky (S. N.). | Aleut. |
| 1871 | Clare (J. R.). | Eskimo. |
| 1871 | Dall (W. H.). | Eskimo. |
| 1871 | Erdmann (F.). | Labrador. |
| 1871 | Erman (G. A.). | Various. |
| 1871 | Hayes (I. I.). | Greenland. |
| 1871 | Kleinschmidt (S. P.). | Greenland. |
| 1871 | Kleinschmidt (S. P.). | Greenland. |
| 1871 | Kragh (P.). | Greenland. |

www.ingramcontent.com/pod-product-compliance
Lightning Source LLC
Chambersburg PA
CBHW030625270326
41927CB00007B/1314